Palgrave Studies of Marketing in Emerging Economies

Series Editors
Robert E. Hinson, Ghana Communication Technology University, Accra, Ghana
Ogechi Adeola, Pan-Atlantic University, Lagos Business School, Lagos, Nigeria

This book series focuses on contemporary themes in marketing and marketing management research in emerging markets and developing economies. Books in the series cover the BRICS (Brazil, Russia, India, China and South Africa), MINT (Mexico, Indonesia, Nigeria and Turkey), CIVETS (Colombia, Indonesia, Vietnam, Egypt, Turkey, and South Africa); EAGLE economies (those which are expected to lead growth in the next ten years, such as Brazil, China, India, Indonesia, South Korea, Mexico, Russia, Taiwan, and Turkey) and all other African countries (classified under developing countries), taking into consideration the demographic, socio-cultural and macro-economic factors influencing consumer choices in these markets. The series synthesizes key subject areas in marketing, discuss marketing issues, processes, procedures and strategies across communities, regions and continents, and also the way digital innovation is changing the business landscape in emerging economies.

Palgrave Studies of Marketing in Emerging Economies presents a unique opportunity to examine and discuss marketing strategy and its implications in emerging economies, thereby filling a gap in current marketing literature.

All chapter submissions to the series will undergo a double blind peer review and all book proposals will undergo a single blind peer review.

Ayantunji Gbadamosi · Charles Blankson ·
Simon P. Sigué
Editors

Contemporary Marketing Practices in Africa, Volume 1

Technological and Strategic Perspectives

palgrave
macmillan

Editors
Ayantunji Gbadamosi
Royal Docks School of Business and Law
University of East London
London, UK

Charles Blankson
G. Brint Ryan College of Business
University of North Texas
Denton, TX, USA

Simon P. Sigué
Faculty of Graduate Studies
Athabasca University
Athabasca, AB, Canada

Wits School of Business Sciences
Johannesburg, South Africa

ISSN 2730-5554 ISSN 2730-5562 (electronic)
Palgrave Studies of Marketing in Emerging Economies
ISBN 978-3-032-27125-9 ISBN 978-3-032-27126-6 (eBook)
https://doi.org/10.1007/978-3-032-27126-6

Cover credit: 2AYCEKE/Alamy Stock Photo

This Palgrave Macmillan imprint is published by the registered company Springer Nature Switzerland AG
The registered company address is: Gewerbestrasse 11, 6330 Cham, Switzerland

Preface

Tribute to Professor Kofi Q. Dadzie

The Academy of African Business and Development (AABD) is honored to sponsor this two-volume edited series, *Contemporary Marketing Practices in Africa*, in celebration of Professor Kofi Q. Dadzie, whose distinguished career and exemplary service have profoundly shaped scholarship, professional practice, and institutional development across the African business and development landscape. This tribute recognizes not only his immense and enduring impact but also his visionary leadership, mentorship, and decades-long dedication to strengthening business research capacity in Africa and elevating the global visibility of African scholarship.

For over four decades, Professor Dadzie has been an influential figure in marketing, logistics, supply chain management, and institutional development. His scholarly journey began at the University of Ghana Business School, followed by advanced training at The Ohio State University, where he earned both an MBA and a Ph.D. in Business Administration. From his earliest appointments, including his tenure as a lecturer in marketing at the University of Ghana Business School and his subsequent roles at North Carolina Central University, Duke University, University of North Carolina–Chapel Hill, Texas Southern University, Morehouse College, Clark Atlanta University, and North Carolina A&T State University, Professor Dadzie developed a reputation for rigorous scholarship, pedagogical excellence, and unwavering commitment to preparing the next generation of marketing and logistics academics and business leaders with an interest in African business and development.

Since arriving at Georgia State University in 1988, where he held the positions of Assistant Professor and Associate Professor, Professor Dadzie has found an academic home that has enabled him to influence business scholarship at the highest levels. His contributions span graduate and undergraduate teaching, doctoral supervision across Africa and the United States, and innovative curriculum development. His visiting professorships at the Ghana Institute of Management and Public Administration (GIMPA) further demonstrate his dedication to strengthening management education in Africa.

Professor Dadzie's scholarly impact is both extensive and pioneering. His publications in highly regarded journals, including *Journal of the Academy of Marketing Science, Journal of Business & Industrial Marketing*, *Journal of Macromarketing*, *Journal of African Business*, *Journal of Public Policy and Marketing*, *Journal of Business Logistics, Journal of Business Research, Journal of Small Business Management, Journal of Marketing Theory and Practice,* and *International Journal of Logistics Management,* to name a few have shaped understanding of marketing practices, logistics adoption, supply chain management, institutional dynamics, and consumer behavior as a whole and in particular in African markets. A gifted intellectual bridge-builder, he has advanced comparative scholarship linking African markets with global contexts, contributed foundational insights on market orientation, and developed frameworks for understanding marketing, logistics, and supply chain transformation across Africa. A complete list of his publications is included in this volume.

Beyond his personal scholarship, Professor Dadzie stands out for his tireless service to academic communities. His leadership roles include serving as Editor of the *Journal of African Business* and as Regional Editor for Africa for the *Journal of Business & Industrial Marketing*. He has also been a guest editor of several influential special issues that helped define and elevate African perspectives in marketing and macro marketing research. His editorial and reviewing responsibilities, as well as his board memberships, reflect an unwavering commitment to strengthening African scholarship within the global academic community.

The AABD has been one of the greatest beneficiaries of Professor Dadzie's wisdom, passion, and leadership. As one of the founding fathers of the Academy in the early 2000s, he has served in numerous capacities, including Conference Chair (2004, 2017), Track Chair, member of the Board of Governors (2020–2025), and most notably, President of AABD (2014–2019). As President, AABD annual conferences continued to thrive as premier global platforms for African business and development scholarship. Within AABD, he worked to strengthen the business research capacity and the membership drive, encompassing canvassing members with an interest in African business and development. His invitation of the renowned African American leader, Mr. Andrew Young, a former US Ambassador to the United Nations, as the guest of honor at the Atlanta AABD conference raised AABD's profile across the United States. These immense works earned him the AABD Presidential Service Award in 2024.

Equally remarkable is Professor Dadzie's legacy of mentorship. He has supervised, examined, and guided doctoral students across Ghana, Côte d'Ivoire, Kenya, Uganda, South Africa, the United States, and beyond. Many of these scholars now occupy influential academic and professional roles, carrying forward his intellectual traditions and values. His mentorship extends informally to countless young scholars across the United States and throughout Africa who have benefitted from his generosity, thoughtful guidance, warmth, and unyielding belief in the potential of African research.

Professor Dadzie's impact also reaches far beyond the academy. Through numerous externally funded research projects supported, among others, by USAID, the Ghana Cocoa Marketing Board, the United States Information Agency, and other international development organizations, he has contributed meaningfully to development policy, rural finance, agricultural marketing, supply chain modernization, and entrepreneurial support systems across West Africa. These interventions have strengthened inclusive growth, sustainable economic development, and institutional capacity in countries such as Ghana and Ivory Coast.

In recognition of Professor Dadzie's decades of scholarship, leadership, and mentorship, these volumes stand as a tribute to a scholar whose work has shaped not only academic thought, but also the evolution of business practice and research capacity in Africa and the United States. His intellectual capability, research rigor, humility, a yearning to help young students, and his steadfast commitment to African business and development exemplify the highest ideals of the AABD.

We celebrate Professor Kofi Q. Dadzie for his extraordinary contributions, his exemplary service to the AABD and the *Journal of African Business*, his impactful presidency of the AABD, and his distinguished career as one of the most influential scholars of African business and development of his generation.

London, UK — Ayantunji Gbadamosi
Denton, TX, USA — Charles Blankson
Athabasca, AB, Canada — Simon P. Sigué

Contents

Editors and Contributors

About the Editors

Ayantunji Gbadamosi (BSc (Hons), MSc, PhD, FCIM, FCMI, SFHEA, CMBE) is an Associate Professor of Marketing and Chair of the School Research Ethics Committee at the Royal Docks School of Business and Law, University of East London (UK). He previously served as Research Coordinator and Chair of the Research and Knowledge Exchange Committee in the school. He is the current President of the Academy of African Business and Development (AABD) and a Visiting Professor at the University of Fort Hare, South Africa. He earned his PhD from the University of Salford, UK. Dr. Gbadamosi has authored over 140 publications, with articles in leading journals such as International Marketing Review, Journal of Electronic Commerce Research, World Development, and Journal of Brand Management. He has also written/edited 14 other books, including *Auto-Psychology, Psychological Marketing, Well-Being and the Workplace* (2026); *Brands, Branding, and Consumerism* (2025), and *Consumer Behaviour and Digital Transformation* (2024). *As of the time of this publication, he* has supported 98 doctoral candidates in various capacities. In this, he has supervised 15 to completion, examined 57, and served as viva Chair for 26 others. His research interests include Consumer Behaviour, SME Marketing, Marketing to Children, and Marketing Communications.

Charles Blankson (Ph.D., Kingston University, London, UK) is a Professor of Marketing and Chair of the Department of Marketing at the G. Brint Ryan College of Business, University of North Texas, Denton, Texas, USA. Dr. Blankson's current research interests include marketing strategy—positioning, branding, and marketing practices; industrial/B2B marketing; services marketing; small business marketing; subsistence marketplaces and poverty alleviation; and international marketing. Dr. Blankson is an Associate Editor of the *International Journal of Bank Marketing*. His research has appeared in the *Journal of Public Policy and Marketing*, *Journal of Macromarketing*, *Journal of Advertising Research*, *Journal of Business Research*, *Industrial Marketing Management*, *European Journal of Marketing*, *International Journal of Operations and Production Management*, *Journal of Services Marketing*, *Journal of Strategic Marketing*, *International Journal of Bank Marketing*, *Journal of African Business*, *Africa Journal of Management*, and others.

Simon P. Sigué is Interim Dean of the Faculty of Graduate Studies, Athabasca University, Canada, and Visiting Professor of Marketing at the Wits Business School of Sciences, South Africa. He is a past President of the Academy of African Business and Development and a former Editor-in-Chief of the *Journal of African Business*. His research focuses on marketing strategy, franchising, and international marketing, and has earned multiple distinctions, including the Best PhD Thesis Award at HEC Montréal, the Best Conference Paper Award from the Academy of Marketing Science, and a nomination for the *Journal of Service Research* Best Article Award.

List of Contributors

Nazifatu Mohammed Abdulai Department of Marketing and Entrepreneurship, University of Ghana Business School, Accra, Ghana; College of Humanities, University of Ghana, Accra, Ghana

Sadick Abubakari Department of Marketing and Entrepreneurship, University of Ghana Business School, Madina, Ghana;
College of Humanities, University of Ghana, Accra, Ghana

Kwame Adom School of Business, Burman University, Lacombe, AB, Canada

Golda Anambane Institute of Statistical, Social and Economic Research (ISSER), University of Ghana, Legon, Ghana

Charles Blankson Department of Marketing, G. Brint Ryan College of Business, University of North Texas, Denton, TX, USA

Kwabena G. Boakye Department of Enterprise Systems and Analytics College of Business Administration, Georgia Southern University, Statesboro, GA, USA

Jhinuk Chowdhury Department of Marketing, G. Brint Ryan College of Business, University of North Texas, Denton, TX, USA

Nicholas Oblitei Commey School of Business and Leadership, Department of Management Studies, Heritage Christian University, Accra, Ghana

Esi A. Elliot Vackar College of International Business and Entrepreneurship, University of Texas, Austin, USA

Ayantunji Gbadamosi Royal Docks School of Business and Law, University of East London, London, UK

Robert E. Hinson Department of Marketing and Entrepreneurship, University of Ghana Business School, Madina, Ghana;
College of Humanities, University of Ghana, Accra, Ghana

Oladapo Jayeola Business School, University of Wolverhampton, University of Wolverhampton, Wolverhampton, UK

Yvonne Karasi Tshwane University of Technology, Pretoria, South Africa

Nnamdi O. Madichie Bloomsbury Institute, London, UK;
Woxsen University, Telangana, India

Mahmoud Abdulai Mahmoud Department of Marketing and Entrepreneurship, University of Ghana Business School, Accra, Ghana;
College of Humanities, University of Ghana, Accra, Ghana

Ntswaki Matlala University of Johannesburg, Johannesburg, South Africa

Kobby Mensah Ghana Tourism Development Company Limited (GTDC), Accra, Ghana;
Business School, University of Ghana, Legon, Ghana

Gilbert Kofi Mensah Business School, University of Ghana, Legon, Ghana

Louicius Michel School of Business, Burman University, Lacombe, AB, Canada

Julius A. Nukpezah Department of Political Science and Public Administration, College of Arts & Sciences, Mississippi State University, Starkville, USA

Raphael Odoom Department of Marketing and Entrepreneurship, University of Ghana Business School, Accra, Ghana;
College of Humanities, University of Ghana, Accra, Ghana

Michael Ogunseyin Business School, University of Wolverhampton, University of Wolverhampton, Wolverhampton, UK

Robert A. Opoku Donald School of Business, Red Deer Polytechnic, Red Deer, AB, Canada

Richard Afriyie Owusu School of Business and Economics, Linnaeus University, Kalmar, Sweden

Fanny Adams Quagrainie Ghana Institute of Management and Public Administration (GIMPA), Achimota, Ghana

Kareem Folohunso Sani Business School, University of Wolverhampton, Wolverhampton, UK

Per Servais School of Business and Economics, Linnaeus University, Kalmar, Sweden

Chido Shambare University of the Western Cape, Cape Town, South Africa

Richard Shambare University of Fort Hare, Alice, South Africa

Knowledge Shumba Stellenbosch University, Stellenbosch, South Africa

Simon P. Sigué Faculty of Graduate Studies, Athabasca University, Athabasca, AB, Canada;
Wits School of Business Sciences, Johannesburg, South Africa

Chloe Weir School of Education, Burman University, Lacombe, AB, Canada

List of Figures

List of Tables

PART I

Introduction

CHAPTER 1

Grounding Technological and Strategic Perspectives in African Marketing Practices

Ayantunji Gbadamosi, Charles Blankson, and Simon P. Sigué

Introduction

Whether in Africa or other contexts, contemporary marketing revolves around customer value. Value can be defined as the perceived benefits minus the costs incurred in the transaction, such as money, time, and emotion (Bowman & Ambrosini, 2000; Mosca et al., 2025; Solomon et al., 2013). This definition explains why consumers' perceptions of

A. Gbadamosi (✉)
Royal Docks School of Business and Law, University of East London, London, UK
e-mail: A.Gbadamosi@uel.ac.uk

C. Blankson
Department of Marketing, G. Brint Ryan College of Business, University of North Texas, Denton, TX, USA
e-mail: Charles.Blankson@unt.edu

S. P. Sigué
Faculty of Graduate Studies, Athabasca University, Athabasca, AB, Canada

Wits School of Business Sciences, Johannesburg, South Africa

A. Gbadamosi et al. (eds.), *Contemporary Marketing Practices in Africa, Volume 1*, Palgrave Studies of Marketing in Emerging Economies,
https://doi.org/10.1007/978-3-032-27126-6_1

value can vary across individuals and consumer segments. In the research conducted by Zeithaml (1988) to gauge some consumers' definition of value, the respondents offered four different definitions or patterns of understanding of value to be 'whatever they want from the products', 'what they get from what they give', and 'the quality for the price paid'. Ultimately, to succeed in the marketplace, marketing will have to focus on how the target market defines value. This is because, with increasing competition in the marketplace, no marketer is guaranteed success. They will have to satisfy the target market, which is invariably linked to such market's definition of value.

There are numerous challenges confronting marketing practitioners as they seek to deliver value to African consumers (Elliot et al., 2026). These include social inequalities, economic uncertainties, climate change, new disruptive technologies, competition, infrastructure, international trade tensions, regulatory barriers, and bureaucracy (Kant et al., 2026; Muhammad et al., 2026; Paumgarten et al., 2012; Petzer & De Meyer, 2013). Some of these have been a clog in the wheel of successful marketing practices on the continent over the years, and recurring, while others are relatively recent. Clearly, there is a need to reinforce marketing practices and theories in Africa to address these upheavals, improve organizational market performance and consumer well-being, and support sustainable development.

Conversely, it is noteworthy that there are numerous marketing opportunities in Africa through which a firm could offer value, as globalization and technology are bringing the African continent closer to the world. At the broad level, economic growth in Sub-Sharan Africa for 2026–2027 is projected at 4.3%, notably different from the 3.5% projected for 2025 (World Bank, 2025). This is evident in the activities of several local businesses and multinational companies in many industries over the years. These companies create, deliver, and co-create value with African consumers in various ways. Marketing activities involving fast-moving consumer goods (FMCGs), fashion products, and electronic and electrical products, as well as services such as tourism, entertainment, banking, and consultancy, continue to thrive in various ways across Africa.

S. P. Sigué
e-mail: simons@athabascau.ca

Within this broader framework, contemporary marketing practices in Africa are unfolding within a fast-changing environment shaped by demographic growth, socio-economic transitions, and deepening global connectivity. While marketing theory has long drawn on Western contexts, African markets present distinctive dynamics, rooted, among others, in informality, cultural diversity, institutional complexity, and uneven technological adoption, that call for new and endogenous perspectives. This two-volume series responds to that need by offering an integrated account of the forces that shape value creation and marketing practice across the continent, advancing a broader agenda for context-sensitive African marketing scholarship.

Although previous research in leadership and several other business disciplines has underscored the importance of Africa-specific knowledge (e.g., Carlowitz & Züfle, 2024; Ogbechie & Ogah, 2024; Sigué, 2020), similar existing marketing volumes, such as Anani-Bossman et al. (2025), often focus on single themes or isolated perspectives. As a result, comparable marketing publications frequently fall short of capturing the full interplay of structural constraints, cultural influences, strategic behavior, and technological change that defines African markets today. Together, the two volumes of this series address this gap by situating African marketing within its complex realities and by highlighting the plurality of factors that shape both opportunities and challenges for firms and drive consumer behavior.

This first volume makes its distinctive contribution by highlighting the technological and strategic forces driving marketing transformation across the continent. The chapters that follow offer a multidisciplinary exploration of how technological changes, shifting consumer cultures, and evolving competitive dynamics are reshaping consumer behavior, marketing activities, and firm and political strategies in Africa. Collectively, they lay the foundation for the series, providing insights that prepare the ground for the ethical and sustainability debates taken up in Volume 2 (Gbadamosi et al., 2026) and demonstrating why a holistic, context-rooted approach is essential to understanding contemporary marketing in Africa.

Technology in African Marketing

There has been a marked upward change in the adoption of technology in recent times. The data given for the internet users as of February 2025 is 5.56 billion (Petrosyan, 2025). It is therefore not surprising that digital transformation now permeates consumers' daily activities with various implications for the marketplace dynamics. Artificial intelligence (AI) is a notable aspect of technological development that is increasingly occupying center stage in marketing systems today. In a simple definition, it can be conceptualized as a machine that behaves in a manner that can be described as intelligent if it were human (McCarthy et al., 1955). This explains why it aids consumers in their purchase activities and decision-making processes in various ways, and assists marketers in monitoring and analyzing consumer behavior, leading to efficiency and effectiveness in the marketing system (Gbadamosi, 2024; Gołąb-Andrzejak, 2023). The current state of AI is highly relevant, and its future is bright. For example, it is reported that investment in Generative AI has grown markedly to $ 2.1 bn since 2020 (Pennington, 2023). Similarly, its global market is estimated at around $267 billion by 2027, indicating a projected healthy increase in adoption (Gbadamosi, 2024; Lin, 2020; Mogaji & Nguyen, 2022). Evidently, AI takes many forms, with varying functions and impacts in marketing. For example, there is Explainable Artificial Intelligence (XAI), which is machine learning capable of producing human-understandable explanations for AI-based information systems (Ahmed et al., 2021; Ncube et al., 2024).

This also has implications for marketing activities in Africa. For instance, the average broadband download speed in Africa, which was 2.68 megabits per second in 2019, increased to 8.68 megabits per second in 2022 (World Bank Group, 2023). This is a noteworthy positive trend regarding marketing practices on the continent. Although certain issues, such as cultural differences, constitute peculiarities of African societies, consumer behavior in that context is also gradually influenced by technology (Gbadamosi, 2024). Schoeman and Haines's (2023) study, conducted in the South African context, shows that teleradiology is perceived as potentially influencing societal, personal, and operational functioning in a positive way. Similarly, Erasmus and Ondoa's (2023) study, which focuses on digital health and Artificial intelligence in Africa, shows advancements in the use of digital data in laboratory medicine, support for decision-making in clinical settings, and patient safety. Despite significant changes in consumption and marketing activities driven by digital transformation in African countries, the digital divide between consumer segments remains evident and a concern for scholars and marketing practitioners.

Accordingly, the chapters in this section address key questions about how digital technologies are reshaping marketing across Africa. They highlight the transformative potential of technology and the structural barriers that foster its impact on African markets.

Sani, Gbadamosi, Ogunseyin, and Jayeola examine how digital inclusion can expand access to rural consumers by analyzing enablers such as mobile internet availability, broadband affordability, digital literacy, and emerging tools like mobile money and e-commerce. They describe how enterprises, governments, and non-profits engage rural communities through digital technologies, while also recognizing infrastructural gaps, gender disparities, and affordability challenges that continue to limit digital transformation and inclusion.

Adom, Commey, and Anambane explore the integration of modern technology to achieve sustainable marketing practices in the contemporary business landscape. As businesses face increasing pressure to adopt environmentally and socially responsible strategies, technology becomes pivotal in facilitating this transition. The chapter examines various technological tools and channels, including digital marketing, data analytics, and others, to understand how firms can improve their marketing strategies to align with sustainable goals.

Abdulai, Mahmoud, and Odoom show that the increasing environmental impact of traditional cooking practices necessitates a transition toward more sustainable solutions. The introduction of clean cooking appliances opens the door to a green cooking revolution by enhancing efficiency, reducing waste, and promoting sustainable behaviors. This chapter provides insights into how perceived ease of use, perceived usefulness, resource integration, actors' interaction, and value co-creation can induce positive or negative attitudes toward the adoption of sustainable clean cooking practices.

Together the above chapters show that while technology is transforming marketing across Africa, its impact depends heavily on the social, cultural, and institutional contexts in which it is applied. Digital tools alone cannot account for how consumers interpret value or how firms navigate complex market conditions.

Consumer Behavior and Strategic Perspectives in Africa

Consumer behavior is an intriguing phenomenon. Marketers in Africa face the challenge of unraveling this to achieve successful operations on the continent. Hence, an adequate understanding of the environmental factors is key to this process. There have been many changes in the legal environment of African countries over the years. Some of these changes are beneficial to marketers. For example, Ojah et al. (2010) provide robust evidence that property rights, as well as external and internal finance channels and factors from the legal environment, influence firms' decisions to invest in fixed capital in the East African Community study. This has been reported as a considerable development in the marketing environment, especially in strengthening the local economy.

Many developments in the legal environment in some African countries pose challenges. In a study exploring opportunities and challenges for Petroleum and liquefied petroleum gas in sub-Saharan Africa, Matthews (2014) observes that Burkina Faso, Côte d'Ivoire, Mali, and Niger rely on incongruent texts from French colonial times and have not updated their legal and regulatory frameworks in decades but highlights South Africa and Botswana positively in terms of their legal system in the context of the products under consideration. These mixed results in sub-Saharan African countries are symptomatic of the weak enforcement and monitoring of marketing activities in some countries. As governments change, the rules and regulations governing marketing activities change as well. Hence, the rules governing marketing activities must be monitored and enforced, as unchecked commercial malpractice can take over the market and discourage efficient marketers in the system (Matthews, 2014). The social and cultural environment in Africa is remarkable. Culture has been identified as a defining factor influencing consumption. It explains what we buy, how we buy them, where we buy them, and how often we buy them (Gbadamosi, 2024). There are some specific cultural values in Africa that differentiate the context from others. For example, Hofstede's model of cultural dimensions identifies power distance, individualism/collectivism, masculinity/femininity, uncertainty avoidance, long-term/short-term orientation, and restraint/indulgence (Gallego-Álvarez & Pucheta-Martínez, 2021; Hofstede, 1980, 2001) in explaining how nations can be culturally diverse. African societies tend to be collectivist, which influences their consumption and how marketing strategies can be applied to the target market on the continent. An example of this is the Ubuntu value in Africa, which states that an individual is who he or she is, being part of a community. It is underpinned by mutual relationships and kindness, serving as the glue that holds African economies together (Ndhlovu, 2024). Due to several factors, including educational factors, the social-cultural influences on consumption in Africa are changing. For example, the role of women as homemakers with limited economic power in the household is gradually changing as more women across the continent enter the workforce and contribute in different ways to their countries' economies. Moreover, the children's role in family consumption in Africa is evolving from mere consumers or users of products to active members of the family buying system, where they serve as initiators, influencers, deciders, and buyers. Findings show that children in Nigeria are involved in decisions not only on products and services meant for them but, in some cases, on other transactions pertaining to the entire family's consumption, such as family foodstuffs and household electronics (Gbadamosi, 2012).

The dynamics of the activities of the actors in the microenvironmental factors, such as suppliers, channel members, competitors, and consumers, are interesting. Local and international suppliers of raw materials have been instrumental in enabling businesses to offer value to consumers. Although competition is often viewed negatively, it can strengthen market systems. Marketing practices and competition in Africa drive innovation, as firms feel compelled to design goods and services that keep them relevant and keep their brands in consumers' minds. In a study of marketing efficiency and determinants of marketing channel choice among rice farmers in rural Tanzania, Mgale and Yunxian (2020) found that shorter distribution channels are more efficient than longer ones and yield the greatest benefits to producers. The study suggests strengthening farmers' associations' capacity. Besides, it also suggests the need for market information systems, rural infrastructure, prudent credit use, smallholder access to productive assets, and to enhance collective action via well-organized farmer groups in the country. Given the challenges of marketing in Africa, operating in this environment has necessitated the use of segmentation, targeting, and positioning for successful marketing practices.

The following chapters therefore explore core questions about how Africa's legal, cultural, and socio-economic environments affect consumer behavior and strategic marketing. They ask how regulatory frameworks influence firms' decisions, how cultural values and shifting family roles redefine consumption, and how crises disrupt traditional decision-making patterns. They also examine how political processes function as forms of branding, how consumer research can be decolonized, and how firms enhance performance through market orientation, innovation, and cross-national positioning. They offer a streamlined yet multifaceted view of Africa's evolving market landscape.

Mensah, Madichie, and Mensah examine how traditional consumer decision-making processes were altered during the crisis, proposing a revised four-stage model comprising need recognition, purchase, ownership, and satisfaction, omitting the information search and alternative evaluation stages. They also reassess the relevance of the 4Ps marketing mix, emphasizing that Product and Place gained heightened importance, while Price and Promotion became less influential. Notably, within the promotional mix, public relations played a significant role, whereas branding became less relevant.

Blankson, Nukpezah, Elliot, and Mensah investigate how important is democracy in the context of an emerging African economy. They conceptualize elections as electoral brands presented to voters, who must choose among various political parties, candidates, and policy preferences, especially during general elections. Through a qualitative ethnographic study in Ghana, they show how political messaging, social context, and institutional shifts influence voter perceptions, offering a broader understanding of political marketing in emerging African democracies.

Opoku, Michel, Adom, and Weir challenge traditional marketing paradigms, rooted in Western epistemologies, arguing that they perpetuate systemic inequities by overlooking contextual power dynamics and information asymmetries that shape consumption patterns. They propose that marginalization stems from structural knowledge disparities, varies across contexts, and is shaped by social hierarchies. This chapter contributes to transformative marketing scholarship by advocating for more equitable and context-grounded consumer research.

Hinson, Mahmoud, and Abubakari test the direct impact of market orientation on firm performance and the mediating effect of new product development. They find that customer orientation, competitor awareness, and inter-functional coordination significantly enhance performance, with new product development acting as a key mediating factor. The findings stress the importance of innovation in informal-sector markets.

Blankson, Boakye, and Chowdhury evaluate how brand positioning strategies operate in cross-national settings by comparing Ghana and the United States. They argue that existing frameworks are outdated and lack comprehensiveness for modern markets. Their findings show that effective sub-positioning strategies can be generalized across developed and developing open-market economies, enhancing brand performance.

Quagrainie, Owusu, and Servais analyze how entrepreneurial identity shapes women's capacity to identify international business opportunities. They identify multiple identity dimensions, including autonomous, transition, know-how, and solution-seeker orientations that drive internationalization pathways. Their findings offer insights into how women entrepreneurs navigate global markets and highlight policy implications for supporting micro-enterprises.

Shumba, Matlala, Karasi, Shambare, and Shambare examine the influence of culture, particularly Ubuntu, on Africa's youth marketing, emphasizing the growing strategic importance of this demographic. They show how cultural values shape young consumers' identities, preferences, and buying behaviors, arguing that youth marketing remains underexplored despite the continent's predominantly youthful population.

In summary, the chapters in this section show that consumer behavior in Africa is shaped by a complex mix of cultural norms, legal structures, and strategic firm decisions. They highlight the need for marketing approaches that recognize these contextual realities and adapt to them.

Conclusion

Contemporary issues in Africa constitute a complex phenomenon, underpinned by a myriad factors and faced with numerous challenges. Hence, for effective marketing in Africa, there will have to be a paradigm shift in the approach. For example, marketers targeting African consumers will have to position notions of value creation, value delivery, and value co-creation with consumers in ways that are more deeply rooted than ever before. This is because the road signs in the marketing system in Africa and other contexts are changing by the day. A typical example of this is the relevance of technology in the consumption and marketing systems. Digital transformation has shifted the conventional pattern. Constructs such as the internet, consumer avatars, electronic word-of-mouth (eWOM) communications, artificial intelligence (AI), mobile money, and social media have now systematically become major aspects of the template for contemporary society, including Africa. Moreover, it is argued that African contexts are underrepresented in the mainstream marketing literature. Unfortunately, Western-centric marketing models have limitations in their suitability for African socio-economic environments. For instance, issues such as community-based validation, which impact affordability, trust, digital literacy, and social proof, are of paramount relevance to consumer behavior in a digitally mediated African market and to the discourse on consumption and marketing activities in Africa. This is another key pointer to the uniqueness of this volume on Contemporary Marketing in Africa. Accordingly, it is imperative to give strategic marketing precedence over tactical options for effectiveness in the contemporary marketing context.

As this volume demonstrates, understanding contemporary marketing in Africa requires attention to the technological, cultural, and strategic forces that drive consumer behavior and foster value creation across the continent. Yet, technology, consumer behavior, and strategy alone cannot fully account for the responsibilities and societal expectations that now frame marketing practice. Readers seeking a deeper examination of the ethical dilemmas, sustainability imperatives, and broader questions of accountability that increasingly influence African markets will find these issues taken up in detail in the second volume of this series (Gbadamosi et al., 2026). This last volume of the series extends the insights developed here and helps the reader gain a fuller, more holistic appreciation of the challenges, opportunities, and responsibilities that define marketing practice in Africa today.

References

Ahmad, W., Kutan, A. M., & Gupta, S. (2021). Black swan events and COVID-19 outbreak: Sector-level evidence from the US, UK, and European stock markets. *International Review of Economics & Finance, 75*, 546–557.

Anani-Bossman, A., Mudzanani, T. E. Pillay, D. (Eds). (2025). *Sustainability marketing in emerging economies: Conceptual and empirical perspectives*. Palgrave Macmillan.

Bowman, C., & Ambrosini, V. (2000). Value creation versus value capture: Towards a coherent definition of value in strategy. *British Journal of Management, 11*(1), 1–15.

Carlowitz, P., & Züfle, S. (Eds). (2024). *Business success in Africa: Academic and managerial insights*. Springer.

Elliott, J., Alexander, B., & Varley, R. (2026). Optimising omnichannel: The case of South African fashion retail. *International Journal of Retail & Distribution Management*, *54*(1), 18–44.

Erasmus, R., & Ondoa, P. (2023). Taking the train of digital health and artificial intelligence to improve medical laboratory service in Africa: Key considerations. *African Journal of Laboratory Medicine, 12*(1), 1–2.

Gallego-Álvarez, I., & Pucheta-Martínez, M. C. (2021). Hofstede's cultural dimensions and R&D intensity as an innovation strategy: A view from different institutional contexts. *Eurasian Business Review, 11*(2), 191–220.

Gbadamosi, A. (2012). Exploring children, family, and consumption behaviour: Empirical evidence from Nigeria. *Thunderbird International Business Review, 54*(4), 591–605.

Gbadamosi, A. (2024). *Consumer behaviour and digital transformation*. Routledge.

Gbadamosi, A., Blankson, C., & Sigué, S.P. (Eds). (2026). Contemporary marketing practices in Africa: Ethical and sustainability perspectives (Vol. 2). Palgrave Macmillan (In press).

Gołąb-Andrzejak, E. (2023). AI-powered digital transformation: Tools, benefits and challenges for marketers-case study of LPP. *Procedia Computer Science, 219*, 397–404.

Hofstede, G. (1980). Culture's Consequences International differences in work-related values (Vol. 5). Sage.

Hofstede, G. (2001). Culture's consequences: Comparing values, behaviors, institutions and organizations across nations. Sage.

Kant, S., Terefe, A., Niguse, T., Adula, M., Alemu, Z. K., & Takaro, G. S. (2026). Social media effect on destination market promotion by mediation of influencer marketing in the Horn of Africa. In *Maximizing destination marketing strategies in the digital era* (pp. 251–278). IGI Global Scientific Publishing.

Lin, Y. (2020). *10 Artificial Intelligence statistics you need to know in 2021.* Available at: www.oberlo.com/blog/artificial-intelligence-statistics

Matthews, W. G. (2014). Opportunities and challenges for petroleum and LPG markets in sub-Saharan Africa. *Energy Policy, 64*, 78–86.

McCarthy, J., Minsky, M. L., Rochester, N., & Shannon, C. E. (1955). A proposal for the Dartmouth summer research project on artificial intelligence. *AI Magazine, 27*(4), 12–14.

Mgale, Y. J., & Yunxian, Y. (2020). Marketing efficiency and determinants of marketing channel choice by rice farmers in rural Tanzania: Evidence from Mbeya region, Tanzania. *Australian Journal of Agricultural and Resource Economics, 64*(4), 1239–1259.

Mogaji, E., & Nguyen, N. P. (2022). Managers' understanding of artificial intelligence in relation to marketing financial services: Insights from a cross-country study. *International Journal of Bank Marketing, 40*(6), 1272–1298.

Mosca, F., Civera, C., Chiaudano, V., & Shakil, H. (2025). Phygital Museums as catalysts for inclusivity, well-being, and human-centric cultural experiences across physical and digital spaces. *Journal of Macromarketing*, 02761467251403943.

Muhammad, A. U., Murtala, S., & Yusuf, A. (2026). Legal and regulatory challenges of Islamic banking in Africa: Finding a balance between Sharia governance and regulatory frameworks. In *Legal and regulatory aspects of Abrahamic finance* (pp. 67–92). IGI Global Scientific Publishing.

Ncube, M., Sibanda, M., & Matenda, F. R. (2024). Investigating the effects of the covid-19 pandemic on stock volatility in sub-Saharan Africa: Analysis using explainable artificial intelligence. *Economies, 12*(5), 112.

Ndhlovu, G. N. (2024). Structural violence and the perpetuation of women's poverty: Exploring the issue of child maintenance in South Africa. *Development Studies Research, 11*(1), 2400895.

Ogbechie, R. & Ogah, M. (Eds). (2024). *Sustainable and responsible business in Africa: Studies in ethical leadership*, Palgrave Macmillan.

Ojah, K., Gwatidzo, T., & Kaniki, S. (2010). Legal environment, finance channels and investment: The East African example. *The Journal of Development Studies, 46*(4), 724–744.

Paumgarten, F., Kassa, H., Zida, M., & Moeliono, M. (2012). Benefits, challenges, and enabling conditions of collective action to promote sustainable production and marketing of products from Africa's dry forests. *Review of Policy Research, 29*(2), 229–250.

Pennington, C. (2023, January 17), Generative AI: The new frontier for VC investment. *Forbes*. www.forbes.com/sites/columbiabusinessschool/2023/01/17/generative-ai-the-new-frontier-for-vc-investment/?sh=5f51154e519c (Accessed, 16th June, 2023).

Petrosyan, A. (2025). 'Number of internet and social media users Worldwide as of February, 2025', Statista, April 1, 2025. www.statista.com/statistics/617136/digital-population-worldwide/ (Accessed, 19th April, 2025).

Petzer, D. J., & De Meyer, C. F. (2013). Trials and tribulations: Marketing in modern South Africa. *European Business Review, 25*(4), 382–390.

Schoeman, R., & Haines, M. (2023). Radiologists' experiences and perceptions regarding the use of teleradiology in South Africa. *SA Journal of Radiology, 27*(1), 1–7.

Sigué, S.P. (Ed.). (2020). *Contemporary issues and prospects in business development in Africa*. Routledge.

Solomon, M. R., Marshall, G. W., Stuart, E. W., & Mitchell, V. (2013). *'Marketing: Real people, reach choices* (7th ed.). Pearson Education Ltd.

World Bank. (2025, April 23). *Economic growth is speeding up in Africa, but uncertainty clouds outlook*. World Bank Press Release. www.worldbank.org/en/news/press-release/2025/04/23/economic-growth-is-speeding-up-in-africa-but-uncertainty-clouds-outlook (Accessed, 26th February, 2026).

World Bank Group. (2023, June 26). *From connectivity to services: Digital transformation in Africa*. Word Bank Group, Results Briefs.. www.worldbank.org/en/results/2023/06/26/from-connectivity-to-services-digital-transformation-in-africa (Accessed, 27th September, 2025).

Zeithaml, V. (1988). Consumer perception of price, quality and value: A means-end model and synthesis of evidence. *Journal of Marketing, 52*(3), 2–22.

PART II

Technology in African Marketing

CHAPTER 2

Digital Inclusion and Its Impact on Reaching Rural African Consumers

Kareem Folohunso Sani, Ayantunji Gbadamosi, Michael Ogunseyin, and Oladapo Jayeola

Introduction

Digital inclusion has emerged as a pivotal subject in contemporary development discourse, particularly in the Global South, as digital technology has rapidly transformed interactions among individuals, markets,

K. F. Sani (✉) · M. Ogunseyin · O. Jayeola
Business School, University of Wolverhampton, Wolverhampton, UK
e-mail: k.sani@wlv.ac.uk

M. Ogunseyin
e-mail: M.ogunseyin@wlv.ac.uk

O. Jayeola
e-mail: O.Jayeola@wlv.ac.uk

A. Gbadamosi
Royal Docks School of Business and Law, University of East London, London, UK
e-mail: A.Gbadamosi@uel.ac.uk.uk

A. Gbadamosi et al. (eds.), *Contemporary Marketing Practices in Africa, Volume 1*, Palgrave Studies of Marketing in Emerging Economies,
https://doi.org/10.1007/978-3-032-27126-6_2

and institutions. Digital inclusion in Africa presents opportunities to address ongoing issues of service accessibility and market inefficiencies, while overcoming geographic barriers for rural residents. The Organisation for Economic Co-operation and Development (OECD, 2022) characterises digital inclusion as an extensive notion that encompasses not only internet access but also vital digital skills, connectivity, affordable tools, and literacy necessary for substantive digital participation. Rural African consumers require these elements to participate successfully in digitised economies and societies. Digital inclusion is of paramount significance for rural consumers in Africa. The World Bank (2023) indicates that over 55% of Africa's population resides in rural areas, where economic participation is constrained by infrastructure deficiencies, inadequate educational opportunities, and poor market integration. Mobile technology, expanding broadband networks, and digital financial services now provide rural people with unparalleled chances to reach broader markets. Innovative methods for inclusion have arisen through advancements such as mobile banking, agricultural e-marketplaces, telemedicine systems, and digital education services (GSMA, 2023). Mobile money services, such as M-Pesa in Kenya and MTN Mobile Money in West Africa, enable rural populations to conduct transactions, safeguard their savings, and access financial services independent of conventional banking institutions (Aker & Blumenstock, 2023).

Despite these advancements, significant inequalities persist. Data from the International Telecommunication Union (ITU) in 2023 indicated that internet connectivity in rural households in Sub-Saharan Africa (SSA) was approximately 36%, compared with over 65% in urban households, a disparity that has persisted over the years. The rural digital divide necessitates immediate intervention (GSMA, 2023). The interplay of gender inequity, insufficient digital knowledge, and higher costs exacerbate the challenges of closing the digital gap. Socio-cultural constraints and diminished financial means render 37% of rural women less likely than rural males to access mobile internet services (GSMA, 2023). Despite the presence of infrastructure, rural consumers perceive digital tools as less beneficial owing to the lack of local content and platforms that cater to their linguistic requirements (Donner & Tewari, 2022). Furthermore, consumer trust, together with the perceived utility of digital platforms, is a crucial factor in digital inclusion. Studies show that rural consumers exhibit increased involvement with digital tools when aided by trustworthy intermediaries or when these products integrate into their social networks (Aker et al., 2021). Initiatives to improve digital inclusion must equally consider the socio-cultural and behavioural circumstances of rural customers.

Digital inclusion offers significant opportunities for firms to engage with customer demographics that have traditionally been marginalised in marketing. Service providers and companies now recognise rural regions as attractive markets, particularly given the growing number of mobile phone users. Digital platforms enable enterprises to gather data and cultivate client interactions while providing individualised solutions in ways previously unattainable. Businesses must tailor their strategies to accommodate the distinct attributes of digital interaction in rural regions to optimise these prospects. Companies must provide user-friendly interfaces, ensure offline functionality, and develop digital advertising that resonates with local audiences and language requirements (World Bank, 2023). Government institutions and development agencies play a crucial role in promoting digital inclusion through policy efforts. Investments in rural broadband infrastructure, along with subsidies for digital devices and community digital literacy initiatives, are crucial strategies for overcoming the digital divide (OECD, 2022). To ensure a lasting positive impact of digital tools on rural users, extensive coordination among government entities, corporate groups, and civil society is essential to make these resources accessible and effective.

The rural African consumer is defined in this chapter as individuals or households residing in spatially isolated, peripheral, and/or low-density regions in Africa, where infrastructure deficiencies, limited connectivity, and scarce market linkages hinder their digital engagement. They are differentiated from urban impoverished consumers, who may be excluded solely on the basis of income but are often closer to physical infrastructure, institutions, and service ecosystems. Rural customers are more susceptible to experiencing a "double" or "triple" disadvantage or marginalisation due to their geographic location, insufficient broadband access, and additional contextual considerations such as socio-cultural elements (GSMA, 2023; World Bank, 2023). Digital exclusion in Africa is mostly a matter of relative location, infrastructure, and context, rather than relative income (Kuteesa et al., 2024).

This chapter adopts the rural consumer as the unit of analysis, focusing on their access to and use of digital platforms, services, and financial instruments. It is contextualised within current circumstances, necessitating a critical evaluation of the impact of digital inclusion on the consumption behaviour of rural Africans and on their use of digital products and services. It aims to (1) analyse the impact of digital inclusion on the consumer behaviour of rural Africans and (2) elucidate the mechanisms facilitating and obstructing digital inclusion. Assessing the role of digital inclusion in rural Africans' consumption patterns is crucial, as it highlights both the opportunities and challenges it presents. Entrepreneurship is acknowledged in rural regions, but this chapter addresses it solely in terms of its influence on the accessibility and consumption of goods and services, as well as the empowerment of rural consumers (Aker & Blumenstock, 2023). This analysis will reveal consumption and inclusion disparities within these communities and facilitate an understanding of the necessary measures to bridge those gaps.

Digital Inclusion in Rural Africa: Opportunities and Barriers

Digital inclusion is a vital element in connecting urban consumers with their rural counterparts across Africa. Oloyede et al. (2022) indicate that digital technologies significantly enhance rural empowerment by facilitating access to information and markets, as well as providing essential services, thereby contributing to the reduction of historical inequalities. Digital literacy programs enhance community development by empowering residents to participate in online activities, thereby promoting increased economic engagement (Puspita, 2024). Educational programs provide individuals with critical access to information and opportunities for engagement in economic activities, leading to enhanced livelihoods. The observed achievements in specific rural areas indicate that digital literacy strategies should be tailored to local contexts to improve community engagement in the digital economy. However, rural areas face challenges in accessing digital infrastructure, underscoring the importance of initiatives that promote digital literacy and financial inclusion to improve economic opportunities (Oloyede et al., 2022). Thus, digital inclusion poses a significant challenge in rural Africa, as disparities in access to technology and digital literacy hinder economic growth and social development. The four primary obstacles to digital inclusion in rural Africa are the insufficient infrastructure, socio-economic disparities, gender, and educational background, which influence individuals' capacity to utilise digital platforms (Kuteesa et al., 2024).

Infrastructure Gaps: Broadband, Electricity, and Connectivity

The primary obstacle to digital inclusion in rural Africa is the insufficient infrastructure. Rural areas often exhibit inferior internet connectivity compared to urban regions, resulting in increased operational costs for service providers and limiting economic opportunities for rural populations. Thus, infrastructure deficiencies in rural Africa remain a significant barrier to digital inclusion, hindering rural consumers from fully benefiting from the digital economy. Inadequate broadband connectivity and inconsistent electricity supply persistently restrict the rural population's ability to utilise online services, including e-learning, telemedicine, and digital financial services (Oloyede et al., 2023; World Bank, 2023). Connectivity rates in rural areas lag those in urban areas, creating a structural disadvantage for rural consumers. The physical remoteness and low population density of the rural areas intensify the high costs for service providers, discouraging investment (GSMA, 2023). If deliberate actions are not taken to close this gap, rural people will continue to face inequitable access to markets and services.

Digital Literacy: The Role of Education and Tailored Programmes

Access to infrastructure is a requisite yet inadequate condition for digital inclusion. Proficiency and assurance in utilising digital tools are also essential for significant engagement in the digital realm. Digital literacy is a multifaceted notion that encompasses more than mere technological skill. It entails comprehending how to access, assess, and utilise information from online sources, executing informed and secure financial transactions online, and leveraging digital technologies to meet practical, everyday needs such as agriculture, healthcare, education, and beyond. In rural Africa, these elements of digital literacy are crucial for leveraging mobile applications, e-commerce platforms, and financial technology services to achieve tangible benefits. Programs tailored to local settings rather than general training appear to have higher adoption rates. Pedagogies that consider linguistic variety, cultural subtleties, and varying levels of exposure have significantly influenced the inclusion of varied consumer groups (Kuteesa et al., 2024; Mwapwele et al., 2019). Local-language adaptations of digital literacy resources or voice-based applications for low-literacy users demonstrate greater acceptance and usability. Conversely, universal training approaches may perpetuate exclusionary tendencies, favouring urban or highly literate demographics.

Educational institutions often lead in developing digital literacy. Initiatives such as ICT programs in schools or digital skills outreach from universities can create avenues for digital literacy; however, they may be hindered by challenges, including underfunding, infrastructural deficiencies, and insufficient teacher training (World Bank, 2023). Enhancing teachers' capabilities and early integration of digital skills in schools are essential for cultivating a digitally literate future generation of rural consumers. Community learning centres, non-governmental organisations, and local cooperatives serve as significant access points for digital literacy. Interventions such as community workshops and peer-learning groups demonstrate that digital education, when integrated into established community frameworks, is more likely to gain trust, encounter less cultural resistance, and foster an environment conducive to learning and experimentation for women, older individuals, and other marginalised groups (Ye & Yang, 2020). Aker and Blumenstock (2023) note analogous trends in their training initiatives in Africa—digital skills training is more widely adopted when delivered by trusted intermediaries, such as microfinance organisations or agricultural extension officers, as the skills and incentives are clearer and tailored to participants' daily needs.

Furthermore, digital literacy should be perceived as an ongoing process rather than a singular action. As digital platforms and technologies advance, rural consumers will necessitate continuous opportunities for education and adaptation. Partnerships that guarantee the training provided is current, scalable, and locally accessible are essential. Perceiving digital literacy as a continuous skill and adaptive process not only empowers individuals but also enhances rural economies by fostering a more informed consumer base, improving home connectivity, and cultivating resilient communities.

Gender Inequalities: Women's Access and Empowerment Through Technology

Gender disparities are a significant obstacle to attaining digital inclusion in Africa. A pronounced gender digital divide exists, with women being less likely than men to use mobile devices, utilise the internet, or benefit from the digital economy, particularly in rural areas (GSMA, 2023). Women in Sub-Saharan Africa are 37% less likely than men to use mobile internet, with a more pronounced disparity in rural regions. The underlying causes of this disparity are intricate and encompass socio-cultural standards, economic disparities, and insufficient digital literacy, all of which contribute to women's exclusion from digital opportunities. Cultural norms may inhibit women's utilisation of technology, particularly in contexts where digital devices are associated with men or where female mobility is restricted. Economic inequality contributes significantly, as rural women, who earn less than their male counterparts, are less able to afford data costs or mobile devices. The absence of digital literacy exacerbates the gender gap, as women are less likely to receive or afford training and are more prone to being marginalised by digital advancements. This exclusion has profound implications for women's empowerment in society.

Digital inclusion enables women to access e-commerce platforms, digital financial services, remote education, and extensive networks. Empirical research indicates favourable socio-economic results not only for individual women but also for their families and communities. Mobile money literacy seminars and microcredit programs, when integrated with mobile money platforms, have enhanced women's financial inclusion, household budgeting, and small business development (Akinyemi & Mushunje, 2020; Sindakis & Showkat, 2024). Women's access to digital agricultural platforms has enhanced productivity and market participation. These instances demonstrate how digital access can directly impact women's livelihoods. Digital inclusion also fosters social empowerment. Women can utilise digital platforms to access educational resources, health information networks, and social media for advocacy and community mobilisation. These actions can enhance women's agency, contest gender stereotypes, and multiply the impact of societal change.

Bridging the gender digital divide is essential for sustainable development and equity in Africa. This challenge necessitates a multifaceted strategy encompassing reducing device and data costs through subsidies and enhancing culturally relevant training programs. Safe environments must be established for women to acquire digital skills, and digital platforms must provide content that is relevant and tailored to women's everyday needs. Collaboration among governments, NGOs, and the corporate sector is crucial to enhance these initiatives, alongside explicit laws to ensure that women are not merely users but also engaged participants in digital economies. Bridging the gender gap in digital access is crucial for achieving the United Nations Sustainable Development Goals

(SDGs), specifically SDG 5 (Gender Equality), SDG 1 (No Poverty), and SDG 8 (Decent Work and Economic Growth). Empowering women with technology is a mutually beneficial approach that enhances the well-being of rural women, their families, and communities, while fostering inclusive growth in Africa.

Affordability and Local Relevance: Cost, Local Language Content, and Trust

Affordability and relevance provide further obstacles, even when infrastructure and skills are established. The cost of data is high, as inexpensive devices are limited, and insufficient funding hinders rural customers from consistently participating in the digital realm (Pan & Mo, 2024). There is a scarcity of local-language material, which often leads rural consumers to perceive digital devices and services as unhelpful, thereby affecting their use and adoption, particularly in low-literacy contexts (Donner & Tewari, 2022). Trust plays a significant role, since rural consumers are more inclined to adopt digital services when endorsed by their local cooperative, community leader, or peer (Aker et al., 2021). It is essential to implement measures that ensure affordable, locally relevant digital access—such as subsidies, support for local content development, and community-driven initiatives—to enhance and expand digital inclusion.

Digital inclusion in rural Africa is significantly pertinent to the United Nations Sustainable Development Goals (SDGs), a crucial development goal, as well as to the consumer agenda. Digital inclusion corresponds with SDG 1 (No Poverty) by facilitating access to mobile money accounts and digital financial services that promote income growth, remittances, and bolster household financial resilience (Aker & Blumenstock, 2023; GSMA, 2023). Initiatives to enhance ICT and connectivity in schools, community learning centres, and other venues promote SDG 4 (Quality Education) by fostering digital literacy and skills, thereby improving the educational outcomes of rural students and youth who encounter obstacles due to inadequate educational infrastructure (Kuteesa et al., 2024; World Bank, 2023). Bridging the gender digital divide and increasing online access for rural women are essential to achieving SDG 5 (Gender Equality), as mobile internet and digital platforms remain largely inaccessible to many women in rural regions due to enduring socio-cultural and economic barriers (Akinyemi & Mushunje, 2020; GSMA, 2023).

Digital technology and services facilitate job creation, entrepreneurship, and enhanced market access, thereby advancing SDG 8 (Decent Work and Economic Growth) through increased, more inclusive engagement in local and regional economies (Sindakis & Showkat, 2024). The expansion of broadband, investment in mobile networks, and community-oriented connectivity solutions advance SDG 9 (Industry, Innovation, and Infrastructure) by strengthening the foundational infrastructure of digital economies and ensuring that rural populations are not marginalised (Pan & Mo, 2024). Thus, digital inclusion in Africa serves not just as a mechanism for consumer empowerment but also as a catalyst for the continent's overarching sustainable development.

To achieve genuine socio-economic empowerment through digital access, it is imperative to ensure and expand access to key digital services, enhance infrastructure and digital literacy, bridge gender disparities, and offer affordable, relevant services. A comprehensive approach that considers all these factors would enable digital inclusion to serve not only as a means of individual consumer empowerment but also as a mechanism for attaining Africa's development objectives.

Modelling Broadband Deployment for Rural Africa's Development

The practical implementation of fixed broadband services in rural Africa necessitates a comprehensive techno-economic model that addresses both infrastructure needs and the socio-economic contexts of the areas. This analysis synthesises results from multiple studies to delineate the essential elements necessary for developing an effective implementation strategy.

Oloyede et al. (2023) present a techno-economic model that analyses capital expenditure (CAPEX) and operational expenditure (OPEX). The research highlights the need to develop this model to understand deployment costs for broadband services in rural African socio-economic contexts. The authors indicate that fixed broadband services can be made viable in underserved regions with appropriate investment and strategic planning. Lehtonen (2020) shows that broadband deployment in rural areas serves as a balancing mechanism, generating economic opportunities comparable to those in urban settings. The author demonstrates that broadband infrastructure is crucial in rural areas for regulating access to economic opportunities and managing resources. Similarly, Ivus and Boland (2015) posit that broadband deployment enhances rural employment growth by reducing operational costs and facilitating business activities in remote regions. These indicate that improved broadband services facilitate advancements across sectors, including agriculture and healthcare, through economic and social benefits. For example, Sanders et al. (2022) found that affordable broadband access enhances agricultural practices, thereby increasing productivity in rural areas where farming constitutes the economic foundation. Development initiatives in Africa aimed at improving the lives of rural consumers through superior agricultural practices and increased market access are fundamentally based on this concept.

Therefore, the frameworks focused on community engagement, as examined by Gwaka et al. (2018), illustrate the effectiveness of localised strategies in addressing digital access challenges. Gwaka et al. (2018) demonstrate that community-specific initiatives can effectively address digital inequality. The authors explain that community networks are essential for broadband deployment in resource-constrained areas, aligning with Oki and Lawrence's (2022) recommendation to implement a shared-cost model for fibre optic technology. Limbach et al. (2016) advocate for the utilisation of existing infrastructures to sustain these initiatives. The authors indicate that network optimisation yields synergistic results and reduces deployment costs. Research suggests that optimising network structures can decrease deployment costs in rural areas. As discussed by Henderson and Roche (2019) in their study, the implementation of broadband infrastructure faces persistent challenges, particularly in policy and regulatory frameworks. The authors assert that informed policy measures are crucial for dismantling access barriers to broadband and ensuring that rural consumers have equitable access to technological advantages. Therefore, the successful implementation of fixed broadband systems in rural Africa requires a thorough techno-economic framework that analyses capital and operational factors alongside socio-economic consequences. The integration of community engagement, shared funding models, and robust policy support will significantly enhance the deployment of broadband infrastructure, thereby promoting rural development throughout Africa.

Entrepreneurship as a Pathway to Consumer Empowerment

Although this chapter primarily emphasises the rural African consumer, it is essential to acknowledge the pivotal role of entrepreneurship in enhancing access to digital goods and services. Rural entrepreneurs frequently serve as intermediaries between rural consumers and digital goods and services, linking rural individuals who might otherwise be marginalised to mobile money services, e-commerce platforms, agricultural information systems, and localised digital applications. These entrepreneurs offer cost-effective access to digital services, connecting individuals and households who are unable to obtain them directly. Facilitating access through entrepreneurship can reduce transaction costs, mitigate market frictions, and expand consumer choice, leading to a more efficient provision of essential services and products to rural families.

Nonetheless, entrepreneurship in rural regions presents its own distinct hurdles. Rural entrepreneurs face numerous access and affordability challenges, just as the people they intend to assist do. Inadequate broadband access, inconsistent electricity supply, and high data costs constrain rural small enterprises' ability to deliver digital products and services to their clientele (GSMA, 2023). Access to financing constitutes a significant obstacle, as most rural entrepreneurs initiate ventures with minimal or no collateral or credit history, hindering their ability to secure loans from conventional financial institutions. Regulatory frameworks may be inadequate or ambiguous, resulting in confusion for small business owners and hindering innovation. Moreover, rural start-ups frequently encounter insufficient access to entrepreneurial training and mentorship, hindering their capacity to grow and commercialise digital solutions.

At the same time, it is indisputable that entrepreneurship has frequently emerged as a direct mechanism to enhance consumer empowerment. Mobile money agents exemplify this phenomenon, initiated at the grassroots level by entrepreneurs who understand the market and consumer demographics, and have facilitated creative avenues for digital financial inclusion in Africa. These grassroots agents offer a range of financial services that enable households to send and receive remittances, safely save, and access funds with greater ease and convenience. This access has enhanced financial inclusion, leading to more effective control over household expenditures and greater security for rural families. Local e-commerce start-ups have enhanced consumer access to essential commodities and agricultural inputs by enabling trade between rural and urban markets. Digital platforms linking rural consumers to health and education services have experienced notable advancement, featuring many initiatives that provide telemedicine and online learning materials (Aker & Blumenstock, 2023; Kuteesa et al., 2024). These are but a few examples of how entrepreneurship has been employed to foster social and economic resilience in rural areas.

Entrepreneurship in rural communities should be regarded not as an end in itself, but as a means to enhance consumer access and participation in the digital economy. The efficacy of rural entrepreneurship should be assessed not only through economic measures but also by its impact on the cost, relevance, and reliability of services for rural consumers. Strategies that enhance digital infrastructure, reduce entry barriers for rural entrepreneurs, and promote inclusive business models can have a cascading positive effect on consumers. Encouraging the development of women-led and youth-led enterprises can enhance consumer empowerment via entrepreneurship, as these entrepreneurs often possess a deeper understanding of the needs of underserved communities (Akinyemi & Mushunje, 2020; Sindakis & Showkat, 2024).

In conclusion, it is essential to recognise and harness entrepreneurship as a catalyst for consumer empowerment in rural areas. By redefining our perspective on entrepreneurship to encompass not only innovation and value creation but also a viable solution to the access and affordability challenges faced by rural consumers, we can more effectively align digital inclusion initiatives with the needs of these frequently marginalised groups. Rural entrepreneurship, when nurtured with consideration for rural consumers, can significantly enhance the availability, accessibility, affordability, and relevance of digital services, thereby making them more inclusive and pertinent to the communities they aim to serve.

Harnessing Digital Innovation for Rural Entrepreneurship

Digital innovation enables rural entrepreneurial ventures to compete and grow more effectively, opening new opportunities for growth (Lekhanya, 2018; Räisänen & Tuovinen, 2020). The latest developments in technology tools and capabilities have led to several research efforts examining how digitalisation affects rural entrepreneurship, with a primary focus on information and communication technology (ICT), e-commerce, and digital financial services. A study by Barnett et al. (2019) demonstrated that mobile phone and Internet usage positively affect rural entrepreneurship in China by enhancing social networking capabilities and information acquisition. The study recognised the potential reverse relationship between entrepreneurship development and ICT utilisation, while demonstrating that individuals who use mobile phones and the Internet have higher entrepreneurship rates than those who do not. Meanwhile, Tang et al.'s (2022) study showed that digital innovations help boost tourism entrepreneurship in rural areas. Technological advancements decreased innovation costs, which in turn promoted innovative behaviour and expanded entrepreneurial activities beyond traditional sectors.

Market Expansion

Digital innovation offers significant opportunities for rural entrepreneurs by enhancing market expansion capabilities. By utilising social media and e-commerce platforms, rural artisans and small-scale producers can access global markets, extending their reach beyond local boundaries and enhancing their income possibilities (Tang et al., 2022). Take, for example, China's e-commerce powerhouse, Alibaba. Alibaba demonstrates how e-commerce platforms can use digital channels to extend their market reach into rural areas through strategic approaches. Alibaba's rural expansion program establishes service centres across rural regions to help local entrepreneurs learn online sales techniques for their products and services. The management of rural service centres is often entrusted to young people from the villages, who also educate local populations about the benefits of online purchasing to those who lack sufficient knowledge or interest (Bhatia-Kalluri, 2021). According to Leong et al. (2016), rural entrepreneurs in China have successfully transformed idle resources into adaptable business opportunities through Taobao village, while connecting developing markets to global value chains. The creation of Taobao Village in rural China facilitated business start-ups among rural residents, enabling them to achieve industrial growth and agglomeration through low-cost digital innovation.

Access to Finance

According to Jalil (2021), rural entrepreneurs need access to financial resources to expand and succeed. Microenterprises primarily utilise internal funds for their operations because acquiring external funding is challenging, often leading to business failure (Fadil & St-Pierre, 2021). Owens (2013) assert that industry practitioners, alongside financial institutions, can tackle these challenges by adopting digital finance technologies to provide rural entrepreneurs with improved access to capital while meeting market consumers' growing financial needs efficiently and securely, Online payment systems represent another significant advancement in digital finance, enabling e-commerce platforms to operate smoothly and effectively (Li et al., 2020). Through digital payment services and mobile banking applications, rural businesses find it simpler to interact with customers across different regions. Payment systems that offer easy, secure transaction methods enhance consumer trust, improve customer convenience, and increase purchasing activity (Oyelami et al., 2020). The Rural and Regional Development Ministry of Malaysia initiated the Rural Entrepreneurs Digitalisation program as part of the Desamall initiative to teach rural entrepreneurs about digital innovation applications with a focus on financial digitalisation and payment gateway management (Bernama, 2024). The combination of training and real-world exposure teaches rural entrepreneurs to effectively utilise digital applications, enhancing productivity and efficiency and supporting the expansion of entrepreneurship.

Business Development and Networking

Small and medium-sized enterprises in rural areas experience better business performance when they utilise social media platforms for networking, which provides them with valuable assistance and advice (Roberts et al., 2017). Bosworth's (2012) study emphasises the importance of networking for rural entrepreneurs, as they often display strong loyalty to their rural consumers. Rural entrepreneurs utilise online business networks to establish connections between enterprises and expand their customer reach (Moyes et al., 2012). Tiwasing (2021) recognises the convenience and effectiveness of social media as a platform for networking and social connection. Research into Malaysian rural Internet centres shows that social networking applications enable rural entrepreneurs to build and strengthen their social capital (Noor et al., 2020). Popular social media platforms, such as Facebook, Instagram, and X (formerly Twitter), offer cost-effective, straightforward ways for customers to connect directly with new products, services, and brands

(Aswani et al., 2018). Rural entrepreneurs can use online reviews and feedback to understand consumer preferences, thereby tailoring their products and marketing efforts to serve a broader customer base. Those who adopt digital tools can extend their market reach and improve their position in the global marketplace. The research by Soluk et al. (2021) found that digital innovation is a key driver of entrepreneurial activity among rural residents in developing countries, such as India. Microbusiness owners employ various methods to grow their operations and adapt their business models based on their observations. Today, entrepreneurs expand their market reach by using digital platforms to sell handcrafted sarees internationally, rather than limiting sales to nearby villages and communities (Nipo et al., 2024).

Local self-help organisations taught shrimp farmers how to maintain proper pH levels in their shrimp basins, thereby boosting productivity. Digital sensor technology, combined with Internet-based applications, enables shrimp farmers to monitor the pH levels of their basins, supporting their long-term commercial shrimp farming operations. Entrepreneurial education combined with training and skills development supports the growth of rural entrepreneurial initiatives in remote, underdeveloped regions (Lekhanya, 2018). Many nations achieve economic development through entrepreneurial education, which plays a crucial role in enterprise growth and sustainability (Kalyani & Kumar, 2011). Entrepreneurs require education on smartphone and Internet usage before they can effectively utilise digital marketing tools, such as web stores, search engine optimisation, and social media. Räisänen and Tuovinen (2020) found substantial variations in digital proficiency among rural microenterprise owners, with some lacking a basic understanding of digital tools. Rural entrepreneurs can bridge the gap to digital proficiency by utilising online platforms and digital tools that provide access to numerous educational resources and training programs. Through online webinars, courses, and e-books, rural entrepreneurs can access extensive information about market trends, business management best practices, and strategies. Entrepreneurs require access to information and resources to develop their skills and abilities, enabling them to make well-informed decisions and adapt to changing market conditions (Nipo et al., 2024). Digital platforms would allow entrepreneurs to network and collaborate with researchers and industry experts. The connectedness enables rural entrepreneurs to exchange experiences, seek advice, and form partnerships that drive the development of innovative business solutions. A wider community network enhances resourcefulness and promotes collaboration, which is essential for entrepreneurial success in rural settings (Moss et al., 2022).

Barriers to the Adoption of Digital Innovation in Rural Entrepreneurship

Studies on the adoption of digital innovation by rural entrepreneurs indicate that their demand for support and resources exceeds that of their urban counterparts (Fanelli, 2021). Alabdali et al. (2023) identify three primary barriers to advanced digital transformation in rural entrepreneurship: inadequate infrastructure, resistance to change, and a lack of knowledge and skills in adopting digital technologies. Rural areas in Malaysia face significant challenges in adopting digital technology, with only 32% of rural small businesses utilising digital tools, compared to over 60% in urban regions (Economic Planning Unit, 2021). Research highlights three primary barriers to digital adoption among rural entrepreneurs: limited access to technological infrastructure (Morris et al., 2022; Rosnan & Yusof, 2023), resistance to change stemming from digital literacy issues (Alabdali et al., 2023; Fanelli, 2021; Ismail et al., 2023), and insufficient regulatory and institutional support systems (Rosnan & Yusof, 2023).

Barriers in Technological Infrastructure

The main barrier to the adoption of digital innovation in rural enterprises is inadequate infrastructure. Studies show that rural entrepreneurs face significant challenges in adopting digital technologies due to unreliable internet connectivity and inconsistent power supplies (Ferrari et al., 2022; Rani et al., 2022). Inadequate infrastructure hinders the effective implementation of digital technologies essential to contemporary business operations, disrupting daily routine activities. Studies indicate that rural regions in developing countries encounter difficulties with internet connectivity, which restricts their ability to engage in digital entrepreneurship (Morris et al., 2022; Rosnan & Yusof, 2023).

Socio-Cultural Barriers

Prior studies indicate a strong relationship between entrepreneurs' attitudes in rural regions and their adoption of digital technologies. Research by Fahmi and Savira (2023) demonstrates that business owners with positive attitudes towards digital technology are more likely to adopt information and communication technology (ICT) solutions. Nipo et al. (2024) indicate that enhanced owner attitudes correlate with increased ICT adoption. The challenges rural entrepreneurs face in adopting digital tools are exacerbated by their reluctance, rooted in insufficient digital literacy and a general distrust of technology. Previous studies indicate that entrepreneurs with inadequate knowledge and experience in digital technology tend to exhibit low engagement in digital innovation activities. Rural entrepreneurs exhibit considerable resistance to adopting digital innovations, stemming from scepticism towards digital technologies, concerns regarding fraud and privacy, mistrust of unfamiliar systems, and inadequate digital literacy skills (Ramdani et al., 2021). The resistance to digital innovation increases due to insufficient training and support, which are crucial for dismantling digital literacy barriers and fostering technology adoption. Fahmi and Savira (2023) conducted research on rural entrepreneurs in South Indonesia, indicating that small businesses adopt digital innovation more when the owner-manager or founder understands the potential benefits of digital technology. Räisänen and Tuovinen (2020) demonstrate that the workshop method effectively disseminated information among rural micro-entrepreneurs, fostering a positive perception of digital innovations and facilitating their planning.

Regulatory and Institutional Constraints

According to Ferrari et al. (2022), entrepreneurs in rural areas with limited local policy support, including financial and technical incentives, are less likely to implement digital innovations in their businesses successfully. Existing regulatory frameworks do not adequately address the needs of rural entrepreneurs, resulting in ineffective policy measures and insufficient support (Rani et al., 2022). Multiple studies investigating the digital transition in SMEs have identified government assistance as a crucial factor in digital adoption, facilitated by digital capital incentives and sponsorship (Saruchera & Mpunzi, 2023). According to the Economic Planning Unit (2021), rural entrepreneurs face challenges in accessing government programs for digital adoption, primarily due to the complexity of application processes and inadequate local infrastructure support. The disparity between governmental policy intentions and the practical needs of rural entrepreneurs highlights the need for more precisely targeted policy interventions. Fanelli (2021) argues that rural enterprises necessitate tailored regulatory frameworks to implement digital innovations, thereby addressing the digital divide and fostering inclusive digital development. The integration of governmental and community support yields favourable results for digital transformation initiatives that include cognitive training and psychological support mechanisms (Geng et al., 2023; Thomas, 2023). Addressing the challenges to digital innovation adoption in rural entrepreneurship requires a focus on both technological and economic obstacles, as well as social factors such as knowledge, experience, training, education, and motivation, alongside institutional support mechanisms. Institutional support encompasses managerial endorsement and financial aid. Entrepreneurs' networks and government support can bridge the digital access divide, and rural entrepreneurship can generate new opportunities, enhance operational efficiency, and stimulate innovation in rural regions. Malaysia aims to lead the regional digital economy. Addressing these challenges is essential to ensure that the benefits of digital transformation are equitably distributed between urban and rural communities (Economic Planning Unit, 2021).

Challenges in Scaling Digital Innovation for Rural Entrepreneurship

Rural entrepreneurship promotes inclusive development by generating employment opportunities across diverse rural economic sectors. Greenberg et al. (2018) postulate that rural development activities contribute to economic growth, thereby enhancing the quality of life in the areas. Businesses in rural areas, characterised by lower population density, frequently face challenges due to insufficient infrastructure. Rural areas face significant challenges in achieving digital transformation, primarily due to limited technological resources and expertise (George, 2023).

Technological Knowledge and Expertise

Rural consumers face numerous challenges in integrating digital innovation. Digital solutions should be able to expand and adapt to meet heightened business demands (Bharadwaj et al., 2013; Ravichandran, 2018). Scaling presents a significant challenge in the absence of adequate technological knowledge, as it requires comprehensive planning and execution. Davenport (2005) asserts that technical knowledge enables organisations to enhance their infrastructure for improved data management, facilitating the implementation of new features without disrupting existing systems and ensuring system performance during periods of high demand. Addressing potential bottlenecks while optimising resources and ensuring data integrity during system expansion involves complex challenges that require a thorough understanding of the technology system and its limitations. Teece's (2018) research suggests that businesses lacking this knowledge are likely to experience operational inefficiencies and increased costs, potentially leading to system failures and hindering their capacity for expansion and innovation.

Financial Limitations

Financial considerations in digital transformation are critical, as they encompass challenges and decisions that shape the potential for positive investment outcomes. Businesses should initiate significant investments in new technologies, infrastructure enhancements, and personnel training. Entrepreneurs in rural areas often face significant financial challenges due to limited resources and the daily expenses required to maintain their infrastructure (Patel & Chavda, 2013). Companies may face budget overruns and financial instability due to mismanagement or underestimation of related costs. Ijomah et al. (2024) discusses the challenges small and medium enterprises in rural areas face in projecting returns from digital initiatives. These enterprises must anticipate long-term benefits amid rapidly changing technological landscapes and market dynamics. Comprehensive financial planning is essential for budget management, while ongoing cost–benefit analysis is crucial for effectively overseeing the intricate financial aspects of digital transformation.

Identification of Skill Gaps and Training Requirements

The absence of technical expertise represents a significant barrier to digital transformation, largely due to existing skill gaps and the need for necessary training. Räisänen and Tuovinen (2020) demonstrate that deficiencies in basic digital literacy among most rural entrepreneurs hinder the successful adoption and utilisation of new technologies. The implementation and management of digital systems require comprehensive training programs because there is a shortage of personnel with advanced technical skills for these tasks. As noted by Iwasaki (2023), businesses must engage in continuous upskilling to stay current with the latest digital tools and processes. To sustain a constant learning curve, companies must allocate resources towards workforce development, enabling employees to effectively leverage digital innovations. Tosheva (2020) cautions that rural enterprises may forfeit the advantages of digital transformation and experience competitive disadvantages if comprehensive training initiatives do not address their skill deficiencies.

Compliance with Regulations and Government Policies

Digital transformation presents a significant challenge for rural entrepreneurs, who must navigate compliance with standards and government policies while ensuring their digital operations align with relevant legal frameworks. The framework outlined by Chukwurah et al. (2024) requires businesses to understand data privacy laws, cybersecurity requirements, and industry-specific standards, which exhibit considerable variation across regions and sectors. Organisations must continuously monitor and adapt their operations to ensure compliance with evolving regulations, which often require specialised legal and technical expertise. Government policies play a dual role in digital transformation, offering financial and infrastructure support through favourable provisions while also imposing additional costs through stringent regulations (Bürer et al., 2022; George, 2023). Rural entrepreneurs must ensure compliance with government regulations and industry standards in their digital initiatives to avoid legal issues and operational challenges while safeguarding their reputations. Rural entrepreneurship faces considerable obstacles in adopting digital technologies, which are essential for enhancing business operations, facilitating market access, and driving economic growth through digital transformation. This process must address specific issues, including insufficient infrastructure, a lack of technical expertise, and slow internet connectivity, to effectively implement digital solutions. Rural entrepreneurs face challenges stemming from limited financial resources, regulatory requirements, and a lack of understanding of the benefits of digital innovation. Rural entrepreneurs require targeted support to address these challenges, which includes government financial incentives or subsidies, community training programs, partnerships with technology firms, and enhanced investments in rural infrastructure. Meeting these specific needs will enable rural businesses to harness digital innovation, resulting in sustainable growth and competitive advantages within rural areas and their communities.

Overcoming Barriers to Digital Innovation for Rural Entrepreneurship

Rural entrepreneurs face various challenges in their attempts to utilise digital technologies. An effective resolution of these challenges necessitates a strategic approach. The strategy emphasises investments in technology and infrastructure, alongside the promotion of digital literacy and financial assistance, and the establishment of robust policies and regulatory frameworks to facilitate digital innovation. These strategic initiatives enable rural consumers to bridge the digital divide, thereby allowing them to fully leverage the digital economy for sustainable economic growth.

Improving Digital Infrastructure

Rural entrepreneurs require enhanced digital infrastructure to effectively compete in the digital economy and address the digital divide. These strategies emphasise improving connectivity alongside service quality and the efficient utilisation of digital technologies to reduce obstacles and challenges. Improvements in digital infrastructure address connectivity issues and mitigate economic disparities. Enhanced digital infrastructure enables rural business owners to participate more effectively in the digital economy. Rural business owners' participation in the digital economy enhances economic opportunities, promotes job creation, and reinforces community development. Improving digital infrastructure primarily requires expanding internet access coverage, as this is the most crucial step towards advancement (García-Mora & Mora-Rivera, 2023). Telecommunications providers must collaborate with governments to ensure rural areas are not neglected. A thorough evaluation of rural regions is crucial to identify areas with inadequate internet connectivity. Service providers and policymakers should focus their attention on these areas.

This chapter primarily focuses on rural African customers; however, it offers valuable analogies and insights from consumer experiences in Asia. Sindakis and Showkat (2024) provides insights into India's rural digital initiatives, demonstrating that a dual strategy combining government-driven broadband infrastructure development with community-oriented digital literacy programs can promote the adoption of mobile banking and e-commerce solutions in rural areas. The "BharatNet" initiative in India aims to eliminate the rural digital divide and stimulate economic development by providing high-speed Internet access to isolated villages (Sindakis & Showkat, 2024). Although the emphasis is on India, the rural adoption tactics discussed reflect the issues and possible solutions in rural Africa. India's model emphasises the necessity for infrastructure development to be accompanied by digital skills training and community awareness initiatives to address trust and literacy obstacles (GSMA, 2023; Kuteesa et al., 2024). A case study from Malaysia, as noted by Pan and Mo (2024), examines rural broadband efforts characterised by public–private partnerships and targeted incentives. These initiatives have been crucial in enhancing connections to regions previously considered commercially impractical due to sparse populations and high implementation costs (Pan & Mo, 2024). Similar physical and economic barriers to private-sector investment are prevalent across Africa (International Telecommunication Union, 2023; World Bank, 2023). These Asian case studies are not intended as direct blueprints for Africa, as each region has distinct socio-economic and infrastructural circumstances. They offer illustrative examples of solutions, such as community-driven digital literacy programs, infrastructure co-investment models, and targeted affordability interventions, that have been tested and tailored to the local settings in Asia. African governments, in their pursuit of inclusive digital development, may utilise these lessons to create interventions that are contextually relevant and internationally informed, thereby empowering rural consumers in Africa to engage with the digital economy (Aker & Blumenstock, 2023).

In addition to improved network coverage, rural areas require faster, more reliable internet to effectively utilise digital technologies (Ford et al., 2023). Various applications, including online learning platforms, telehealth services, and effective business operations, necessitate high-speed

Internet access. The installation of fibre-optic cables improves infrastructure capabilities and provides superior speed and reliability compared to traditional copper line connections (Briglauer et al., 2024). Government funding can support the construction of rural broadband infrastructure. Increased competition among internet service providers (ISPs) leads to improvements in service quality and lower prices. The South Korean government has promoted competition among Internet service providers, enabling rural populations to access fast internet connections at affordable prices (Lee et al., 2023). Rural entrepreneurs should establish digital marketplaces and platforms to expand their customer base and increase revenue opportunities (Heeks et al., 2021). Private enterprises should collaborate with government entities to establish digital marketplaces that meet the needs of rural businesses. The Thai government has established a "Smart Digital Hub" to support rural farmers and artisans in promoting their products online, thereby expanding their customer base and business reach (Iwasaki, 2023).

Developing Digital Literacy and Competencies

Rural consumers require digital skills to utilise digital tools and technologies effectively, independent of their access to high-speed internet. Rural business owners require additional resources beyond digital infrastructure to thrive in the digital economy. The effective utilisation of digital tools and technologies is crucial for optimising the advantages of digital innovations (Freeman et al., 2020; Liu et al., 2020). Digital literacy encompasses the competencies required to create and manage online retail platforms, utilise social media for marketing, and implement digital payment systems. Digital literacy enhances business productivity by facilitating smoother operations, improving communication, and enabling the automation of tasks. This system enables entrepreneurs to strengthen business management by automating manual tasks and increasing overall efficiency. Digital tools facilitate the optimisation of supply chain operations, real-time inventory monitoring, and enhanced customer relationship management for entrepreneurs. Rural entrepreneurs must acquire proficiency in digital tools and technologies to maximise the advantages of widespread coverage and high-speed internet access.

Rural entrepreneurs require additional resources beyond digital infrastructure to succeed in the digital economy. As noted by Nikou and Aavakare (2021), to optimise technological advancements, entrepreneurs require digital literacy, defined as the capacity to utilise digital tools and technologies effectively. Digital literacies encompass managing customer markets, handling business relationships, developing marketing strategies, managing cybersecurity, and accessing online financial support and programs. Business owners with digital literacy skills can access resources and information to stay informed about consumer preferences, market trends, and emerging business opportunities. Digital literacy empowers entrepreneurs to conduct competitive analyses and acquire market research, thereby facilitating data-driven decision-making (Liu et al., 2020). Effective business planning relies on obtaining information to meet the dynamic demands of the market. Business owners proficient in digital tools can adopt strategies such as digital marketing campaigns, smartphone applications, and e-commerce platforms to expand customer reach and maintain a competitive edge. The effective use of digital tools enhances networking and collaboration, enabling business owners to establish vital alliances and professional relationships. A thorough understanding of digital security is essential for safeguarding business information and transactions against online threats (Thakur, 2024). Business owners must implement best practices to safeguard their online presence, including data encryption, the use of strong passwords, and regular software updates to mitigate security vulnerabilities.

According to Chohan and Hu (2022), digital literacy facilitates the utilisation of online financial services and government programs. Business owners knowledgeable in digital processes can submit online applications for financial support, thereby streamlining the application process and increasing funding success rates. Rural business owners who employ digital literacy will navigate the digital landscape more effectively, thereby enhancing their companies' competitiveness and resilience in the rapidly evolving digital economy. Collaboration between governments and academic institutions can facilitate the delivery of digital literacy training through community centres, schools, and non-governmental organisations. PMGDISHA is a component of India's Digital India initiative that aims to deliver digital literacy training to rural households (Sivakumar, 2018). The eUsahawan program in Malaysia offers online courses focused on social media management, digital marketing, and e-commerce fundamentals, designed to help rural entrepreneurs enhance their digital presence and expand their market reach (Holroyd, 2019). Specialised training programs, along with coaching and mentoring, provide personalised support, while online learning platforms facilitate ongoing skill development. Several Asian nations have implemented programs to enhance digital literacy among rural consumers. Google collaborates with Vietnam's "Digital 4.0" initiative to provide complimentary training in digital marketing and online business strategies for small and medium-sized enterprises (SMEs). The Digital Economy Promotion Agency (DEPA) of Thailand offers training in digital marketing, e-commerce, and data analytics to rural businesses. The a2i (Access to Information) program in Bangladesh employs Digital Centres to provide practical training for rural entrepreneurs (Dolar Kar et al., 2020). Implementing these strategies allows stakeholders to assist rural entrepreneurs in overcoming challenges while efficiently utilising digital technologies.

Financial Support and Capital Accessibility

Improvements in digital infrastructure and literacy must be accompanied by financial support to enable rural entrepreneurs to fully leverage digital innovations. Insufficient financial resources hinder rural entrepreneurs from obtaining essential digital tools and infrastructure (Freeman et al., 2020). Rural enterprises face financial challenges in acquiring the necessary digital technology, including computers and high-speed internet, due to insufficient funding (Räisänen & Tuovinen, 2020). The ongoing expenses associated with maintaining and upgrading digital marketing will persist as a financial burden for rural business owners, even with access to certain digital tools. Ongoing financial pressures impose constraints on businesses with restricted budgets, complicating the sustainability of long-term digital innovation efforts. Financial aid is essential for overcoming these challenges and barriers. Assistance programs may partially subsidise initial implementation costs for digital technology. Government grants and subsidies help companies overcome financial obstacles related to acquiring essential digital tools (Chen et al., 2021). Grants are utilised for the development of e-commerce platforms, enhancements to internet infrastructure, and the acquisition of digital devices. As noted by Khai et al. (2020), the Malaysian government has facilitated the digitalisation of rural businesses via initiatives such as the SME Digitalisation Grant. Digital projects necessitate financial backing to sustain operations after the initial funding period. Subsidies for internet access and digital marketing services enable rural business owners to maintain and enhance their online presence by lowering ongoing operating expenses. Microfinance funds are essential financial resources for rural enterprise operations (Jalil, 2021; Rasheed et al., 2019). Business owners may secure small loans under favourable conditions through these initiatives to invest in digital technologies and infrastructure. Grameen Bank's lending activities have facilitated access to digital technology for rural entrepreneurs in Bangladesh, enabling business growth (Kandie & Islam, 2022).

Simplifying Digital Regulations

The need for restructuring digital regulations is as critical as financial support, infrastructure enhancements, and the advancement of digital literacy. Government efforts to reduce bureaucratic burdens may stimulate digital entrepreneurship and innovation in rural areas (Ajayi-Nifise et al., 2024). Streamlining digital business regulations fosters a conducive business environment essential for rural areas. Enterprises located in remote regions, which often lack sufficient regulatory guidance, encounter bureaucratic obstacles that hinder their ability to establish and sustain digital businesses effectively. Simplified digital regulations enable entrepreneurs to allocate more time to business activities, rather than navigating complex regulatory systems. Streamlined regulations facilitate the initiation and management of businesses by entrepreneurs. This strategy facilitates rural economic development by strengthening digital infrastructure, expanding literacy programs, and supporting funding initiatives. Indonesia implemented the "Omnibus Law" to strengthen investment and entrepreneurship by standardising legal frameworks, including regulations for digital businesses (Nipo et al., 2024; Novadina, 2024).

Digital Inclusive Finance (DIF) in Rural Africa

Over the past decade, digital inclusive finance (DIF) has emerged as a transformative force across rural Africa. Defined as the provision of accessible, affordable, and secure financial services through digital technologies, DIF holds the promise of bridging the financial divide between urban centres and remote, often marginalised, rural consumers. It leverages tools such as mobile money platforms, digital banking applications, and e-wallets to bring financial services closer to populations historically excluded from formal banking systems. From enabling farmers to access microloans to empowering women entrepreneurs, DIF has catalysed socio-economic inclusion and supported grassroots development. Its potential has been recognised not only for alleviating poverty but also for driving intra-African trade, expanding the tax base, and fostering long-term resilience.

Digital inclusive finance (DIF) in rural Africa has, over time, proven to be a sustainable force in financial transformation by bridging economic access gaps for those previously underserved by financial services. The widespread adoption of financial products, such as mobile money and digital banking, has significant potential to reduce poverty and promote economic empowerment (Mwakalila & Kasongwa, 2024). The rapid growth and proliferation of these services have the potential to accelerate intra-African trade and payments (World Bank, 2023). This financial inclusion addresses gaps in financial services in rural areas by utilising digital technologies, which are key to making services accessible to all, regardless of economic status. Rural areas pose their unique challenges, characterised by geographic remoteness, low population density, and limited infrastructure. These factors, combined with others, result in the exclusion of the rural population from financial systems (Sustainability Directory, 2025).

DIF has been successful in reaching and creating opportunities for women, the poor, and those historically excluded from financial services. Digital banking enables rural consumers to engage in secure transactions, access microcredit, and save (Home Pride Bank, 2025). Despite these advancements, large areas of underserved and unreached rural regions persist due to the high cost of technical support and maintenance (Eton et al., 2025). Hence, there must be policies that focus on digital infrastructure, especially in rural areas, to address the limited access to technology and digital literacy, thereby helping consumers build trust in digital finance (Azeez et al., 2025). Access to previously inaccessible financial products, such as microcredit, small loans, and savings, has empowered farmers to purchase equipment, fertilisers, and other essentials, thereby increasing productivity and incomes. With access to this financing, entrepreneurs in rural areas can expand their business reach, create local jobs, and foster economic growth in their respective communities (Microfinancing Partners in Africa, 2023). Being able to save digitally comes with ease, making consistency easier; this provides rural households with the backdrop to grow financial resilience, help cope with emergencies, and break cycles of poverty (Sustainability Directory, 2025).

Government spending on these infrastructure developments would serve dual purposes: on the one hand, increasing digital financial inclusion, and on the other, providing an opportunity to broaden the tax base and increase revenue collection. By bringing in an increased portion of the rural population, who mainly operate in the informal economy, into the traceable digital transactions, the government would be able to capture financial activities that were previously outside the tax net, through the use of digital IDs, these IDs help in taxpayer identification, efficient filing and increased compliance (International Centre for Tax and Development, 2024). However, caution should be exercised; while these taxes aim to improve government revenue, concerns exist that they may hurt rural areas that heavily rely on these financial services, thereby encouraging a return to cash-based transactions and reversing the gains made in financial inclusion (UNCDF, 2022). DFI holds immense promise to foster social and economic development in rural Africa. A holistic approach that combines investment in technology, targeted policy interventions, and ongoing education on digital literacy is crucial for harnessing the full potential of digital finance.

Nevertheless, digital inclusive finance (DIF) is transforming the financial landscape for rural consumers. It addresses rural financial exclusion by enhancing residents' access to essential credit, savings, and insurance services (Wang & Fu, 2021). The integration of digital technology into financial services enables rural populations to overcome the barriers posed by traditional banking systems. Ma et al. (2025) suggest that providing financial services to remote areas increases income levels and enhances economic resilience among vulnerable populations. Enhanced access to financial services facilitates regular transactions and fosters business development, thereby contributing to the expansion of rural economies. Nonetheless, disparities continue to exist. Research indicates that DIF enhances household income and consumption patterns in rural areas; however, the effects differ significantly based on local development conditions. Digital financial inclusion projects yield more significant outcomes in areas with greater access to education and economic resources, suggesting that equitable access to technology and educational opportunities is crucial for optimising the impact of digital financial inclusion (Yi et al., 2024). A significant challenge remains in ensuring that digital financial services effectively reach marginalised rural populations, rather than inadvertently benefiting individuals who are already financially secure (Liu et al., 2023). Policymakers should collaborate with local governments and community organisations to develop frameworks that enhance access to technology and improve digital literacy among rural consumers. These initiatives will enhance rural economies by improving infrastructure and education, thereby fostering equitable growth in the digital era.

The Promise and Progress of DIF

The widespread adoption of mobile financial services has been a game-changer for many rural African consumers. Initiatives such as M-Pesa in Kenya and similar models in Tanzania and Rwanda have significantly increased access to savings, credit, and insurance for those previously excluded. Scholars like Mwakalila and Kasongwa (2024) argue that the proliferation of digital finance platforms can accelerate poverty reduction and promote inclusive economic empowerment. The World Bank (2023) has also emphasised the value of DIF in supporting intra-African trade by facilitating seamless cross-border payments. Such innovations not only enhance business efficiencies but also integrate fragmented rural markets into broader regional economies. Yet, despite these advancements, rural Africa still faces significant barriers. Geographic isolation, inadequate digital infrastructure, and low literacy rates persist as significant challenges (Sustainability Directory, 2025). Many rural areas are underserved or entirely excluded due to the high costs of technical support and limited market incentives for financial institutions.

Financial Inclusion and Rural Empowerment

One of the most remarkable outcomes of DIF is its ability to extend financial services to women, smallholder farmers, and informal entrepreneurs—groups that formal financial systems have traditionally sidelined. Digital finance enables rural users to conduct secure transactions, access micro-credit facilities, and build savings (Home Pride Bank, 2025). These services have practical economic impacts. Small loans and savings options have enabled farmers to invest in fertilisers, equipment, and improved seeds, resulting in increased yields and higher incomes. Meanwhile, entrepreneurs can expand their businesses, create jobs, and contribute to local economies (Microfinancing Partners in Africa, 2023). Equally important is the financial resilience that digital savings mechanisms foster. Access to secure, convenient savings platforms enables rural households to manage risks, respond to emergencies, and plan for future needs, thereby breaking the cycle of vulnerability and poverty.

Infrastructure, Trust, and Policy Support

Despite these benefits, gaps in infrastructure and digital literacy continue to limit DIF's reach and effectiveness. The high cost of digital infrastructure in remote areas discourages investment, while limited education restricts consumers' ability to navigate financial technologies confidently (Azeez et al., 2025). Governments must therefore prioritise investment in rural digital infrastructure. Expanding network coverage, improving electricity access, and investing in affordable devices are essential components. Moreover, fostering trust in digital systems through financial education campaigns and user-friendly platforms will be key to sustained adoption. There are also implications for government revenue. As digital financial services expand, they offer a pathway to formalising informal economies. Through digital IDs and traceable transactions, tax systems can capture previously untaxed income, potentially broadening the tax base (International Centre for Tax and Development, 2024). However, policymakers must balance this opportunity with the risk of overburdening low-income users. Imposing digital transaction taxes in fragile rural economies could deter adoption and reinforce a reliance on cash-based systems (UNCDF, 2022).

DIF, Economic Resilience, and Local Variation

A growing body of research affirms that DIF contributes to income growth and economic resilience among rural populations. Studies by Ma et al. (2025) highlight the role of digital finance in boosting household incomes and fostering entrepreneurial activity. However, these impacts are not uniform. The extent to which DIF enhances livelihoods varies depending on local infrastructure, education levels, and economic opportunities (Yi et al., 2024). This indicates a need for place-sensitive policy frameworks that account for these disparities and ensure that digital finance reaches the most marginalised. Digital Inclusive Finance (DIF), economic resilience, and local variation are closely linked, particularly for regional development and planning. Digital Inclusive Finance enhances local economic resilience by increasing the accessibility of financial services through digital means. The economic volatility stemming from events such as the 2008 financial crisis and the COVID-19 pandemic makes this connection increasingly vital for regional navigation. Regions exhibiting robust DIF have enhanced capacity to cultivate economic resilience, as evidenced by empirical studies. The research by Sun et al. illustrates how DIF enhances local economic stability by improving financial accessibility for micro and small enterprises (MSMEs). Sun et al. (2024) demonstrate how DIF fortifies local economic stability by improving access to financial resources for MSMEs, which serve as essential catalysts for employment and innovation in local markets. Li et al. (2021) demonstrate that DIF methods enhance financial inclusion, thereby fostering economic growth and promoting green economic practices through access to green funding. The twin benefits of DIF illustrate its strategic role in enhancing economic resilience against external economic disruptions.

Giannakis and Papadas' research reveals notable regional disparities in economic resilience across Europe (Giannakis & Papadas, 2021). Research findings indicate that local development outcomes are profoundly influenced by national economic trends, as a substantial portion of economic productivity variability at the NUTS-3 level stems from national factors. Zhang et al. demonstrate that the geographical and temporal attributes of urban economic resilience in China suggest that local conditions and infrastructure significantly influence resilience capability (Jie et al., 2023; Zhang et al., 2023). Choei et al. (2020) propose that municipal planning practices can enhance the delivery of public goods by utilising DIF solutions that mitigate system inefficiencies. Lee and Wang's (2022) research advocates for municipalities to adopt tailored initiatives to address disparities in intra-regional resilience, thereby promoting equitable economic recovery following the Great Recession (Lee & Wang, 2022).

Formulating sustainable resilience policies requires a comprehensive awareness of local disparities. Oprişan et al. (2023) demonstrate that understanding variations in economic resilience among counties facilitates the identification of risks and opportunities, thereby enhancing the effectiveness of resource allocation. Numerous investigative studies indicate that successful governance frameworks must endorse localised approaches to create sustainable resilience mechanisms, as noted by Latif et al. (2023). The relationship between Digital Inclusive Finance and economic resilience, along with regional disparities, underscores the need for policies tailored to regional needs. Regions seeking to develop economic resilience must integrate Digital Inclusive Finance with comprehensive planning and governance frameworks to attain sustainable growth.

Therefore, digital inclusive finance is not just a tool—it is a strategic pillar for rural revitalisation in Africa. It empowers marginalised populations, strengthens local economies, and integrates the rural poor into the national and continental financial ecosystems. Nonetheless, its potential will only be fully realised through deliberate, inclusive, and context-sensitive interventions. The road ahead requires collaboration between governments, financial institutions, technology providers, and rural consumers. With the right investments in infrastructure, education, and innovation, DIF can become a cornerstone of sustainable development across rural Africa.

Conclusion

Digital inclusion has the potential to serve as a paramount empowerment tool for African consumers, many of whom have been systematically marginalised from fully engaging in the digital economy. This chapter has highlighted the substantial obstacles faced by African customers, particularly in rural areas, including insufficient infrastructure, inconsistent electricity supply, affordability concerns, limited digital literacy, and enduring gender disparities. It has also emphasised emerging prospects, such as mobile money platforms, e-commerce access, digital education initiatives, and community-based broadband solutions, which illustrate the potential benefits of inclusive digital systems.

The chapter emphasises the need to reconceptualise entrepreneurship as a means of consumer empowerment. Entrepreneurship is pivotal to the discourse on empowering rural African consumers, as entrepreneurs provide the financial, economic, and educational services essential for consumers to access digital technology and markets. Consequently, entrepreneurship should not be perceived as an end in itself, but rather as a mechanism that helps customers overcome the obstacles of distance, cost, and trust. Focusing on the rural African customer is crucial for ensuring that the chapter's argument remains aligned with the needs of policy and investment end-users in the entrepreneurship sector.

Moreover, the chapter has contextualised the discourse on digital inclusion in reference to the United Nations Sustainable Development Goals

(SDGs). Access to financial technologies advances the objectives of SDG 1 (No Poverty) by enabling households to augment their income and enhance their resilience; the integration of ICT in educational institutions and community centres is a method to fulfil SDG 4 (Quality Education); addressing the digital gender gap would facilitate progress towards SDG 5 (Gender Equality); digital platforms that create economic opportunities and foster innovation could aid in realising SDG 8 (Decent Work and Economic Growth) and SDG 9 (Industry, Innovation, and Infrastructure). This establishes that digital inclusion is a fundamental component of sustainable development.

The issue of digital inclusion presents both practical and policy challenges, while also offering an opportunity to gain insights from African contexts and other nations and regions. This chapter on digital inclusion and the empowerment of African consumers offers new insights into the interests and experiences of people marginalised within our economic and social systems.

In summary, advancing digital inclusion for rural African consumers requires a comprehensive strategy that encompasses infrastructure investment, affordability policies, digital literacy programs, and measures to address gender disparities. This approach must be integrated into local communities, formulated through active engagement, and aligned with global development objectives. With appropriate dedication and coherence, the advantages of digital inclusion will transcend mere connectivity, enhancing the sustainable livelihoods of consumers, fortifying resilient households, and invigorating rural African economies.

References

Ajayi-Nifise, A. O., Tula, S. T., Asuzu, O. F., Mhlongo, N. Z., Olatoye, F. O., & Ibeh, C. V. (2024). The role of government policy in fostering entrepreneurship: A USA and Africa review. *International Journal of Management & Entrepreneurship Research, 6*(2), 352–367. https://doi.org/10.51594/ijmer.v6i2.775

Aker, J. C., & Blumenstock, J. E. (2023). *Connectivity and consumption: Mobile access in African markets*. Review of Development Economics.

Aker, J. C., Blumenstock, J. E., & Dillon, B. (2021). Mobile technology and rural markets in Africa. *Journal of Development Economics, 152*, Article 102681.

Akinyemi, B., & Mushunje, A. (2020). Determinants of mobile money technology adoption in rural areas of Africa. *Cogent Social Sciences, 6*(1). https://doi.org/10.1080/23311886.2020.1815963

Alabdali, S. A., Pileggi, S. F., & Cetindamar, D. (2023). Influential factors, enablers, and barriers to adopting Smart Technology in rural regions: A literature review. *Sustainability, 15*(10), 7908. https://doi.org/10.3390/su15107908

Aswani, R., Kar, A. K., Ilavarasan, P. V., & Dwivedi, Y. K. (2018). Search engine marketing is not all gold: Insights from Twitter and SEOClerks. *International Journal of Information Management, 38*(1), 107–116. https://doi.org/10.1016/j.ijinfomgt.2017.07.005

Azeez, O. K., Yu, P., & Sesay, B. (2025). The role of digital trade and technological advancements in shaping financial resilience in Sub-Saharan Africa. *Sustainability*, 1–29.

Barnett, W. A., Hu, M., & Wang, X. (2019). Does the utilisation of information communication technology promote entrepreneurship? Evidence from rural China. *Technological Forecasting and Social Change, 141*, 12–21. https://doi.org/10.1016/j.techfore.2019.01.007

Bernama. (2024, February 26). KKDW allocates RM1.7 million to help rural entrepreneurs to master digitalisation. *Bernama*. https://www.bernama.com/en/news.php?id=2273615

Bharadwaj, A., El Sawy, O. A., Pavlou, P. A., & Venkatraman, N. V. (2013). Digital business strategy: Toward a next generation of insights. *MIS Quarterly*, 471–482. https://doi.org/10.25300/MISQ/2013/37:2.3

Bhatia-Kalluri, A. (2021). *E-commerce for rural micro-entrepreneurs: Mapping restrictions, ecologies of use and trends for development*. Proceedings of the 1st Virtual Conference on Implications of Information and Digital Technologies for Development. https://doi.org/10.48550/arXiv.2108.09759

Bosworth, G. (2012). Characterising rural businesses—Tales from the paperman. *Journal of Rural Studies, 28*(4), 499–506. https://doi.org/10.1016/j.jrurstud.2012.07.002

Briglauer, W., Krämer, J., & Palan, N. (2024). Socioeconomic benefits of high-speed broadband availability and service adoption: A survey. *Telecommunications Policy, 48*(7), Article 102808. https://doi.org/10.1016/j.telpol.2024.102808

Bürer, M. J., de Lapparent, M., Capezzali, M., & Carpita, M. (2022). Governance drivers and barriers for business model transformation in the energy sector. In *Swiss energy governance: Political, economic and legal challenges and opportunities in the energy transition* (pp. 195–243). https://doi.org/10.1007/978-3-030- 80787–0_10

Chen, C. L., Lin, Y. C., Chen, W. H., Chao, C. F., & Pandia, H. (2021). Role of the government to enhance digital transformation in small service businesses. *Sustainability, 13*(3), 1–26. https://doi.org/10.3390/su13031028

Choei, N., Kim, H., & Kim, S. (2020). Improving infrastructure installation planning processes using procedural modelling. *Land, 9*(2), 48. https://doi.org/10.3390/land9020048

Chohan, S. R., & Hu, G. (2022). Strengthening digital inclusion through e-government: Cohesive ICT training programs to intensify digital competency. *Information Technology for Development, 28*(1), 16–38. https://doi.org/10.1080/02681102.2020.1841713

Chukwurah, N., Ige, A. B., Adebayo, V. I., & Eyieyien, O. G. (2024). Frameworks for effective data governance: best practices, challenges, and implementation strategies across industries. *Computer Science & IT Research Journal, 5*(7), 1666–1679. https://doi.org/10.51594/csitrj.v5i7.1351

Davenport, T. H. (2005). *Thinking for a living: how to get better performances and results from knowledge workers*. Harvard Business Press.

Dolar Kar, T. M. R., Islam, N., & Gani, M. O. (2020). Leveraging the youth to a sustainable development: A case study on A2i Innovation Lab. *Thu Dau Mot University Journal of Science, 2*(4), 373–388. https://doi.org/10.37550/tdmu.EJS/2020.04.082

Donner, J., & Tewari, A. (2022). The relationship between internet access and customer trust remains a significant concern among low-income market segments. *Information Technology for Development, 28*(1), 1–16.

Economic Planning Unit. (2021). *Malaysia digital economy blueprint*. Perpustakaan Negara Malaysia.

Eton, M., et al. (2025). Exploring the effect of digital finance on financial inclusion in Uganda, a reflection from Lira City. *Journal of Electronic Business and Digital Economics, 4*(1), 183–199.

Fadil, N., & St-Pierre, J. (2021). Growing SMEs and internal financing: The role of business practices. *Journal of Small Business and Enterprise Development, 28*(7), 973–994. https://doi.org/10.1108/JSBED-11-2019-0375

Fahmi, F. Z., & Savira, M. (2023). Digitalisation and rural entrepreneurial attitude in Indonesia: A capability approach. *Journal of Enterprising Communities: People and Places in the Global Economy, 17*(2), 454–478. https://doi.org/10.1108/JEC-06-2021-0082

Fanelli, R. M. (2021). Barriers to adopting new technologies within rural small and medium enterprises (SMEs). *Social Sciences, 10*(11), 430. https://doi.org/10.3390/socsci10110430

Ferrari, A., Bacco, M., Gaber, K., Jedlitschka, A., Hess, S., Kaipanen, J., Koltsida, P., Brunori, G., et al. (2022). Drivers, barriers, and impacts of digitalisation in rural areas from the viewpoint of experts. *Information and Software Technology, 145*. https://doi.org/10.1016/j.infsof.2021.106816

Ford, S., Buscemi, J., Hirko, K., Laitner, M., Newton, R. L., Jonassaint, C., Klesges, L. M., et al. (2023). Withdrawn as duplicate: Society of Behavioural Medicine (SBM) urges Congress to ensure efforts to increase and enhance broadband internet access in rural areas. *Translational Behavioural Medicine, 13*(6), 420–422. https://doi.org/10.1093/tbm/ibz035

Freeman, J., Park, S., & Middleton, C. (2020). Technological literacy and interrupted internet access. *Information, Communication & Society, 23*(13), 1947–1964. https://doi.org/10.1080/1369118X.2019.1623901

García-Mora, F., & Mora-Rivera, J. (2023). Exploring the impacts of Internet access on poverty: A regional analysis of rural Mexico. *New Media & Society, 25*(1), 26–49. https://doi.org/10.1177/14614448211000650

Geng, L., Hui, H., Liang, X., Yan, S., & Xue, Y. (2023). Factors affecting intention toward ICT adoption in rural entrepreneurship: Understanding the differences between business types of organisations and previous experience of entrepreneurs. *Sage Open, 13*(3). https://doi.org/10.1177/21582440231197112

George, A. S. (2023). Evaluating India's economic growth: Challenges and opportunities on the path to 5 trillion dollars. *Partners Universal International Innovation Journal, 1*(6), 85–109. https://doi.org/10.5281/zenodo.10307006

Giannakis, E., & Papadas, C. (2021). Spatial connectivity and regional economic resilience in turbulent times. *Sustainability, 13*(20), 11289. https://doi.org/10.3390/su132011289

Greenberg, Z., Farja, Y., & Gimmon, E. (2018). Embeddedness and growth of small businesses in rural regions. *Journal of Rural Studies, 62*, 174–182. https://doi.org/10.1016/j.jrurstud.2018.07.016

GSMA. (2023). *The mobile economy: Sub-Saharan Africa 2023.*

Gwaka, L., May, J., & Tucker, W. (2018). Towards low-cost community networks in rural communities: the impact of context using the case study of Beitbridge, Zimbabwe. *The Electronic Journal of Information Systems in Developing Countries, 84*(3). https://doi.org/10.1002/isd2.12029

Heeks, R., Gomez-Morantes, J. E., Graham, M., Howson, K., Mungai, P., Nicholson, B., & Van Belle, J.-P. (2021). Digital platforms and institutional voids in developing countries: The case of ride-hailing markets. *World Development, 145*, Article 105528. https://doi.org/10.1016/j.worlddev.2021.105528

Henderson, D., & Roche, N. (2019). Examining the policy mix for broadband deployment in wales: The role of informal coordination in the last mile. *Local Economy the Journal of the Local Economy Policy Unit, 35*(1), 48–67. https://doi.org/10.1177/0269094219883396

Holroyd, C. (2019). Digital content promotion in Southeast Asia: Government strategies for a new economic sector. *Journal of Asian Public Policy, 12*(1), 15–33. https://doi.org/10.1080/17516234.2018.1477029

Home Pride Bank. (2025). *Digital banking: Transforming rural finance* [Online]. https://www.homepridebank.com/learn/the-role-of-digital-banking-in-rural-communities [Accessed 6 June 2025].

Ijomah, T. I., Idemudia, C., Eyo-Udo, N. L. & Anjorin, K. F. (2024). Innovative digital marketing strategies for SMEs: Driving competitive advantage and sustainable growth. *International Journal of Management & Entrepreneurship Research, 6*(7), 2173–2188. https://doi.org/10.51594/ijmer.v6i7.1265

International Centre for Tax and Development. (2024). *The digital transformation of tax administrations: What's in ot for low-income countries?* [Online]. https://www.ictd.ac/blog/digital-transformation-of-tax-administrations-whats-in-it-for-low-income-countries/ [Accessed 6 June 2025].

Ismail, N. A., Bakar, M. A., & Hilmi, M. I. (2023). Encouraging factor for ICT usage in agriculture from supplier view: A case study in Southern Region, Malaysia. *ESTEEM Journal of Social Sciences and Humanities, 7*(2), 240–253.

Ivus, O., & Boland, M. (2015). The employment and wage impact of broadband deployment in Canada. *Canadian Journal of Economics/revue Canadienne D Économique, 48*(5), 1803–1830. https://doi.org/10.1111/caje.12180

Iwasaki, K. (2023). Chinese firms driving digitalisation in the ASEAN region. *Pacific Business and Industries, 23*(90), 2–31. https://www.jri.co.jp/en/MediaLibrary/file/english/periodical/rim/2023/90.pdf

Jalil, M. F. (2021). Microfinance towards micro-enterprises development in rural Malaysia through digital finance. *Discover Sustainability, 2*(1), 55. https://doi.org/10.1007/s43621-021-00066-3

Jie, H., Li, Q., Du, M., & Chen, X. (2023). Spatial and temporal variation of economic resilience and its drivers: Evidence from Chinese cities. *Frontiers in Environmental Science, 11*. https://doi.org/10.3389/fenvs.2023.1109857

Kalyani, B., & Kumar, D. (2011). Motivational factors, entrepreneurship and education: Study with reference to women in SMEs. *Far East Journal of Psychology and Business, 3*(2), 14–35.

Kandie, D., & Islam, K. J. (2022). A new era of microfinance: The digital microcredit and its impact on poverty. *Journal of International Development, 34*(3), 469–492. https://doi.org/10.1002/jid.3607

Khai, K. G., Onn, Y. W., Zulkifli, R. B., Kandasamy, S., & Ahmad, A. B. (2020). The necessity to digitalise SMEs' business model during the COVID-19 pandemic period to remain sustainable in Malaysia. *Journal of Education and Social Sciences, 16*(1), 73–81.

Kuteesa, K., Akpuokwe, C., & Udeh, C. (2024). Theoretical perspectives on digital divide and ICT access: comparative study of rural communities in Africa and the United States. *Computer Science & It Research Journal, 5*(4), 839–849. https://doi.org/10.51594/csitrj.v5i4.1045

Latif, N., Safdar, N., Liaquat, M., Younas, K., Nazeer, N., & Rafeeq, R. (2023). The role of institutional quality in assessing the environmental externality of financial inclusion: A DCE approach. *Frontiers in Environmental Science, 11.* https://doi.org/10.3389/fenvs.2023.1071149

Lee, H., Jeong, S., & Lee, K. (2023). The South Korean case of deploying rural broadband via fibre networks by implementing a universal service obligation and a public-private partnership-based project. *Telecommunications Policy, 47*(3), Article 102506. https://doi.org/10.1016/j.telpol.2023.102506

Lee, S., & Wang, S. (2022). Impacts of political fragmentation on inclusive economic resilience: Examining American metropolitan areas after the Great Recession. *Urban Studies, 60*(1), 26–45. https://doi.org/10.1177/00420980211064455

Lehtonen, O. (2020). Population grid-based assessment of the impact of broadband expansion on population development in rural areas. *Telecommunications Policy, 44*(10), Article 102028. https://doi.org/10.1016/j.telpol.2020.102028

Lekhanya, L. M. (2018). The digitalisation of rural entrepreneurship. In *Entrepreneurship-Trends and challenges*. IntechOpen. https://doi.org/10.5772/intechopen.75925

Leong, C., Pan, S. L., Newell, S., & Cui, L. (2016). The emergence of self-organizing e-commerce ecosystems in remote villages of China: A tale of digital empowerment for rural development. *MIS Quarterly, 40*(2), 475–484. https://doi.org/10.25300/MISQ/2016/40.2.11

Li, G., Fang, X., & Liu, M. (2021). Will digital inclusive finance make economic development greener? Evidence from China. *Frontiers in Environmental Science, 9.* https://doi.org/10.3389/fenvs.2021.762231

Li, J., Wu, Y., & Xiao, J. J. (2020). The impact of digital finance on household consumption: Evidence from China. *Economic Modelling, 86*, 317–326. https://doi.org/10.1016/j.econmod.2019.09.027

Limbach, F., Kuebel, H., & Zarnekow, R. (2016). Improving rural broadband deployment with synergistic effects between multiple fixed infrastructures. *Australasian Journal of Information Systems, 20.* https://doi.org/10.3127/ajis.v20i0.1191

Liu, C., Chen, L., Li, Z., & Wu, D. (2023). The impact of digital financial inclusion and urbanisation on agricultural mechanisation: Evidence from counties of China. *PLoS One, 18*(11), Article e0293910. https://doi.org/10.1371/journal.pone.0293910

Liu, Z. J., Tretyakova, N., Fedorov, V., & Kharakhordina, M. (2020). Digital literacy and digital didactics as the basis for new learning models development. *International Journal of Emerging Technologies in Learning, 15*(14), 4–18. https://doi.org/10.3991/ijet.v15i14.14669

Ma, Y., Wei, R., & Bi, H. (2025). How does digital inclusive finance enhance rural economic resilience?—A study based on provincial panel data in China. *PLoS One, 20*(4), Article e0321630. https://doi.org/10.1371/journal.pone.0321630

Microfinancing Partners in Africa (2023). *Loans for African farmers* [Online]. https://microfinancingafrica.org/micro-financing-solutions-for-agriculture-transforming-farming-practices-in-africa/ [Accessed 6 June 2025].

Morris, M., Morris, W., & Bowen, R. (2022). Implications of the digital divide on rural SME resilience. *Journal of Rural Studies, 89*, 369–377. https://doi.org/10.1016/j.jrurstud.2022.01.005

Moss, T. W., Loor, A. D., & Parada, F. D. (2022). Partnerships as an enabler of resourcefulness in generating sustainable outcomes. *Journal of Business Venturing, 37*(1), Article 106089. https://doi.org/10.1016/j.jbusvent.2020.106089

Moyes, D., Whittam, G., & Ferri, P. (2012). A conceptualisation of the relationship capital of rural small service firms. *Local Economy, 27*(2), 136–151. https://doi.org/10.1177/0269094211428867

Mwakalila, E., & Kasongwa, L. (2024). The transformative impact of digital financial inclusion among marginalised groups on economic growth. *Journal of Social Development, 14*(1).

Mwapwele, S., Marais, M., Dlamini, S., & Biljon, J. (2019). Teachers' ICT adoption in South African rural schools: a study of technology readiness and implications for the South Africa Connect broadband policy. *The African Journal of Information and Communication, 24*. https://doi.org/10.23962/10539/28658

Nikou, S., & Aavakare, M. (2021). An assessment of the interplay between literacy and digital Technology in Higher Education. *Education and Information Technologies, 26*(4), 3893–3915. https://doi.org/10.1007/s10639-021-10451-0

Nipo, D. T., Lily, J., Fabeil, N. F., & Jamil, I. A. A. (2024). Transforming rural entrepreneurship through digital innovation: A review on opportunities, barriers and challenges. *Journal of Management and Sustainability, 14*(2), 114. https://doi.org/10.5539/jms.v14n2p114

Noor, M. M., Hashim, N., & Jamin, R. M. (2020). Implications of ICT for development on enhancing rural entrepreneur program (REP) at Telecentres in Malaysia. *International Journal of Business and Society, 21*(2), 629–642. https://doi.org/10.33736/ijbs.3275.

Novadina, F. (2024). Fundamentals of Omnibus law in legal studies. *Enigma in Law, 1*(2), 45–50. https://doi.org/10.61996/law.v1i2.37
OECD. (2022). *Addressing the digital divide: Comprehensive digital transformation in Africa.*
Oki, O., & Lawrence, M. (2022). Cost-effectiveness of fibre optic technology deployment in rural area. *Journal on Innovation and Sustainability RISUS, 13*(2), 111–123. https://doi.org/10.23925/2179-3565.2022v13i2p111-123
Okunade, B., A, O., Adediran, F., Adewusi, O., Daraojimba, R., & Igbokwe, J. (2024). Community development programs in rural Africa: An effectiveness review. *International Journal of Science and Research Archive, 11*(1), 1217–1226. https://doi.org/10.30574/ijsra.2024.11.1.0185
Oloyede, A. A., Fark, N., Noma, N., & Tebep, E. (2022). Measuring the impact of the digital economy in developing countries: A systematic review and meta-analysis. *SSRN Electronic Journal.* https://doi.org/10.2139/ssrn.4106167
Oloyede, A., Grace, D., & Faruk, N. (2023). A techno-economic model for future deployment of fixed broadband services to stimulate development across rural Africa. *International Journal of Mobile Communications, 21*(2), 181. https://doi.org/10.1504/ijmc.2023.128819
Oprişan, O., Pîrciog, S., Ionaşcu, A., Lincaru, C., & Grigorescu, A. (2023). Economic resilience and sustainable finance: A path to development and convergence in Romanian counties. *Sustainability, 15*(19), 14221. https://doi.org/10.3390/su151914221
Owens, J. (2013). Offering digital financial services to promote financial inclusion: Lessons we've learned. *Innovations: Technology, Governance, Globalisation, 8*(1–2), 271–282. https://doi.org/10.1162/INOV_a_00179
Oyelami, L. O., Adebiyi, S. O., & Adekunle, B. S. (2020). Electronic payment adoption and 'consumers' spending growth: Empirical evidence from Nigeria. *Future Business Journal, 6*, 1–14. https://doi.org/10.1186/s43093-020-00022-z
Pan, C., & Mo, X. (2024). *Impact of digital financial inclusion development on rural income levels*, 274–281. https://doi.org/10.2991/978-94-6463-408-2_31
Patel, B., & Chavda, K. (2013). Rural entrepreneurship in India: Challenge and problems. *International Journal of Advance Research in Computer Science and Management Studies, 1*(2).
Puspita, I. (2024). The impact of digital literacy programs on information access in rural African communities in Indonesia. *African Journal of Information and Knowledge Management, 2*(1), 13–26. https://doi.org/10.47604/ajikm.2266

Räisänen, J., & Tuovinen, T. (2020). Digital innovations in rural micro-enterprises. *Journal of Rural Studies, 73*, 56–67. https://doi.org/10.1016/j.jrurstud.2019.09.010

Ramdani, B., Raja, S., & Kayumova, M. (2021). Digital innovation in SMEs: A systematic review, synthesis and research agenda. *Information Technology for Development, 28*(1), 1–25. https://doi.org/10.1080/02681102.2021.1893148

Rani, N. Z. A. A., Ismail, M. K., Kumaran, V. V., Muhamad, M. Z., & Shaupi, N. S. A. (2022). Analysing the challenges in adopting digitalisation among SMEs: A case study in Malaysia. *Res Militaris, 12*(4), 500–509.

Rasheed, R., Siddiqui, S. H., Mahmood, I., & Khan, S. N. (2019). Financial inclusion for SMEs: Role of digital micro-financial services. *Review of Economics and Development Studies, 5*(3), 429–439.

Ravichandran, T. (2018). Exploring the relationships between IT competence, innovation capacity and organisational agility. *The Journal of Strategic Information Systems, 27*(1), 22–42. https://doi.org/10.1016/j.jsis.2017.07.002

Roberts, E., Beel, D., Philip, L., & Townsend, L. (2017). Rural resilience in a digital society: Editorial. *Journal of Rural Studies, 54*, 355–359. https://doi.org/10.1016/j.jrurstud.2017.06.010

Rosnan, H., & Yusof, N. (2023). Digital technologies and small-scale rural farmers in Malaysia. In B. Alareeni, A. Hamdan, R. Khamis & R. E. Khoury (Eds.), *Digitalisation: Opportunities and challenges for business* (p. 620). ICBT 2022. Lecture Notes in Networks and Systems. Springer, Cham. https://doi.org/10.1007/978-3-031-26953-0_72

Sanders, C., Gibson, K., & Lamm, A. (2022). Rural broadband and precision agriculture: A frame analysis of United States federal policy outreach under the Biden administration. *Sustainability, 14*(1), 460. https://doi.org/10.3390/su14010460

Saruchera, F., & Mpunzi, S. (2023). Digital capital and food agricultural SMEs: Examining the effects on SME performance, inequalities and government role. *Cogent Business & Management, 10*, 1–22. https://doi.org/10.1080/23311975.2023.2191304

Sindakis, S., & Showkat, G. (2024). The digital revolution in India: Bridging the gap in rural technology adoption. *Journal of Innovation and Entrepreneurship, 13*(1), 29. https://doi.org/10.1186/s13731-024-00380-w

Sivakumar, B. (2018). Digital India—A key to transform India. *International Journal of Creative Research Thoughts, 6*(2), 1368–1375. https://doi.org/10.36106/paripex/3707557

Soluk, J., Kammerlander, N., & Darwin, S. (2021). Digital entrepreneurship in developing countries: The role of institutional voids. *Technological Forecasting and Social Change, 170*, Article 120876. https://doi.org/10.1016/j.techfore.2021.120876

Sun, J., Liu, T., & Zhao, R. (2024). The effect of digital finance on inclusive green growth: Evidence from China's urban agglomerations. *Managerial and Decision Economics, 45*(7), 4851–4865. https://doi.org/10.1002/mde.4303

Sustainability Directory. (2025). *Rural digital financial inclusion* [Online]. https://prism.sustainability-directory.com/term/rural-digital-financial-inclusion/

Tang, G. N., Ren, F., & Zhou, J. (2022). Does the digital economy promote innovation and entrepreneurship in rural tourism in China? *Frontiers in Psychology, 13*, Article 979027. https://doi.org/10.3389/fpsyg.2022.979027

Teece, D. J. (2018). Profiting from innovation in the digital economy: Enabling technologies, standards, and licensing models in the wireless world. *Research Policy, 47*(8), 1367–1387. https://doi.org/10.1016/j.respol.2017.01.015

Thakur, M. (2024). Cyber security threats and counter measures in digital age. *Journal of Applied Science and Education, 4*(042), 1–20. https://doi.org/10.54060/a2zjournals.jase.42

Thomas, B. (2023). Exploring the facilitators of e-commerce adoption among rural entrepreneurs in Sabah. *Journal of BIMP-EAGA Regional Development, 9*(1), 1–11. https://doi.org/10.51200/jbimpeagard.v9i1.4365

Tiwasing, P. (2021). Social media business networks and SME performance: A rural–urban comparative analysis. *Growth and Change, 52*(3), 1892–1913. https://doi.org/10.1111/grow.12501

Tosheva, E. (2020). Economic and social benefits of digital economy and digital transformation in The Republic of North Macedonia. *İzmir Sosyal Bilimler Dergisi, 2*(2), 42–51.

UNCDF. (2022). *Ghana announces electronic levy: Possible scenarios for the progress of digital financial inclusion* [Online]. https://www.uncdf.org/article/7408/ghana-electronic-levy [Accessed 6 June 2025].

Wang, X., & Fu, Y. (2021). Digital financial inclusion and vulnerability to poverty: Evidence from Chinese rural households. *China Agricultural Economic Review, 14*(1), 64–83. https://doi.org/10.1108/caer-08-2020-0189

World Bank. (2023). Digital financial inclusion in Africa interview series. *Settor Amediku* [Online]. https://www.worldbank.org/en/news/feature/2023/09/28/digital-financial-inclusion-in-africa-interview-series-settor-amediku [Accessed 6 June 2025].

Ye, L., & Yang, H. (2020). From digital divide to social inclusion: A tale of mobile platform empowerment in rural areas. *Sustainability, 12*(6), 2424. https://doi.org/10.3390/su12062424

Yi, S., Ying, Q., Ya, Y., Shi, J., & Cui, Y. (2024). The impact of China's digital inclusive financial development gap on the optimisation of rural consumption structure. *PLoS One, 19*(8), Article e0308412. https://doi.org/10.1371/journal.pone.0308412

Zhang, J., Zhang, S., Huang, X., Zhang, Z., & Jin, C. (2023). Spatiotemporal evolution of coordinated development between economic resilience and green finance under the background of sustainable development. *Sustainability, 15*(11), 9101. https://doi.org/10.3390/su15119101

CHAPTER 3

Tech for Good: The Future of Sustainable Marketing

Kwame Adom, Nicholas Oblitei Commey, and Golda Anambane

Background of the Study

The nexus of digital technology and sustainable marketing presents a pivotal, yet largely understudied, frontier for development in Sub-Saharan Africa (Anning-Dorson & Zulu, 2025). The continent is characterized

K. Adom (✉)
School of Business, Burman University, Lacombe, AB, Canada
e-mail: kwameadom@burmanu.ca

N. O. Commey
School of Business and Leadership, Department of Management Studies, Heritage Christian University, Accra, Ghana
e-mail: noco17a@hcu.edu.gh

G. Anambane
Institute of Statistical, Social and Economic Research (ISSER), University of Ghana, Legon, Ghana
e-mail: ganambane001@st.ug.edu.gh

A. Gbadamosi et al. (eds.), *Contemporary Marketing Practices in Africa, Volume 1*, Palgrave Studies of Marketing in Emerging Economies,
https://doi.org/10.1007/978-3-032-27126-6_3

by a rapidly expanding digital economy and a dynamic young population, offering unprecedented opportunities for innovation, economic growth, and development. Concurrently, it faces immense environmental and social challenges, including climate change impacts and the transition from traditional, resource-intensive economic models to a more technological approach. Over the last two decades, the demand for technological integration in marketing practices has reached astronomical levels. The reason is that it enables firms to achieve sustainability goals. Since the beginning of the twenty first Century, organizations have altered how they conduct their marketing activities in response to technological advancements. Marketing scholars have also extended this conversation over the years. The marketing world has experienced significant changes during these years due to rapid technological developments, shifting consumer tastes and preferences, and emerging platform technologies (social media). The evaluation of dominant marketing trends in 2025 draws on current industry data and research (Rodionov, 2021; Musa et al., 2024). Modern marketing strategies undergo their most notable changes by implementing artificial intelligence alongside personalized consumer experiences, short-form video content, and authentic brand community development (Olanrewaju et al., 2025).

Organizations must respond quickly to changes in consumer behavior and technological developments, as these factors determine their market success in a dynamic business environment. The chapter argues that while a growing body of academic and professional literature exists on technology adoption and sustainable business practices in the region, a critical analysis of their intersection reveals profound and systemic research gaps. Some of these gaps are highlighted in this chapter. Particularly, the chapter focuses on three main gaps.

First, the behavioral nexus examines the critical disconnect between consumer awareness of sustainability and their actual purchasing behavior. There is limited research on how digital platforms can move beyond simple information dissemination to actively influence and incentivize pro-sustainability actions.

In addition, scaling for the Informal Economy needs attention. The information economy represents the vast majority of economic activity in the region. However, the informal economy has a particularly low level of productive use of digital technology. Available research on sustainable marketing focuses on formal firms, leaving a significant portion of the market understudied.

Finally, it is worth noting that bridging the digital divide calls for more research: available studies seldom provide a cohesive framework for designing sustainable marketing strategies to overcome the widespread infrastructural and socio-economic barriers to the digital divide, including high costs, limited skills, and the persistent gender gap.

In addressing the gaps identified, the following are the objectives of the chapter:

- To investigate how technological innovations support sustainable marketing practices to boost environmental responsibility and business competitiveness.
- To examine specific technologies (e.g., data analytics, AI, blockchain) that can be leveraged to enable and enhance sustainable marketing strategies.
- To document the current productive use of basic digital technologies (especially mobile phones, USSD, SMS, and social messaging apps like WhatsApp, Instagram, and the like) within informal business operations.
- To assess the accessibility and usability of existing digital sustainability initiatives among users with low literacy and limited technical skills.
- To identify specific examples of companies implementing successful sustainable marketing strategies integrated with technology within various sectors.

Sub-Saharan Africa is on the precipice of a transformative era, driven by the dual forces of technological innovation and a growing global imperative for sustainable development. The continent's digital sector is experiencing rapid expansion, with its internet economy projected to contribute over US$700 billion to the GDP by 2050 (Olanrewaju et al., 2025). This growth is not merely an abstract economic trend; it is manifesting in the daily lives of millions, with mobile phone usage and social media engagement reaching unprecedented levels (Olanrewaju et al., 2025). This proliferation of digital tools has the potential to redefine traditional business models, facilitate market access, and drive new forms of social and economic organization. Technology integration serves two purposes: solving environmental issues and enabling businesses to succeed in markets that prioritize sustainability.

The term technology in this study primarily refers to digital technologies most relevant to the African context. This includes mobile and internet-enabled devices, social media platforms, mobile money systems, and data analytics. These tools drive the current wave of innovation and have the most significant potential to bridge the gap between firms and consumers in the sustainable marketplace. While other technologies are mentioned, the focus remains on the digital ecosystem due to its pervasive and transformative nature in the region.

As Rosdionov (2021: 132) puts it, "the marketing environment is characterized by a high degree of complexity, mobility and unpredictability". Therefore, organizations that succeed in this light can study this environment and devise strategies to remain relevant to their customers, shareholders, and other stakeholders. The current marketing trends require businesses to adapt strategies to changing consumer behaviors while using digital platforms to boost customer engagement and market competitiveness. Therefore, businesses must adopt innovative marketing strategies to stay relevant and practical in the fast-changing market environment (Robertsone & Lapiņa, 2023). Beyond this, firms must develop adaptive capabilities and monitor emerging digital technologies and consumer preferences since these factors strongly impact marketing effectiveness. Understanding consumer behavior and integrating digital marketing tools enables businesses to develop effective strategies that connect with their target audience and generate desired results (Shaw, 2024). Firms must be intentional about regularly updating their marketing strategies to align with consumer expectations as technological progress advances in the current digital environment.

Businesses can use technology not only to understand sustainable marketing practices but also to align their operations with consumer needs and societal standards, thereby achieving brand loyalty and market leadership. Implementing technology in sustainable marketing strategies becomes vital for building strong consumer connections and improving brand loyalty in today's environmentally aware market.

The rest of the paper focuses on the context of sustainable marketing in Sub-Saharan Africa (SSA), the evolution of marketing in the digital age, understanding sustainable marketing—the historical development, current trends, role of digital technology in SM, digital marketing, big data analytics, emerging technologies, and clever sustainable marketing, and integration of technology, employees, and customers. The chapter ends with practical lessons/recommendations for companies integrating technology to achieve Sustainable Marketing in Sub-Saharan Africa, followed by a conclusion.

The Context of Sustainable Marketing in Sub-Saharan Africa: A Foundation of Promise and Paradox

Although nascent, academic inquiry into sustainable marketing in Sub-Saharan Africa has already yielded valuable insights highlighting promise and paradox. A study conducted among 391 manufacturing enterprises in Tanzania found that a strategic green marketing orientation significantly and positively influences environmental sustainability (Ismail et al., 2023). The research further found that this effect is moderated by a firm's "green absorptive capacity". Its ability to acquire, assimilate, and apply environmental knowledge underscores the importance of internal capabilities in driving sustainable outcomes. These findings are crucial, as they provide an empirical basis for the argument that incorporating environmental considerations into business strategy is not merely a social obligation but a source of competitive advantage in a global market. The analysis of consumer behavior reveals a critical and underexplored paradox. Another study of tertiary students in South Africa found that customer awareness of sustainability matters and sustainable marketing efforts are indeed linked to sustainable behavior (Masocha, 2018). This finding confirms a positive correlation between knowledge and action. However, the same study found that, despite recognizing the importance of sustainability, consumers frequently purchase environmentally harmful products. This contradictory behavior suggests that a simple lack of information is not the primary barrier to sustainable consumption. More complex, systemic factors that prevent a positive attitude from translating into a pro-environmental purchasing decision are at play. The limited scope of these studies, focused on a single sector in one country and a specific consumer demographic in another, further underscores a significant gap in our understanding of these dynamics across the continent's diverse regions and economies.

Methodology

This conceptual paper conducted a comprehensive synthesis and critical analysis of existing literature to understand how digital technologies can be leveraged to bridge the intention-behavior gap in sustainable consumption, with particular attention to scalability in the informal economy and accessibility across the digital divide. The research is guided by a **pragmatic philosophy**, prioritizing practical outcomes and solution-oriented findings. It employed an **interpretivist approach** to understand the nuanced social and behavioral dynamics reported in the literature.

Research Design

This is a **qualitative-dominant, systematic desktop study**. The design is structured to be transparent and replicable, involving sequential phases of data collection, analysis, and synthesis.

Data Sources and Search Strategy

A multi-layered search strategy captures academic, practical, and contextual insights. The primary academic databases engaged are Scopus, Web of Science, Science Direct, JSTOR and Google Scholar for peer-reviewed journal articles. Other sources include Reports from the World Bank, International Telecommunication Union (ITU), United Nations Development Programme (UNDP), and UN Environment Programme, as well as relevant publications from McKinsey, World Economic Forum, World Resources Institute, and NGOs focused on digital inclusion (e.g., Alliance for Affordable Internet). A systematic search was conducted using predefined Boolean search ("OR" and "AND") strings tailored to the three research gaps.

Inclusion and Exclusion Criteria: Inclusion: Sources published within the last 10 years (2015–2025) to ensure relevance; sources focusing on or with significant applicability to the target region; sources available in English; empirical studies, theoretical reviews, and high-quality case studies.

Exclusion: Sources older than 10 years (unless seminal works); sources not peer-reviewed or from non-credible publishers; sources with a primary focus on developed economies with no transferable insights.

Academic integrity was maintained through rigorous citation and the avoidance of plagiarism. The potential biases of source authors and publishers (e.g., corporate reports) were critically evaluated.

Systematic Literature Review

The Evolution of Marketing in the Digital Age

From traditional to digital marketing, marketing has undergone significant evolution over the last several decades, particularly since the emergence of digital technology. The evolution shows businesses establishing audience connections and generating value while adjusting to shifting consumer behavior. From the selling concept to customer relationship management, marketing has gradually moved toward the digital landscape. With the advances in Information Communication Technology (ICT), how businesses conduct marketing activities has changed dramatically. The change starts with marketing communications, customer acquisition, engagement, and relationship building. There is a quantum shift from traditional media (radio, television, billboards, and so on) to a more technology-based platform (the Internet and social media). Increasingly, among academics and scientific researchers, the conversation about digital transformation and digitalization continues (Robertsone & Lapiņa, 2023). Organizations undergo significant change through digital transformation (DT) by implementing digital technologies to transform their value-creation processes and adapt to the business landscape (Robertsone & Lapiņa, 2023; Vial, 2021). The transformation process delivers improved operational efficiency while creating innovative solutions that lead to market competitiveness in today's fast-changing business environment. The improved operational efficiency and innovative capabilities help organizations stay competitive and increase shareholder value.

Businesses traditionally use broad marketing strategies to attract as many customers as possible, according to Bhayani and Vachhani (2014). During this time, the focus was on achieving maximum reach and repetition, despite a lack of precise knowledge about who their marketing messages influenced.

In the 1990s, the Internet gained prominence, marking the onset of the digital age (Curran, 2012; Ryan, 2010). The outcome was that organizations now need websites to develop their digital footprint. As a result, email marketing has emerged as an innovative method for businesses to communicate directly with their customers (Hartemo, 2016). Over the period, companies treated their websites as digital catalogues instead of fully utilizing their web capabilities. The discovery of search engine optimization (SEO) became vital when Google introduced its search engine in the late 1990s (Levene, 2011; Seymour et al., 2011). Furthermore, customer needs became essential as search engines began helping users find products and services through their search results. At the same time, companies adopted content marketing, seeking valuable content to improve search engine positions and attract natural website visitors or to boost online traffic.

The growing influence of social media platforms has changed marketing from one-way communication into a two-way dialogue between businesses and their customers (Kaplan, 2015; Smith, 2009). Through social media platforms, brands can directly connect with consumers for instant feedback while developing product-based communities. In this direction, a new phase of marketing, influencer marketing, emerged as a method for product promotion through trusted voices. The advancement of technology has led to improved capabilities for companies' data collection and analysis. Launching analytics tools gave marketers unprecedented abilities to monitor consumer activities more precisely (Grandhi et al., 2021). The marketing strategies shifted toward highly targeted approaches, allowing businesses to customize their messages based on customer preferences, interaction history, and personal information. This has been achieved through automation tools that help businesses create personalized email marketing campaigns and remarketing initiatives to boost customer interaction (Rosário & Dias, 2023).

Mobile marketing has become essential for businesses as part of the digital revolution, given the widespread adoption of smartphones. Mobile devices have evolved into essential tools for consumer activities, from research to purchase decisions (Kumar & Mittal, 2020; Ström et al., 2014). The shift demanded that marketers improve their website's accessibility and create mobile advertising solutions. The development of location-based services enabled precise marketing campaigns that delivered messages to specific customers when they were physically present in particular locations. Today's marketing strategies combine artificial intelligence and machine learning as core elements, especially in the Industry 4.0 era (Mathew, Brintha, & Jappes, 2023). The application of artificial intelligence delivers predictive analytics, strengthening customer understanding and producing better recommendations (Boozary et al., 2024). Real-time customer service operations use chatbots and virtual assistants to improve consumer interactions and experiences. Automating social media posting and advertising buying processes enables marketers to allocate their time to strategy development rather than performing routine operations.

There is a need for ethical considerations and transparency as the marketing environment continues to evolve. As marketing progresses, consumer expectations regarding ethical practices and transparency in business operations also evolve. Consumer worries about privacy and data security motivate brands to disclose their data collection methods openly. Implementing the General Data Protection Regulation (GDPR) (a comprehensive EU law enacted on May 25, 2018, focused on data privacy). There is also a growing focus on trustworthy marketing practices, leading to greater demands for market transparency. The digital era has brought about a swift evolution in marketing through revolutionary technological developments. In this regard, the path to future success depends on businesses that demonstrate adaptability alongside a deep understanding of consumer behavior. In this dynamic business environment, successful marketing requires marketers to advance their practices through technological innovation while building profitable, authentic relationships with their audiences. Understanding marketing in the digital age has influenced the concept of sustainable marketing, promoting more ethical and responsible business practices. The discussion turns on the historical development of sustainable marketing.

Historical Development of Sustainable Marketing (SM)

Kumar et al. (2013) follow the development of sustainable marketing from ecological and societal marketing concepts. Their study demonstrates the necessity of integrating sustainability principles with marketing practices through strategies that protect the environment while also generating profits. The field of sustainability marketing shows growing interest but needs further research and development, as identified gaps reveal substantial potential for future studies. Integrating sustainability into marketing began more than 40 years ago, when companies began linking their marketing activities to environmental and social objectives

(Bhattacharyya, 2023). During this time, the business's focus has been to fulfill current customer requirements without sacrificing future customer needs. Using this approach, businesses achieve better marketing efficiency. The field of SM research has faced conceptual challenges over the last 20 years, leading to the creation of the Green Framework, which established a unified framework for sustainable marketing research (Lunde, 2018). Sono performed a bibliometric analysis in 2023, which shows marketing sustainability research has explored multiple themes, while sustainability variables from a marketing perspective stand out as a primary focus (Sono, 2023).

The evolution of sustainable marketing shows that businesses now recognize their interconnected relationship with societal well-being, so they must develop innovative strategies that align consumer values with environmental targets (Barraco, 2024; Lunde, 2018). The evolution enables companies to become sustainable market leaders while strengthening brand loyalty to meet consumer needs and address environmental challenges (Navaratne, 2023). Companies that focus on sustainability differentiate themselves from competitors, build consumer trust, and achieve enduring success and societal benefits (Navaratne, 2023; Udeh & Dugba, 2025). It shows that brands must demonstrate genuine, transparent communication to establish trust-based consumer loyalty (Navaratne, 2023). Adopting green marketing practices by businesses strengthens their market position and supports public objectives, creating a mutually beneficial connection between corporate achievements and environmental protection (Barraco, 2024; Lunde, 2018). The connection between sustainability and marketing functions is key because it enables businesses to build stronger relationships with customers who value ethical purchasing and social responsibility. Companies with effective sustainability communication gain improved brand loyalty and market perception while achieving financial success and environmental benefits (Navaratne, 2023; Udeh & Dugba, 2025). Sustainability efforts align with global climate change mitigation efforts, responsible consumption initiatives, and consumer demand.

White et al. (2025) explain the historical development of sustainability marketing, starting from resource conservation and green marketing. The current trends have expanded the scope to include the circular economy, anti-consumption, regulatory frameworks, and social and ethical considerations. The analysis predicts that future sustainability marketing will develop through system-driven, business-driven, and consumer-driven changes to enhance understanding and create innovative solutions for a sustainable future. The paper provides an extensive analysis of the development of sustainability marketing throughout history. It demonstrates how sustainability marketing has expanded its focus from resource conservation and green marketing to encompass multiple subjects that mirror the changing sustainability issues in marketing practices (White et al., 2025). The research further examines current sustainability marketing practices by focusing on circular-economy principles, anti-consumption strategies, regulatory standards, and innovative approaches.

The strategic partnership provides businesses with sustainable innovation opportunities that help them stay current in their market while positively affecting society and the environment. Sustainable marketing strategies must adapt continuously because stakeholders must understand how sustainability integration works with core business operations. Companies must base their sustainability engagement on authentic communication because fake environmental marketing, known as greenwashing, remains a concern for consumers. Businesses adopted sustainable marketing practices because they realized the impact of their operations on social welfare. Thus, they needed new methods to unite environmental targets with consumer values. Developing sustainable marketing methods enables businesses to establish sustainable market growth that satisfies consumer demands and environmental standards. Organizations dedicated to sustainability achieve market recognition and consumer trust, thereby establishing enduring business success and creating positive social impact.

Understanding Sustainable Marketing (SM).

Sustainable Marketing (SM) helps protect the environment while fulfilling social responsibilities and establishing sustainable profitability for organizations that adopt this approach. It integrates ecological and social aspects into complete marketing strategies that link financial goals to ethical and environmental standards. The conversation around climate change and its catastrophic environmental impact is raging. The environmental protection approach requires organizations to reduce their ecological impact across all stages of product and service development, including production, packaging, distribution, and disposal. Businesses should implement policies on renewable energy sources, waste reduction, and sustainable product design, including the use of recyclable and biodegradable materials.

It is also incumbent on businesses to follow ethical guidelines under social responsibility principles, which protect human rights, establish ethical workplaces, and generate positive social effects in their operational areas. The organization must operate supply chains free from exploitation while investing in community development by supporting diversity, equity, and inclusion initiatives. In doing so, organizations achieve long-term profitability through establishing themselves as responsible brands that build loyal customers while differentiating themselves in the market. Sustainable marketing creates value for all stakeholders, including shareholders, by addressing societal issues while anticipating regulatory shifts and changes in consumer preferences.

Companies create environmental friendliness through green branding using eco-friendly messaging and sustainable packaging (Lunde, 2018) while promoting green certifications such as Fair Trade and Energy Star. Companies must practice ethical sourcing by obtaining raw materials responsibly through fair worker compensation, safe working conditions, and sustainable farming and mining practices. Marketers conduct product lifecycle analysis to evaluate and reduce the environmental impacts products generate from design through to disposal. To do this, businesses partner with social and environmental organizations through cause-related marketing to raise awareness and raise funds for essential social causes. Trust is essential to conducting business; as a result, any organization that reports its sustainability progress and goals to stakeholders builds trust with them and consumers. Therefore, SM requires more than selling green products, because organizations must change their operational methods to achieve sustainable profitability and human and planetary well-being for enduring success.

Current Trends in Sustainable Marketing

Recent technological advancements have spurred a new trend in SM. Organizations are leveraging the Internet of Things (IoT) to transform how they conduct marketing and gain a competitive advantage. Some of these new trends in SM are discussed in this section. Organizations are developing complete digital-age strategies to handle today's fast-changing marketing environment. The digital age transformed business communication and consumer relationships, leading to new SM strategies that align with contemporary consumer values (Widiastuti et al., 2024). These strategies now combine social media platforms, digital advertising, and advanced analytics to achieve successful engagement with the target audience. Organizations use Instagram, TikTok, LinkedIn, and other social media platforms to display their products and services while promoting their sustainability initiatives, corporate social responsibility, and ethical practices (Widiastuti et al., 2024).

These digital platforms help companies increase brand visibility while enabling direct consumer interaction, which builds trust and community connections. Businesses use user-generated content, influencer partnerships, and interactive digital campaigns to boost their sustainability initiatives while showing supply chain transparency and environmental and social commitment. Any organization that implements these efforts establishes better relationships with environmentally aware consumers, strengthens brand loyalty, and drives growth, supporting a sustainable future. However, the successful implementation of SM depends on interactive content and consumer participation, as these elements help consumers build stronger connections and better understand sustainability issues (Widiastuti et al., 2024). Brands in this direction turn to establish meaningful connections through interactive consumer experiences, which include online quizzes, social media challenges, and virtual events. As a result, consumers gain the power to actively support sustainability goals through interactive experiences that enable them to express their opinions, showcase their eco-friendly choices, and support their preferred causes.

The positive outcome is when consumers co-create content or join brand-initiated sustainability challenges, developing a sense of community feeling and shared mission with the business. The participatory approach strengthens brand loyalty while making consumers feel they are essential partners in shaping a brand's sustainability path. These strategies help brands increase their impact by transforming one-way communication into engaging dialogue, strengthening trust, and promoting sustainable consumption behaviors.

The traditional approach to SM emphasizes minor or gradual improvements by promoting specific eco-friendly products and running recycling initiatives. These important initiatives operate at the system's edges, yet they fail to challenge established practices while addressing fundamental problems such as climate change, biodiversity decline, and global social disparities. The current trend in SM also focuses on transformative SM, which involves embedding sustainability principles directly into business core strategies, product lines, and value proposition frameworks (Uyanik, 2024). This method surpasses basic consumer expectations by aligning a company's fundamental mission with environmental and social objectives. A company must transform its supply chain operations while developing circular economies through industry partnerships to create solutions with stakeholders, including consumers, employees, and policymakers (Uyanik, 2024).

The growing recognition of SM demonstrates how industry leaders, scholars, and consumers now understand that isolated actions will not solve global challenges. Evidently, transformative change serves both environmental protection and business sustainability because climate change impacts worsen while consumer demands shift. There is an urgent requirement for marketing to evolve from basic sustainability message delivery to active leadership of transformative change (Uyanik, 2024). SM has made significant advancements but continues to face challenges in developing comprehensive solutions to global sustainability issues. The transition needs creative thinking, innovative approaches, and business model challenges to establish brands as social change agents (Widiastuti et al., 2024). According to Widiastuti et al. (2024), future research and practice should address these challenges to realize the full potential of SM.

The Role of Digital Technology in SM

According to Rosário, Lopes, and Rosário (2023), businesses' adoption of digital technologies has transformed SM strategies. Companies can implement targeted, sustainable initiatives by integrating social media platforms with content management systems and data analytics. The literature shows that digital marketing strategies promote sustainable development. This is achieved through their ability to encourage sustainable consumption patterns and evaluate how green marketing campaigns affect consumer attitudes and purchasing choices (Rosário et al., 2023). Digital platforms enable brands to maintain ongoing dialogues with consumers who provide feedback, driving continuous improvement in sustainability practices.

Technology has become the fulcrum around which SM revolves heavily. It enables businesses to reach customers effectively while promoting green products and sustainable operations. The digital era has transformed marketing practices because digital platforms and tools are essential for promoting sustainability awareness and product adoption. The effectiveness of SM strategies is supported by technological advancements, which include digital marketing, big data analytics, and artificial intelligence. The following sections delve into the specific roles and contributions of technology in SM. The digital transformation process affects business sustainability through its impact on marketing operations. The systematic literature review by Qing and Jin (2023) shows that digital transformation enables sustainable practices throughout supply chain management, product development, and customer service operations. Digital technology adoption enables companies to achieve transparency while minimizing environmental impact and strengthening stakeholder engagement, both of which are essential for sustainable marketing. Areas such as direct marketing and big data analytics are discussed.

Digital Marketing

The dynamic nature of digital marketing enables businesses to establish powerful connections with consumers to promote sustainable products and services. Through websites, social media platforms, email marketing, and online advertising, companies can leverage digital channels to raise awareness of sustainability issues and promote environmentally friendly products (Dube et al., 2023). This multi-channel strategy enables diverse audience engagement, extending the sustainability messaging reach. Dube et al. (2023) demonstrate the essential role of digital marketing in achieving sustainable marketing targets. Digital marketing serves as a flexible platform that enables sustainable product and service promotion, underscoring its importance for academic research and business operations. There is concrete evidence through real-world examples to demonstrate how digital marketing strategies can support corporate sustainability objectives (Dube et al., 2023).

The significance of social media alongside other digital platforms remains extremely imperative. These platforms are essential educational resources that teach consumers about sustainability topics such as climate change, waste reduction, ethical sourcing, and social responsibility. Companies can build trust through transparency by allowing consumers to communicate directly. Through these interactions, businesses can build sustainable values into their marketing strategies, resulting in long-term brand loyalty and positive consumer attitudes (Widiastuti et al., 2024). The outcome is that digital marketing is the critical link between sustainability programs and customer actions, helping companies promote their sustainable practices and drive significant marketplace change.

Big Data Analysis

Big data analysis drives essential changes in SM decision-making by enabling businesses to understand consumer behavior patterns, emerging trends, and preference dynamics. It enables firms to understand consumer behavior by analyzing large datasets, including social media data, online transaction records, customer feedback, and IoT device data. It has been observed that it enhances a business's ability to create marketing strategies that effectively connect with sustainability-focused consumers through understanding consumer behavior (Widiastuti et al., 2024). Not only does it help companies achieve better marketing results through data-based campaign development, but it also strengthens their relationships with environmentally aware consumers. Big data analysis enables organizations to continuously track their marketing initiatives, ensuring their strategies remain aligned with market requirements and sustainable development targets. The data-driven approach helps organizations identify innovative opportunities, improve resource utilization, and enable prompt responses to changing consumer needs. According to Widiastuti et al. (2024), big data organizations can embed sustainability elements into their core marketing decisions, strengthening their commitment to sustainable business practices and supporting positive societal and environmental outcomes.

Emerging Technologies and Smart Sustainable Marketing (SSM)

The advancement of SM depends heavily on emerging technologies, which include Artificial Intelligence (AI), the Internet of Things (IoT), and Blockchain. The Greek business market study demonstrates that these technologies boost SSM through real-time data analysis, personalized customer experiences, and efficient resource management (Kalogiannidis et al., 2023). AI analytics enables companies to analyze consumer sustainability behavior, thereby creating marketing campaigns that connect with environmentally aware consumers (Kalogiannidis et al., 2023). AI technologies, including chatbots, augmented reality, and natural language processing systems, have become essential assets for SM strategies. These technologies are essential for boosting consumer engagement by delivering interactive, personalized, and dynamic experiences that appeal to today's audiences. Chatbots deliver sustainability feature information through instant consumer communication while recommending eco-friendly products to individual customers, according to Yadav and Sondhi (2023). Augmented reality applications enable customers to see products in real-life situations, boosting transparency and trust in sustainable product statements.

The SM derives benefits from AI through its ability to provide complex behavioral insights about consumers. By analyzing big data encompassing purchase records, website behaviors, and social media sentiment, AI helps marketers identify consumers who care about sustainability and develop SM messages to target them. For Yadav and Sondhi (2023), using data-driven methods enables better optimization of marketing strategies, resulting in more focused campaigns that align with sustainability objectives and remain relevant.

The field of marketing research now includes AI as an emerging discipline, with ChatGPT and conversational AI chatbots supporting SM development. The tools enable continuous consumer contact and immediate delivery of sustainability information while supporting customer service, strengthening the company's sustainability commitment. Yadav and Sondhi (2023) again examines a decade-long dataset of marketing AI implementation to reveal important patterns alongside difficulties and promising possibilities. The paper suggests that future research should focus on AI's theoretical and practical SM implications, while advocating joint efforts among technology developers, sustainability experts, and marketers (Yadav & Sondhi, 2023). AI transforms digital marketing operations through individualized customer experiences and improved advertising strategies, thereby simultaneously helping achieve sustainability goals (Gündüzyeli, 2024). AI recommendation systems recommend sustainable products to customers based on their personal choices, and programmatic advertising selects environmentally responsible brands for delivery. Research by Gündüzyeli (2024) shows how AI helps establish SM practices by providing dual benefits: enhancing environmental performance and social and economic sustainability metrics. To achieve a comprehensive and robust literature review of these subjects, researchers must consult additional sources, as the AI and SM fields continue to expand across multiple disciplines.

Integration of Technology, Employees, and Customers

The advancement of SM depends heavily on technology, yet employees and customers are essential to achieving sustainability targets. Therefore, SM strategies require synergy between employee support and technological innovation to achieve effective implementation. According to their findings, Kushwaha et al. (2022) explain that employee involvement in sustainable initiatives is key, but employees' impact receives less attention than technological progress.

Kushwaha et al. (2022) stress the essential role of technology in SM, noting that it enhances the effectiveness of marketing strategies while expanding reach and strengthening customer engagement. Technology facilitates sustainable business practices by helping businesses promote green products, optimize operations, and minimize waste, thereby generating substantial environmental benefits. Although the research demonstrates employee support for sustainable initiatives, it also finds that technology is the leading force behind SM strategies. The company can build stronger customer bonds and achieve essential environmental targets through transparency, while maintaining accountability and driving innovation in sustainable products.

Despite the groundbreaking changes technology brings to this field, SM faces multiple obstacles. Consumers face difficulties adopting sustainable products on a large scale because they tend to be expensive (e.g., organic products). The inconsistent nature of product labeling and marketing approaches makes it challenging for consumers to identify sustainable products among non-sustainable alternatives (Dhiman & Singh, n.d.). For example, a bag of apples in a grocery store labeled organic may be difficult for a potential buyer to authenticate. However, organic farming is environmentally friendly and supports SM. The success of SM strategies depends on solving these issues for optimal results.

Applying sustainable marketing through technology requires attention to data privacy concerns, digital access inequalities, and greenwashing risks. Companies must verify that their technological applications meet ethical requirements while delivering sustainability benefits. The rapid evolution of technology demands that marketing professionals stay up to date through continuous learning and adaptation to successfully implement new tools and platforms.

How firms can improve their marketing strategies to align with sustainable goals: A practical Approach

The practical solution involves integrating sustainability into brand identity while delivering transparent, long-term value to customers in line with their social requirements. Integrating sustainability into business operations improves brand equity, builds customer trust and loyalty, and yields social benefits and market success (Udeh & Dugba, 2025). Brands achieve sustainable alignment by demonstrating their commitment to environmentally friendly practices and by developing communication methods that resonate with consumers' ethical beliefs (Navaratne, 2023).

Companies should integrate sustainability into their marketing approach by implementing it through every stage, from product creation to customer relationships, to maintain a comprehensive approach for present-day concerned consumers. This strategy aligns with the research findings, as consumers avoid "greenwashing" while demanding authentic, sustainable marketing practices. Authentic brand connections that address environmental issues foster stronger brand loyalty and positive social impact (Navaratne, 2023). The combined approach helps businesses fulfill consumer demands for ethical practices while building market leadership, which drives sustainable development and business continuity (Agu et al., 2024). Business organizations must continuously assess their marketing strategies to maintain market effectiveness and adapt to environmental changes. A successful sustainable marketing approach depends on stakeholder participation and transparent practices, establishing a sustainable marketplace that benefits consumers and businesses.

Organizational brands need to maintain continuous conversations with their consumers to establish sustainable business practices that become essential for market success. They need to focus on sustainability because consumers now choose companies that demonstrate authentic dedication to sustainability rather than those with fake environmental initiatives. Companies that practice sustainability authentically develop distinct market positions, enabling them to build stronger relationships with customers who prioritize ethical business practices. Through market differentiation, brands build stronger customer relationships and establish a more ethical business environment that emphasizes sustainable practices instead of profit maximization. By addressing environmental challenges, sustainable marketing integration enables brands to succeed within a socially aware economy.

Agu et al. (2024) argue that firms must adopt authentic communication methods about sustainability initiatives to gain consumer trust and maintain customer loyalty. Brands that prioritize open communication while maintaining ethical conduct develop dedicated customer relationships, which lead to market success through sustainable practices (Agu et al., 2024). Sustainable initiatives maintained by companies create both positive brand perception and market competitiveness alongside customer loyalty (Agu et al., 2024). Marketing strategies must align with sustainability initiatives to develop a brand image that appeals to contemporary, socially engaged consumers (Mandung, 2024). Sustainable marketing is an essential business transformation that enables brands to develop enduring consumer connections through mutual values and trust. To build consumer trust and loyalty, brands must deliver effective sustainability messages while implementing these values in operational activities.

It is suggested that firms seeking to succeed in environmentally conscious markets should adopt sustainable marketing approaches that emphasize genuine customer connections and ethical conduct. The strategic importance of sustainable marketing continues to grow because it fulfills customer requirements while generating sustainable business results and positive community outcomes. There is a need to maintain transparency and authenticity to establish trust with their consumers, as these stakeholders now assess brand sustainability and ethical practices with great care. A competitive market demands brands establish deep connections with customers by building authentic relationships to achieve higher brand loyalty. Research shows that transparency and authenticity have become essential to sustainable marketing, as consumers prioritize sustainable brands (Mandung, 2024). The increasing consumer demand for brands that genuinely care about sustainability requires companies to adopt sustainable practices while communicating their environmental values honestly to build long-term consumer loyalty.

Practical Lessons/Recommendations for Companies Integrating Technology to achieve SM in Sub-Saharan Africa

The SM has become part and parcel of the modern marketing system. It is, therefore, urgent for businesses, especially those in the global south and/or Sub-Saharan Africa, to embrace the idea. This last section of the paper provides operational advice to companies about implementing appropriate technology for SM in Sub-Saharan Africa. The successful implementation of SM through technology demands that companies train employees digitally while using social media platforms and data analytics to understand consumer behavior.

The region requires businesses to establish strong data systems and analytical tools to improve their marketing methods and better serve local market needs. In line with this, companies should develop partnerships with local tech startups to create innovative SM solutions for Sub-Saharan Africa. These partnerships will enable businesses to obtain new technologies and creative solutions that will help align marketing strategies with environmental sustainability targets and consumer demands. To achieve this, companies must maintain complete transparency throughout their marketing operations because authenticity is the key factor in fighting greenwashing skepticism in the region. This method strengthens brand reputation and supports the United Nations Sustainable Development Goals by promoting sustainable practices. Consequently, companies that adopt these practices will enhance their market position and create positive social and economic impacts on the region. Implementing technology in SM practices remains vital for Sub-Saharan Africa to achieve economic expansion and environmental targets. Other areas that need attention in navigating the future of SM are discussed.

First, businesses should take advantage of the growing importance of mobile technology for market reach. The reason is the high mobile penetration in SSA. To do this, companies can use SMS (Short Message Service), USSD (Unstructured Supplementary Service Data), and mobile apps to engage rural and urban consumers. For instance, companies can send eco-awareness messages or promote sustainable products through SMS alerts.

The future of SM lies in the promotion of transparency via Blockchain. A blockchain is a decentralized digital ledger system that distributes transaction records across multiple computers to provide secure, transparent, and unalterable data storage. The system operates without central control because multiple nodes (computers) work together to maintain it. The network requires a collective agreement to modify recorded data, which remains unalterable. Blockchain creates a chain through blocks that contain hashes that link each block to its predecessor. The network participants (nodes) validate new blocks through consensus mechanisms such as Proof of Work or Proof of Stake before adding them to the Blockchain. The block becomes an unalterable part of the Blockchain after network confirmation. All participants can view transactions, but they can maintain pseudonymous identities. The system protects data through cryptographic methods, including hashing techniques. The Blockchain is needed to build trust around sustainability claims. More importantly, it can verify supply chains and green sourcing. An example is using certain QR (Quick Response) codes on products that show eco-certification and origin. The QR codes deliver instant access to information when scanned, regardless of the data they contain.

Furthermore, firms should utilize data analytics for targeted campaigns to promote SM. The underlying reason is that it will increase efficiency and minimize waste. To achieve this, AI and data platforms must be used to understand customer preferences and behavior. A classic example would be to tailor promotions or marketing communications based on consumption patterns and reduce unnecessary marketing materials.

SSA businesses need to adopt green digital platforms. It is an online tool, application, and ecosystem that promotes environmental sustainability through carbon footprint reduction, resource optimization, and the promotion of eco-friendly practices. Digital technologies such as AI, IoT, Blockchain, and cloud computing enable sustainable business models, innovative energy management, and circular economy solutions through these platforms. These platforms are helpful because they reduce reliance on physical media such as paper or plastic. The platforms become operational using email, social media, and e-commerce to replace print-based campaigns. Businesses, therefore, must run paperless promotions and/or loyalty programs to deepen the adoption of SM strategies.

Firms must invest in local tech startups to benefit fully from SM strategies. Local tech startups are early-stage companies that use technology to develop solutions to regional or global challenges. The startups use local talent to develop innovative solutions through advanced technologies, including AI, IoT, Blockchain and fintech, which disrupt established industries. This will encourage innovation and local economic sustainability. Businesses can achieve this by partnering with or funding startups that offer green tech or localized digital solutions. An example will be businesses working with AgriTech firms to promote eco-friendly farming through apps.

Finally, businesses must create eco-centric digital content for SM. Eco-centric digital content refers to any online material, including blogs, videos, social media posts, infographics, podcasts, and so on, that makes environmental sustainability, ecological awareness, and responsible consumption its core focus. The strategy requires developing and distributing powerful digital content that educates people about environmental issues while promoting sustainable practices. The content development process will create blog posts, social media campaign videos, infographics, and multimedia assets that motivate people to adopt eco-friendly practices. The organization will develop content that matches its core values while maintaining a consistent brand voice to connect with audience interests, needs and values. In the long term, the strategy will achieve environmental stewardship, community involvement and long-term ecological impact through its educational approach to engagement. This also influences consumer behavior toward sustainability by developing campaigns on climate, recycling, and local sustainability topics. Using influencer-led TikTok and/or other campaigns will promote zero-waste practices.

Author's construction, 2025, based on the review of the SM literature.

Table 3.1 presents a proposed quadrant analytical tool that could help firms in SSA and beyond articulate their sustainable marketing strategies clearly.

The Tale of Two Successful Firms Integrating Technology to Achieve SM in SSA

A few firms have successfully applied modern technology in their businesses to achieve sustainability. In this section, brief information gathered from their websites is presented.

M-KOPA

"M-KOPA is a leading African fintech platform that provides affordable financial and digital products to 'Everyday Earners'—the tenacious

Table 3.1 Sustainable Marketing in Sub-Saharan Africa: A Quadrant Analysis

	Low consumer engagement	*High consumer engagement*
Low Strategic Orientation	**Quadrant 3: Unaware & Unengaged** Majority of the market. Firms rely on traditional business models. Consumers lack access to sustainable alternatives or information. This is the domain of most informal micro-enterprises	**Quadrant 4: Demand–Supply Gap** Consumers are aware of sustainability and are receptive to marketing efforts, but firms have not integrated sustainability into their core strategy. High greenwashing risk
High Strategic Orientation	**Quadrant 2: The Silent Innovators.** Firms are adopting sustainable practices (e.g., the Tanzania study) but are not effectively communicating their value to consumers. The challenge here is to translate internal strategy into external, credible marketing	**Quadrant 1: The Ideal Nexus** Firms have a strategic orientation and successfully engage consumers with transparent, trustworthy, sustainable marketing. This is the aspirational state and a key "how-to" research area

entrepreneurs who are the backbone of the continent's economies. Our mission is to make financing for everyday essentials accessible to everyone. M-KOPA was founded in 2010 on the idea that combining digital micropayments with GSM connectivity could provide affordable access to life-enhancing products. Since then, we've built a financial platform that has deployed over $1.5 billion in credit and enabled over 5 million customers across five countries—Kenya, Uganda, Nigeria, Ghana, and South Africa—to own quality smartphones, access digital services, and progress towards their financial goals. Our innovative model offers affordable daily repayment plans that align with how people earn their money. We offer flexible and locally relevant products to help people achieve progress in their lives". (https://www.m-kopa.com/about).

This firm has successfully applied technology to promote financial inclusion through Fintech in SSA on a sustainable basis.

Twiga Foods

In the last 8 years, Twiga has touched over 140,000 small retailers across Kenya—about 25% of the entire industry. In our journey, we have built a deep understanding of how to innovate in the African retail market. We are embracing independent retailers and giving them greater access to high-quality foods, produce, and consumer goods by leveraging the latest technology, the ubiquity of mobile phones, and modern distribution and logistics.

Bringing Greater Food Security to Africa

According to some estimates, Africans spend up to 10 times more of their disposable income on food than people in developed markets do. This economic challenge to food security is primarily caused by the highly fragmented and inefficient retail market across the continent, where roughly 90% of retailers are small, independent businesses. About 150 years ago, consumers in the United States were spending a similarly exorbitant share of their income on food, but years of private-sector-led investment in retail infrastructure built an efficient supply chain. (https://www.twiga.com).

Other firms could study these and other successful firms and learn from their approach to applying technology to achieve sustainable marketing.

Limitations

Notwithstanding the meticulous work of sifting through data to achieve the highest quality, the study has some limitations. These are highlighted below:

The available literature constrains the study; significant gaps in published research limit the analysis. The analysis was hindered by a shortage of directly relevant, high-quality studies. The available literature is scattered and general, leaving notable gaps in understanding crucial elements of the phenomenon under examination. Therefore, the proposed framework was developed from various, sometimes only loosely related, sources rather than being firmly rooted in a well-established theoretical base. This, in turn, inevitably brings an element of theoretical conjecture into the discussion.

The study did not generate primary empirical evidence to test the proposed framework. This study is theoretical in scope and did not entail the collection or analysis of original empirical data. In the absence of empirical testing, whether through quantitative experiments, qualitative case studies, or fieldwork, the framework's practical applicability, predictive capacity, and effectiveness in real-world contexts are unverified. Thus, it is presented as a foundation for future research rather than as an established, validated instrument.

Direction for Future Research

Future research should focus on an empirical study using a mixed-methods approach to investigate the integration of technology and SM. Academic researchers are encouraged to move beyond single-country or single-sector case studies to comparative, longitudinal research across the diverse regions of Sub-Saharan Africa. A multi-disciplinary approach is essential, integrating insights from marketing, behavioral economics, data science, and political science to develop a more holistic understanding of the issues. Policymakers and development agencies must recognize that addressing the research gaps requires foundational and systemic interventions. The top priority should be strategic investment in robust data-collection systems and statistical capacity-building initiatives. Without a reliable data foundation, all other development efforts and research will be hindered. Furthermore, unified, regional regulatory frameworks are needed to foster a predictable and trustworthy digital environment.

Conclusion

The future of marketing depends on the union of digital progress and environmental responsibility, as the global marketplace continues to transform at an accelerated pace. The strategic adoption of technology in sustainable marketing represents an essential business requirement for organizations to maintain their position as responsible and resilient. Artificial intelligence, together with machine learning. Blockchain, big data analytics, and the Internet of Things (IoT) have revolutionized consumer behavior analysis, supply chain management, and environmental impact evaluation in business operations. Success in technological sustainability needs more than technical ability for its implementation. The approach necessitates firms to transform their business models while redefining their value creation methods and stakeholder relationships. The integration of technology requires marketers to collaborate with various teams to verify that solutions align with organizational social responsibility objectives and regulatory standards. The ethical assessment of data privacy, equitable access, and long-term societal impact should be the basis for integrating technology.

Combining technology with sustainable marketing practices creates a practical approach that enables brands to innovate ethically, operate efficiently, and build meaningful customer relationships. This path requires visionary leadership, financial investment, and responsible accountability, yet it generates substantial rewards for businesses and society.

The overarching aim of this chapter was to investigate how technological innovations support sustainable marketing practices to boost environmental responsibility and business competitiveness. After carefully analyzing the gathered information, it can be said that "digital technology" is permanently rooted in business in SSA. The future of sustainable development in Sub-Saharan Africa is inextricably linked to the strategic and ethical application of digital technologies. While the proliferation of mobile devices and social media has created an unprecedented platform for communication, significant research gaps remain at the intersection of technology and sustainable marketing.

References

Agu, E. E., Iyelolu, T. V., Idemudia, C., & Ijomah, T. I. (2024). Exploring the relationship between sustainable business practices and increased brand loyalty. *International Journal of Management & Entrepreneurship Research, 6*(8), 2463–2475.

Anning-Dorson, T., & Zulu, M. (2025). Digital transformation of sustainability marketing in

Barraco, M. (2024). Characteristics of research on green marketing. Theoretical study. *Marketing Science & Inspirations, 19*(1), 15–25.

Bhattacharyya, J. (2023). The structure of sustainability marketing research: A bibliometric review and directions for future research. *Asia-Pacific Journal of Business Administration, 15*(2), 245–286.

Bhayani, S., & Vachhani, N. V. (2014). Internet marketing vs traditional marketing: A comparative analysis. *FIIB Business Review, 3*(3), 53–63.

Boozary, P., Hosseini, I., Pourmirza, M., GhorbanTanhaei, H., & Sheykhan, S. (2024). The impact of marketing automation on consumer buying behaviour in the digital space via artificial intelligence. *Power System Technology, 48*(1), 1008–1021.

Curran, J. (2012). Rethinking internet history: James Curran. In *Misunderstanding the internet* (pp. 40–71). Routledge.

Dube, M., Tshuma, S., & Mawere, R. A. (2023). The role of digital marketing in sustainable marketing: using digital channels to raise awareness and promote sustainable products and services. In *Sustainable marketing, branding, and reputation management: Strategies for a greener future* (pp. 295–309). IGI Global.

Grandhi, B., Patwa, N., & Saleem, K. (2021). Data-driven marketing for growth and profitability. *EuroMed Journal of Business, 16*(4), 381–398.

Gündüzyeli, B. (2024). Artificial intelligence in digital marketing within the framework of sustainable management. *Sustainability, 16*(23), 10511.

Hartemo, M. (2016). Email marketing in the era of the empowered consumer. *Journal of Research in Interactive Marketing, 10*(3), 212–230.

Ismail, I. J., Amani, D., & Changalima, I. A. (2023). Strategic green marketing orientation and environmental sustainability in sub-Saharan Africa: Does green absorptive capacity moderate? Evidence from Tanzania. *Heliyon, 9*(7).

Kalogiannidis, S., Kalfas, D., Loizou, E., Papaevangelou, O., & Chatzitheodoridis, F. (2023). Smart sustainable marketing and emerging technologies: Evidence from the Greek business market. *Sustainability, 16*(1), 312.

Kaplan, A. M. (2015). Social media, the digital revolution, and the business of media. *International Journal on Media Management, 17*(4), 197–199.

Kumar, V., & Mittal, S. (2020). Mobile marketing campaigns: Practices, challenges and opportunities. *International Journal of Business Innovation and Research, 21*(4), 523–539.

Kumar, V., Rahman, Z., & Kazmi, A. A. (2013). Sustainability marketing strategy: An analysis of recent literature. *Global Business Review, 14*(4), 601–625.

Kushwaha, B. P., Kaur, G., Singh, N., & Sharma, A. (2022). Integrating employees, customers and Technology to build an effective, sustainable marketing strategy. *International Journal of Sustainable Society, 14*(4), 310–322.

Levene, M. (2011). *An introduction to search engines and web navigation*. Wiley.

Lunde, M. B. (2018). Ethical concerns of Un (sustainable) stakeholders: A reexamination of stakeholder theory in sustainable decision-making. In *Marketing Transformation: Marketing Practice in an Ever Changing World: Proceedings of the 2017 Academy of Marketing Science (AMS) World Marketing Congress (WMC)* (pp. 89–95). Springer International Publishing.

Mandung, F. (2024). The impact of sustainability and environmental ethics in product marketing campaigns: A qualitative study with a sociological and economic approach. *Golden Ratio of Data in Summary, 4*(2), 911–922.

Masocha, R. (2018). Sustainable marketing practices and sustainable consumer behaviour of tertiary students in South Africa. *Journal of Economics and Behavioral Studies, 10*(3), 248–257.

Mathew, D., Brintha, N. C., & Jappes, J. W. (2023). Artificial intelligence powered automation for Industry 4.0. In *New Horizons for Industry 4.0 in modern business* (pp. 1–28). Springer International Publishing.

Musa, H. G., Fatmawati, I., Nuryakin, N., & Suyanto, M. (2024). Marketing research trends using technology acceptance model (TAM): A comprehensive review of researches (2002–2022). *Cogent Business & Management, 11*(1), 2329375.

Navaratne, A. (2023). Incorporating sustainability contexts in marketing.

Olanrewaju, G., Omoniyi, L., Adebisi, P., Ayantayo, T., Yange, E., & Boluwaji, V. (2025). Best practice compendium:" Greener tech in Africa.

Robertsone, G., & Lapiņa, I. (2023). Digital transformation as a catalyst for sustainability and open innovation. *Journal of Open Innovation: Technology, Market, and Complexity, 9*(1), Article 100017.

Rodionov, S. O. (2021). Current trends in industry and features of marketing activities. https://doi.org/10.33216/1998-7927-2021-267-3-132-136

Rosário, A. T., & Dias, J. C. (2023). How has data-driven marketing evolved: Challenges and opportunities with emerging technologies. *International Journal of Information Management Data Insights, 3*(2), Article 100203.

Rosário, A. T., Lopes, P. R., & Rosário, F. S. (2023). The digital marketing for sustainable development.

Seymour, T., Frantsvog, D., & Kumar, S. (2011). History of search engines. *International Journal of Management & Information Systems (IJMIS), 15*(4), 47–58.

Shaw, A. (2024). Digital marketing productivity: Assessing what SMEs do and demonstrating how they can improve efficiency. *Available at SSRN* 4863178.

Smith, T. (2009). The social media revolution. *International journal of market research, 51*(4).

Sono, M. G. (2023). Bibliometric analysis of the term "Marketing sustainability.". *West Science Interdisciplinary Studies, 1*(06), 314–325.

Ström, R., Vendel, M., & Bredican, J. (2014). Mobile marketing: A literature review on its value for consumers and retailers. *Journal of Retailing and Consumer Services, 21*(6), 1001–1012.

Udeh, E., & Dugba, A. (2025). An analysis of the potential integration of sustainability into marketing strategies by companies. *European Journal of Management and Marketing Studies, 9*(3).

Uyanik, M. (2024). Sustainability marketing: The intersection of sustainability and marketing for a better world. In *Marketing innovation strategies and consumer behaviour* (pp. 108–128). IGI Global.

Vial, G. (2021). Understanding digital transformation: A review and a research agenda. In *Managing digital transformation* (pp. 13–66).

White, K., Cakanlar, A., Sethi, S., & Trudel, R. (2025). The past, present, and future of sustainability marketing: How did we get here and where might we go? *Journal of Business Research, 187*, Article 115056.

Widiastuti, E., Sukesi, S., & Sarsiti, S. (2024). Sustainable marketing in the digital age: A systematic review of the latest strategies and tactics. *International Journal of Economics, Business and Accounting Research (IJEBAR)*, *8*(1).

Yadav, A., & Sondhi, H. (2023, March). Systematic literature review on sustainable marketing and artificial intelligence. In *2023 10th International Conference on Computing for Sustainable Global Development (INDIACom)* (pp. 583–588). IEEE.

CHAPTER 4

Service-Dominant Logic and the Technology Acceptance Model: A New Frontier for the Adoption of Clean Cooking Practices

Nazifatu Mohammed Abdulai, Mahmoud Abdulai Mahmoud, and Raphael Odoom

Introduction

The global transition to clean cooking technologies remains a critical priority toward achieving sustainable development, climate mitigation, and public health (Ibe & Kollur, 2024; Odoi-Yorke, 2024; Yadav et al.,

N. M. Abdulai · M. A. Mahmoud (✉) · R. Odoom
Department of Marketing and Entrepreneurship, University of Ghana Business School, Accra, Ghana
e-mail: mamahmoud@ug.edu.gh

College of Humanities, University of Ghana, Accra, Ghana

N. M. Abdulai
e-mail: nmohammed_abdulai@stu.ug.edu.gh

R. Odoom
e-mail: rodoom@ug.edu.gh

A. Gbadamosi et al. (eds.), *Contemporary Marketing Practices in Africa, Volume 1*, Palgrave Studies of Marketing in Emerging Economies,
https://doi.org/10.1007/978-3-032-27126-6_4

2024). According to the International Energy Agency (IEA, 2023), more than 2.3 billion people now depend on traditional fuels, generating household air pollution that causes millions of premature deaths every year (World Health Organization (WHO), 2021). The use of traditional cooking methods is not only inefficient but also contributes significantly to environmental degradation and exacerbates ozone layer depletion by emitting excess carbon dioxide and burning fossil fuels (Lacey et al., 2017).

Furthermore, this practice results in significant indoor and outdoor air pollution (Rosário Filho et al., 2021), which has been directly linked to numerous health complications, including cancer, stroke, heart diseases, chronic obstructive pulmonary diseases, and, in most cases, leading to deaths, with children under five being disproportionately affected (WHO, 2022). Advanced fuels such as LPG, ethanol, and biogas are usually cleaner, more efficient, safer, and more appealing to users than traditional solid fuels (Robin & Ehimen, 2024). The last decade, however, has seen quite a few manufacturers modify solid-fuel cookstoves into sophisticated stoves to improve combustion and reduce emissions compared to open fires and traditional stoves. Meanwhile, the policy objective to reduce indoor and outdoor air pollution, to mitigate the long-term and near-term climate change, to reduce deforestation, and others still hang in the balance (Robin & Ehimen, 2024).

A study in Ghana by Karakara and Osabuohien (2021) reveals that 78.82% of the population uses dirty fuels for cooking, indicating that solid fuels are used by most households in Ghana. This indicates that about 21% of households adopt sustainable clean cooking practices. Another data collated by the Ghana Statistical Service in 2022 states that situating health facilities close to domestic household communities in Ghana facilitates the adoption of sustainable cooking practices, as the health professionals, as part of a voluntary service, educate the households around these communities on the dangers of using solid fuels for cooking (Adjei-Mantey, 2024).

The Global Alliance for Clean Cookstoves and the Energy Commission have all launched advocacy campaigns against traditional cooking methods, but more remains to be done, as over 80 percent of the world's population still uses them (Robin & Ehimen, 2024). In 2010, the Global Alliance for Clean Cookstoves, a Public Private Partnership to serve as a catalyst for thriving global market for clean cooking solutions was launched with over 650 partners including 38 countries joining the alliance which saw them raise over $30 million, directly leveraged more than $120 million in new funding from alliance partners and convened over 350 global experts to help develop a forward-looking plan for overcoming the many barriers that hinder the progress of the clean cooking advocacy in the past. The alliance, in its 3rd year, sought to implement action plans in 6 priority countries, namely: Bangladesh, China, Ghana, Kenya, Nigeria, and Uganda, thereby catalyzing private investment into the sector and advancing priority research (Lindgren, 2020).

Despite numerous programs carried out and innovations generated to diffuse clean cooking solutions (Anjanappa et al., 2024; van den Wall Bake et al., 2025), be it liquefied petroleum gas, improved biomass stoves, or electric stoves, the broad adoption of such solutions remains weak, especially in the low and middle-income countries. Therefore, there is a persisting gap between technological availability and actual uptake, due to the shortcomings of adoption models that focus too narrowly on technical features or cost barriers (Puzzolo et al., 2016; Troncoso & Soares da Silva, 2017).

Across many areas, the Technology Acceptance Model (TAM) has been widely applied to explain user adoption of innovations, emphasizing Perceived Usefulness (PU) and Perceived Ease of Use (PEOU) as key determinants of behavioral responses (Davis, 1989). While this foundation model has shown strong predictive capacity (Ezeudoka & Fan, 2024). Its narrow focus on individual cognition and rational decision-making has been criticized for overlooking the broader social, cultural, and institutional dynamics that shape technology adoption (Dwivedi et al., 2015)

In response to these limitations, TAM2 (Venkatesh & Davis, 2000) expanded the model by incorporating social influence factors (e.g., subjective norms, voluntariness, image) and cognitive instrumental processes (e.g., job relevance, output quality, result demonstrability). Similarly, TAM3 (Venkatesh & Bala, 2008) introduced determinants of PEOU such as computer self-efficacy, external control, computer anxiety, and perceived enjoyment, as well as the moderating effects of experience and facilitating conditions. These developments enriched TAM by embedding social contexts and experiential dimensions into adoption research, making the model attuned to socio-economic realities. Nevertheless, even with these extensions, TAM2 and TAM3 continue to conceptualize these factors primarily as external variables influencing individual cognition, leaving the systemic and relational nature of the adoption of sustainable clean cooking practices insufficiently theorized (Taherdoost, 2018).

To address this gap, this study offers a conceptual complement between TAM2 and TAM3 and Service-Dominant Logic (SDL) (Vargo & Lusch, 2003; 2016) to facilitate the adoption of sustainable clean cooking practices in Ghana. SDL shifts the focus from goods to services and from embedded value to value co-creation through actors' interactions, resource integration, and institutional arrangement (Da Silva & Cardoso, 2025; Mele & Russo-Spena, 2025). Under this paradigm, technologies do not carry inherent value; instead, they acquire meaning and utility through use-in-context and collaborative practices within service ecosystems. Users are therefore not passive adopters but active participants who cocreate value by integrating their knowledge, cultural practices, and institutional resources into the adoption process (Akaka & Vargo, 2014).

By opening a dialogue between TAM's cognitive-attitudinal and socio-contextual constructs (social influence, facilitating conditions) and SDL's emphasis on relational value co-creation, this paper charts a novel frontier in clean cooking research. This conceptual view contends that adoption outcomes are forged not just by those technical attributes of clean cooking technologies, but also by residual experiences of users and their socio-cultural meanings (actors' interactions and resource integration), within institutional arrangements in which they are embedded (Sovacool, 2014; Rehfuess et al., 2014). The synthesis in this paper offers an enriched, service-oriented perspective on technology adoption, with users forming the nexus as co-creators of value rather than consumers receiving innovations. Further, this conceptual viewpoint offers practical recommendations for policymakers, practitioners, and designers of clean cooking interventions toward a greater appreciation of sustainable energy transitions.

Methodology

To proceed with this perspective article, a critical review of research that has guided the service-dominant logic and the technology acceptance model was conducted. A search of the Scopus Index and Web of Science was conducted, with an inclusion criterion of the combination of keywords such as service-dominant logic and clean cooking practices, technology acceptance and clean cooking practices, and service-dominant logic and technology acceptance model. This yielded 36 articles from these two databases, including Scopus (25) and Web of Science (11). This perspective paper draws on these 36 papers to provide a proper understanding of the area of clean cooking, the technology acceptance model, and service-dominant logic.

Service-Dominant Logic and Technology Acceptance Model in the Literature

SDL presents a fundamental departure from traditional Goods-Dominant Logic (GDL) by proposing that value is co-created through resource integration and service exchange within the context of existing institutional norms and practices (Vargo & Lusch, 2004, 2016). Whereas GDL views value as embedded in products and brought into realization by market transactions, SDL views value as co-created by multiple actors and determined in use, not in exchange (Vargo & Lusch, 2008, 2016). Over its maturity, SDL has evolved, presenting 11 foundational premises based on 5 core axioms (FP11; Vargo & Lusch, 2016) that uphold the centrality of service, resource integration, institutional arrangements, and phenomenological value determination in value co-creation. SDL has been operationalized in other consumer studies to enhance the sale of goods and services due to its value co-creation nature. This makes SDL a powerful tool to explore how clean cooking is adopted in broader contexts. SDL shifts the focus from user acceptance to value co-creation in the service ecosystem.

Traditionally, developers of clean cooking technologies, especially in Ghana, are concerned with product utility, efficiency, and cost (the GDL way) (Odoi-Yorke, 2024). However, SDL puts the user in the position of value co-creator within the broader service ecosystem. Adoption is shaped not just by product characteristics but also through actor interactions, resource integration, and institutional norms and practices (Chandler & Vargo, 2011; Lusch & Vargo, 2014a, 2014b). From this standpoint, clean cooking technologies constitute a value proposition rather than an off-the-shelf solution, and their integration into communities as part of their routines and experiences is essential to their success (Tregua et al., 2021). For instance, the service delivery platform, which may include community training, after-sales support, or digital engagement, serves as a critical mechanism for adoption (Kunz & Hogreve, 2011). Institutional arrangements such as organizational norms, policy incentives, and local leadership also matter for coordinating value co-creation across households, commercial users, and manufacturers. Consequently, SDL offers an approach that moves away from viewing adoption as a one-off transaction, focusing instead on fostering ongoing value realization, adaptation, and social learning. From this wider perspective, SDL offers a powerful theoretical lens for supporting sustainable, scalable, clean-cooking shifts in underserved communities.

Introduced by Fred Davis in 1985, the TAM is one of the foundational models for predicting the adoption of new technologies by individuals and organizations. TAM addresses many scholars' complaints about user resistance and system non-performance by recognizing specific constructs that influence technology adoption, such as perceived usefulness, perceived ease of use, user attitude, behavioral intention, and actual system use (Dziak Mark, 2024). Davis argued that the system's attributes and capabilities serve as stimuli that shape users' attitudes and motivation, thereby increasing the likelihood of adoption. Further, he went on to suggest that his predictive model posits that technological systems may evoke a response from potential users who assess such systems for compatibility with their needs so that they can either resist or accept engaging with the said technological system on grounds of perceived value and ease of usability (Davis, 1985). The TAM1 was later developed by Venkatesh and Davis (1996), which removed the 'attitude' component seen in the original TAM because it does not fully capture the mediation effect of PU and PEOU on '*behavior*' (Davis, 1989, p. 320).

Over time, scholars identified that technology adoption is not driven solely by technical perceptions but also by social influence and cognitive instrumental processes, such as job relevance, output quality, and result demonstrability (Venkatesh & Davis, 2000). This gave birth to TAM2 as an extension of the TAM, highlighting the constructs of perceived usefulness. The TAM2 also highlights that user acceptance is shaped by both individual cognition and social expectations. Venkatesh later developed the TAM3 model in the same year (2000), integrating computer efficacy, perceptions of external control, computer anxiety, and enjoyment as determinants of perceived ease of use (Venkatesh & Bala, 2008).

By bringing together all the TAM2 and TAM3 in complementarity with SDL, this presents a holistic approach to understanding clean cooking adoption. While the TAM2-TAM3 identifies the cognitive and socio-contextual determinants of individual acceptance, SDL situates these determinants within the broader service ecosystems by capturing how actors, resources, and institutions collectively shape adoption.

Complement of SDL and TAM2-TAM3

While the original TAM as initiated by Davis (1985), which highlights the acceptance of technology using determinants such as perceived usefulness (PU), perceived ease of use (PEOU) and attitude toward use has been criticized for overlooking the larger socio-technical dynamics, (Alquran Balaman & Baş, 2023), this perspective article proposes a complement between the TAM2-TAM3 and SDL to extend the theoretical understanding of clean cooking adoption. The TAM2-TAM3 sought to overcome the cognitive focus by incorporating broader socio-economic and contextual dimensions. TAM2 (Venkatesh & Davis, 2000) introduced social influence constructs (subjective norm, voluntariness, image) and cognitive instrumental processes (job relevance, output quality, result demonstrability), highlighting how social pressure and contextual alignment influence the adoption of sustainable clean cooking practices. TAM3 (Venkatesh & Bala, 2008) further expanded the framework by theorizing about the dimensions of PEOU, including computer self-efficacy, perception of external control, computer anxiety, and perceived enjoyment. This emphasizes the role of experience and facilitating conditions, making the model more open to socio-economic realities in the adoption of sustainable clean cooking.

TAM2 and TAM3 represent a significant step forward in accounting for socio-cultural determinants of adoption. However, they continue to treat these factors as external variables that influence individual cognitive appraisals. This leaves the deeper, relational, and systematic processes through which adoption unfolds unaddressed, especially in areas such as sustainable clean cooking, where technologies are embedded in complex socio-technical and cultural ecosystems. While TAM3 explains how anxiety or facilitating conditions can affect PEOU, it does not capture how adoption is shaped by community engagement, institutional arrangements, and co-creation of value among multiple actors.

Drawing on the weaknesses of the TAM2 and TAM3 in the adoption of sustainable clean cooking, the SDL offers a complementary perspective by reframing the adoption of clean cooking practices as a process of value co-creation within service ecosystems (Vargo & Lusch, 2004, 2016). SDL emphasizes actors' interaction, resource integration, and institutional arrangements as central to how technologies gain meaning and value in practice. For this reason, adoption is not shaped by perceived utility and ease, but a collective system process in which various actors in the value co-creation chain co-shape outcomes (Chandler & Vargo, 2011; Sarno & Siano, 2022). This paper presents a complementary approach combining TAM2-TAM3 and SDL to explore multi-level adoption of clean cooking practices, using multidimensional constructs such as value co-creation, resource integration, and institutional arrangements alongside TAM2-TAM3 to build a collaborative and institutional ecosystem.

This chapter presents a novel contribution that moves beyond treating adoption as a sequence of individual decisions and instead theorizes it as a socially co-created phenomenon, which provides both theoretical and practical depth for designing interventions that address not only user perceptions but also the service ecosystems in which clean cooking solutions are introduced. While previous adoption studies often remain at the level of cognitive determinants, the integration of TAM2-TAM3 and SDL is explicitly designed to address the gap in clean cooking adoption. Tam2-TAM3 explains why users may resist new technologies due to perceptions of low usefulness, limited ease of use, social influence, or facilitating conditions. SDL, however, complements this by situating adoption in a broader service ecosystem, where success depends on the effects of social influence and other facilitating conditions, through the integration of technological know-how by both the producer and the user, herein called actors, value co-creation through training programmes, after-sales service, and policy incentives. This multi-level solution framework offers strategies for overcoming the barriers to TAM2-TAM3 adoption, but does not situate its premise on both actors to facilitate the adoption of sustainable clean cooking practices. Together, both TAM2-TAM3 and SDL provide practical and integrated framework for the adoption of sustainable clean cooking adoption.

Directions for Future Studies

The achievement of the United Nations Agenda 2030 still remains thwarted due to the slow adoption of sustainable cooking practices (WHO, 2022). The ozone layer is being depleted each day by man-made activities, such as the release of carbon dioxide from burning fossil fuels, which continue to pose dangerous health hazards to humans (Anjanappa,

2024). The study on the merger of theories to form other factors of adoption in the clean cooking area has been underexplored, giving room for researchers and academic scholars to consider research into other factors, which are customer centric value-oriented ways of adoption, where the customer feels involved and part of the network of actors in the benefit of value (Lacey et al., 2017). Drawing on the above, we propose expanding this paper to test the listed hypotheses within the domains of domestic and commercial consumers of smart cooking appliances. A qualitative study of this theoretical merger is also important for understanding the concept from the producers' or manufacturers' perspective regarding the proposed factors in the adoption of clean cooking devices. This conceptual paper adapted the TAM 2 and TAM3 constructs and complemented them with the three constructs of the service-dominant logic to form a basis for understanding sustainable clean cooking adoption (Tang & Jiang, 2024; Davis et al., 2024; Vargo & Lusch, 2017). Future studies can also adapt the service-dominant logic framework and expand it into an extended version. Lastly, future studies should also examine how complementing consumer behavior theories with technology-oriented theories influences the adoption and acceptance of new technologies in the context of clean cooking practices.

References

Adjei-Mantey, K. (2024). On clean energy use: The role of health care facilities in improving clean cooking energy adoption in Ghana. *Discover Sustainability, 5*(1), 479.

Akaka, M. A., & Vargo, S. L. (2014). Technology as an operant resource in service (eco) systems. *Information Systems and e-Business Management, 12*, 367–384.

Anjanappa, J. (2024). Unveiling the Green Paradox-Biodiversity Risk in Renewable Energy Investments in India. Available at SSRN 4722554.

Anjanappa, J., Samant, S., & Ullah, H. (2024). Unleashing the potential: Transforming India's clean cooking ecosystem through social value innovation in India. Available at SSRN 4807119.

Tang, L., & Jiang, J. (2024). Enhancing the combined-TAM-TPB model with trust in the sharing economy context: A meta-analytic structural equation modeling approach. *Journal of Cleaner Production, 442*, Article 141168.

Balaman, F., & Baş, M. (2023). Perception of using e-learning platforms in the scope of the technology acceptance model (TAM): A scale development study. *Interactive Learning Environments, 31*(8), 5395–5419.

Chandler, J. D., & Vargo, S. L. (2011). Contextualization and value-in-context: How context frames exchange. *Marketing Theory, 11*(1), 35–49.

da Silva, A. A., & Cardoso, A. J. M. (2025). Harnessing technology to drive coopetition and value co-creation: A service-dominant perspective. *Administrative Sciences, 15*(2), 64.

Davis, F. D., Granić, A., & Marangunić, N. (2024). *The technology acceptance model: 30 years of TAM*. Springer International Publishing AG.

Davis, F. D. (1989). Perceived usefulness, perceived ease of use, and user acceptance of information technology. *MIS Quarterly*, 319–340.

Dwivedi, Y. K., Wastell, D., Laumer, S., Henriksen, H. Z., Myers, M. D., Bunker, D., Elbanna, A., Ravishankar, M. N., & Srivastava, S. C. (2015). Research on information systems failures and successes: Status update and future directions. *Information Systems Frontiers, 17*, 143–157.

Ezeudoka, B. C., & Fan, M. (2024). Determinants of behavioral intentions to use an E-Pharmacy service: Insights from TAM theory and the moderating influence of technological literacy. *Research in Social and Administrative Pharmacy, 20*(7), 605–617.

Ibe, K. K., & Kollur, S. P. (2024). Challenges towards the adoption and use of sustainable cooking methods: A comprehensive review. *Sustainable Environment, 10*(1), 2362509.

Karakara, A. A., & Osabuohien, E. S. (2021). Clean versus dirty energy: Empirical evidence from fuel adoption and usage by households in Ghana. *African Journal of Science, Technology, Innovation and Development, 13*(7), 785–795.

Kunz, W. H., & Hogreve, J. (2011). Toward a deeper understanding of service marketing: The past, the present, and the future. *International Journal of Research in Marketing, 28*(3), 231–247.

Lacey, F. G., Henze, D. K., Lee, C. J., Van Donkelaar, A., & Martin, R. V. (2017). Transient climate and ambient health impacts due to national solid fuel cookstove emissions. *Proceedings of the National Academy of Sciences, 114*(6), 1269–1274.

Lindgren, S. A. (2020). Clean cooking for all? A critical review of behavior, stakeholder engagement, and adoption for the global diffusion of improved cookstoves. *Energy Research & Social Science, 68*, Article 101539.

Mele, C., & Russo-Spena, T. (2025). Agencement of onlife and phygital: Smart tech–enabled value co-creation practices. *Journal of Service Management, 36*(2), 217–240.

Odoi-Yorke, F. (2024). A systematic review and bibliometric analysis of electric cooking: Evolution, emerging trends, and future research directions for sustainable development. *Sustainable Energy Research, 11*(1), 24.

Puzzolo, E., Pope, D., Stanistreet, D., Rehfuess, E. A., & Bruce, N. G. (2016). Clean fuels for resource-poor settings: A systematic review of barriers and enablers to adoption and sustained use. *Environmental Research, 146*, 218–234.

Rehfuess, E. A., Puzzolo, E., Stanistreet, D., Pope, D., & Bruce, N. G. (2014). Enablers and barriers to large-scale uptake of improved solid fuel stoves: A systematic review. *Environmental Health Perspectives, 122*(2), 120–130.

Robin, T., & Ehimen, E. (2024). Exploring the potential role of decentralised biogas plants in meeting energy needs in sub-Saharan African countries: A techno-economic systems analysis. *Sustainable Energy Research, 11*(1), 8.

Rosário Filho, N. A., Urrutia-Pereira, M., d'Amato, G., Cecchi, L., Ansotegui, I. J., Galán, C., Pomés, A., Murrieta-Aguttes, M., Caraballo, L., Rouadi, P., & Annesi-Maesano, I. (2021). Air pollution and indoor settings. *World Allergy Organization Journal, 14*(1), Article 100499.

Sovacool, B. K. (2014). What are we doing here? Analyzing fifteen years of energy scholarship and proposing a social science research agenda. *Energy Research & Social Science, 1*, 1–29.

Taherdoost, H. (2018). A review of technology acceptance and adoption models and theories. *Procedia Manufacturing, 22*, 960–967.

Tregua, M., Brozovic, D., & D'Auria, A. (2021). 15 years of service-dominant logic: Analyzing citation practices of Vargo and Lusch (2004). *Journal of Service Theory and Practice, 31*(4), 563–606.

Trinh, V. L., & Chung, C. K. (2023). Renewable energy for SDG-7 and sustainable electrical production, integration, industrial application, and globalization. *Cleaner Engineering and Technology, 15*, Article 100657.

Troncoso, K., & da Silva, A. S. (2017). LPG fuel subsidies in Latin America and the use of solid fuels to cook. *Energy Policy, 107*, 188–196.

Yadav, A., Nair, V. K., Viswanathan, P. K., Manoj, P., & Raman, R. (2024). Analyzing the journey and future trajectories of clean cooking research in India: A bibliometric analysis and case study research. *Discover Sustainability, 5*(1), 521.

van den Wall Bake, K., Tigabu, A., Talevi, M., van Beukering, P., & Schaafsma, M. (2025). Solar PV and clean cookstove technology diffusion systems: Four case studies from Sub-Saharan Africa. *Renewable Energy, 240*, Article 122201.

Vargo, S. L. & Lusch, R. F. (2014a). Evolving to a new dominant logic for marketing. In *The service-dominant logic of marketing* (pp. 3–28). Routledge.

Vargo, S. L., & Lusch, R. F. (2014b). Inversions of service-dominant logic. *Marketing Theory, 14*(3), 239–248.

Vargo, S. L., & Lusch, R. F. (2016). Institutions and axioms: An extension and update of service-dominant logic. *Journal of the Academy of Marketing Science, 44*, 5–23.

Vargo, S. L., & Lusch, R. F. (2017). Service-dominant logic 2025. *International Journal of Research in Marketing, 34*(1), 46–67.

Venkatesh, V., & Bala, H. (2008). Technology acceptance model 3 and a research agenda on interventions. *Decision Sciences, 39*(2), 273–315.

PART III

Consumer Behaviour and Strategic Perspectives

CHAPTER 5

Crisis-Driven Consumer Behaviour: Navigating Purchasing Patterns and Marketing Implications During the COVID-19 Crisis

Kobby Mensah, Nnamdi O. Madichie, and Gilbert Kofi Mensah

Introduction

This chapter applies social impact theory to analyse consumer behaviour amid global crises, using the Covid-19 pandemic as a case study. The chapter argues that the fear of scarcity significantly altered purchasing patterns, particularly in emerging economies such as Ghana, where supply chain disruptions exposed vulnerabilities in the distribution and marketing of essential goods. The chapter notes a muted five-stage consumer

K. Mensah (✉)
Ghana Tourism Development Company Limited (GTDC), Accra, Ghana
e-mail: kobbymensah@ug.edu.gh

K. Mensah · G. K. Mensah
Business School, University of Ghana, Legon, Ghana
e-mail: gkmensah007@st.ug.edu.gh

A. Gbadamosi et al. (eds.), *Contemporary Marketing Practices in Africa, Volume 1*, Palgrave Studies of Marketing in Emerging Economies,
https://doi.org/10.1007/978-3-032-27126-6_5

decision-making model during the pandemic, giving way to an adaptive four-stage process in most purchase decisions in the study, comprising need recognition, purchase, ownership, and satisfaction. The muted information search and evaluation of alternatives highlight the urgency-driven nature of consumer behaviour in crisis time, and necessity and availability override brand preference and price sensitivity.

The results confirm that during crisis situations, particularly during COVID-19, the information search and evaluation of alternative options collapsed, as consumers prioritised immediacy, survival, and availability over brand preference or comparative analysis. This aligns with findings in the crisis-consumer literature (Hamilton, 2021; Loxton et al., 2020), which show that decision-making heuristics dominate under time pressure and uncertainty. Hence, the revised four-stage model: need recognition, purchase, ownership, and satisfaction, better captures the accelerated and necessity-driven process, providing a more accurate framework than the traditional five-stage model in pandemic contexts.

The study finds that the shift in consumer decision-making has profound implications for marketing strategy. It suggests that the traditional marketing mix of 4Ps—product, price, place, and promotion—would not function at the same level of importance in crisis periods. Product availability and distribution, represented as a place in the marketing mix, became paramount as consumers prioritised access. The product in the marketing mix is also noted as paramount, but from the perspective of what are termed 'essential purchases,' such as food, personal hygiene items, and medical supplies. The Ghanaian market, as with most markets globally, witnessed unprecedented panic buying of essentials, while non-essential purchases were postponed, leading to a de-prioritisation of such goods as luxury consumption. This suggests that the consumer decision-making process was largely dictated by survival needs rather than aspirational consumption—a utilitarian versus a hedonistic purchasing approach. Also noteworthy was the rise in the importance of

N. O. Madichie
Bloomsbury Institute, London, UK

Woxsen University, Telangana, India

N. O. Madichie
e-mail: nnamdi.madichie@bil.ac.uk

e-commerce platforms and mobile payment solutions to the supply chain as a result of the no-contact instructions during the pandemic. This shift has significant implications for marketing, prompting a reassessment of marketing strategies to align with consumer priorities during crises.

Despite its valuable insights, the study faced limitations due to data-collection constraints imposed by the pandemic, which necessitated the use of online surveys and led to incomplete responses, duplicate entries, and inconsistencies, requiring a thorough data-cleaning process to ensure reliability. Post-pandemic consumer behaviour studies must be conducted to explore potential long-term shifts in purchasing patterns.

Literature Review and Hypotheses Formulation

Perceived Scarcity, Uncertainty, and Purchase Intention During Crises

The Covid-19 lockdowns in the first half of 2020 triggered unprecedented shifts in consumer purchase intentions and behaviour, driven by fear of shortages of essential commodities such as personal hygiene products (e.g. toilet paper and hand sanitiser). This reaction was expected, as panic buying often serves as a coping mechanism in times of crisis (Billore & Anisimova, 2021; Yuen et al., 2020), providing consumers with a perceived sense of control over uncertainty. The widespread sense of scarcity, fuelled by mainstream media reports on supply chain disruptions, was characterised by three key emotions: fear, panic, and risk (Arafat et al., 2020; Putri et al., 2021). These emotions shaped consumer purchase decisions, leading many to purchase whatever essentials they could find, while prioritising immediate needs over discretionary spending.

While the 4Ps remain central in marketing, this study observed muted roles of price and promotion. Empirical evidence supports this: during Covid-19, consumers deprioritised price sensitivity (Nistorescu & Puiu, 2009; Tsao et al., 2019) because availability trumped cost. Similarly, promotional messages lost traction, as uncertainty and panic reduced consumers' responsiveness to persuasive advertising (Wong et al., 2021). Instead, product availability and distribution ('place') determined purchase choices. This selective focus highlights an important crisis-induced recalibration of the marketing mix, demonstrating why only product and place retained dominance while price and promotion receded.

According to Social Impact Theory (Latane, 1981), an individual undergoes psychological change in the presence of others, whether real or perceived. Hence, their beliefs, emotions, and actions are shaped by social influences. Consumer purchasing decisions in such crises are dictated by external forces rather than intrinsic needs, as also noted in Naeem (2021) and Kemp et al. (2021), who emphasise the primacy of social influence, herd behaviour, and media-driven narratives in shaping crisis-time decisions.

Another observed shift was that the purchase of non-essential and luxury goods declined, so the 'availability of brands' was prioritised over 'preference for brands.' This shift had significant implications for advertising and promotional activities, as traditional marketing efforts became less effective. Consumers were already highly motivated by the uncertainty of the situation, leaving little room for marketing influence on their buying decisions (Wong et al., 2021).

Another notable behavioural change was self-imposed rationing. Many consumers, uncertain about how long their stockpiled goods would last, adjusted their consumption patterns to stretch supplies. This behaviour highlights how scarcity and uncertainty shape both purchasing and consumption habits. Given these shifts, the study explores how consumer buying behaviour is influenced in times of crisis. Using Social Impact Theory for interpretation, it calls for examining the marketing mix and consumer decision-making frameworks during crisis and uncertain times. Social Impact Theory has been widely applied in social psychology research (Latane & Wolf, 1981; Latane & Nida, 1981). It has also been adapted to explain language evolution (Nettle, 1999), cultural shifts (Harton & Bullock, 2007), and attitude changes in social groups through computational modelling (Nowak et al., 1990).

Latane & Wolf (1981) proposed that social impact is a function of these three variables. As sources become stronger, closer, and more numerous, their influence intensifies (Basset & Latane, 1976; Chang et al., 2018; Jackson & Latane, 1981). Similarly, when individuals experience external pressure from a dominant group, their behaviour aligns with that pressure. For example, panic buying emerges as a direct consequence of increasing social impact. As more people rush to buy goods, the perception of scarcity intensifies, reinforcing panic-driven purchases. This aligns with previous studies demonstrating that social influence intensifies with the growing number of sources (Gerard et al., 1968; Milgram et al., 1969).

Latane and Wolf (1981) describe social impact as both multiplicative and divisive, meaning that a change in any of the three key variables results in a proportional shift in influence. If an individual aligns with the behaviour of an influential group, they are susceptible to both multiplicative (intensifying) and divisive (spreading) effects of social influence. This highlights the power of social environments in shaping behaviour. Components of Social Impact Theory include the following three key factors: (i) Strength—The significance or influence of the source. It refers to the individual characteristics that make a person or entity influential (Latane, 1981). (ii) Immediacy—The proximity of the source to the target. It may also be seen as the closeness of the influencer to the target, which includes physical proximity, clarity of communication, and the absence of barriers or filters. Immediacy inversely correlates with physical distance, meaning the closer the influencer, the stronger the impact. (iii) Number of sources—The total number of individuals exerting influence. Research suggests that social influence impact increases with the square root of the number of people involved (Latane & Harkins, 1976; Latane & Wolf, 1981). More sources amplify influence, while fewer sources weaken it.

Consumers' fear of missing out (FOMO) and desire to avoid future regrets also contribute to panic buying (Loomes & Sugden, 1982). The Regret Theory suggests that when consumers face the possibility of losing access to a product, they feel compelled to buy immediately. This is particularly evident in situations where time-limited offers or sudden product shortages create urgency. In extreme cases, such conditions can lead to hoarding behaviours. Latane (1981) noted that Social Impact Theory applies to various social phenomena, including responses to crises, media influence, and emergency situations. COVID-19 fuelled widespread fear, which, in turn, altered consumer behaviour. Panic buying, initially triggered by a few individuals, quickly escalated as more people joined the trend. As the influence of influencers (panic buyers) increased, their impact grew, reducing others' resistance to engaging in similar behaviour (Tsao et al., 2019). The result was an exponential surge in demand for essential goods, reinforcing the cycle of panic buying.

> ***H1:*** *Perceived scarcity has a significant impact on consumer intention to make bulk purchases.*
> ***H2:*** *Perceived scarcity significantly influences consumers to panic buy.*

H3: Perceived scarcity significantly influences consumer uncertainty during a crisis.

Panic Buying and Consumer Purchase Intention

Sunarto (2018) defines panic purchasing as the consumer's decision to buy, use, and invest in goods or services driven by uncertainty and perceived risk. According to Kulemeka (2010), panic buying is triggered by four key factors: (1) the perception of immediate danger, (2) a belief that limited solutions are available, (3) a sense that existing solutions are obstructed, and (4) crisis-related communication that fuels panic. The literature notes that consumer purchasing behaviour changes significantly during crises, deviating from conventional buying patterns (Sharma & Sonwalka, 2013; Nistorescu & Puiu, 2009). This shift occurs due to heightened 'perceived risk.' In a crisis era, consumers purchase unusually large amounts of products in anticipation of a disaster, real or perceived (Tsao et al., 2019). They prioritise availability and proximity over brand preference and price. Tsao et al. (2019) found that most consumers are willing to accept substitutes for their preferred brands during crises. Additionally, demand for luxury and premium goods declines as consumers shift spending to essential items (Nistorescu & Puiu, 2009). In other studies (Utami, 2020), panic buying is typically characterised by purchases of necessities such as food and fuel due to fears of impending shortages. Helsloot and Ruitenberg (2004) argue that perceived scarcity acts as a catalyst for panic buying, leading consumers to purchase in bulk and alter their normal buying behaviours.

H4: Panic buying significantly affects consumers, leading them to make bulk purchases during a pandemic.

H5: Panic buying significantly mediates the relationship between perceived scarcity and consumers' intention to make bulk purchases during a pandemic.

Perceived Scarcity and Consumer Uncertainty During a Pandemic

Scarcity refers to the actual or perceived shortage of goods and services, which can be either long-term (due to legal restrictions) or short-term (due to stockouts). Scarcity can manifest in two forms: variety scarcity (limited availability of specific models or sizes) and category scarcity (limited access to an entire product category) (Grier & Davis, 2013). Scarcity can affect individuals or entire communities. In times of crisis, community-wide perceived scarcity often drives shifts in purchasing behaviour (Hamilton et al., 2018). Under normal conditions, consumers make purchases based on demand, researching available brands before deciding. However, perceived scarcity creates a sense of urgency, disrupting this process. Hamilton et al. (2018) define perceived scarcity as the threat to one's ability to obtain desired goods or services. This perception leads to increased demand, bulk purchases, and reduced product search efforts (Li, 2020a, 2020b).

Studies have explored perceived scarcity in different perspectives, including supply-induced scarcity (Robinson et al., 2016; Kinata, 2016; Gupta & Gentry, 2016), shelf-based scarcity (Robinson et al., 2016; Parker & Lehmann, 2011), and price-based scarcity (Park et al., 2020). Research confirms that perceived scarcity significantly influences consumer behaviour, leading to increased willingness to pay and a preference for bulk buying (Kinata, 2016; Gupta & Gentry 2016; Parker & Lehmann, 2011). Robinson et al. (2016) found that scarcity cues affect product choice, increasing consumer willingness to select unfamiliar brands. However, consumers react differently when they suspect that scarcity is artificially created by suppliers.

Chen and Teng (2013) found a strong positive correlation between perceived scarcity and purchase intention. Wu et al. (2012) compared two theoretical models, Lynn's Scarcity–Expensiveness–Desirability (S-E-D) model (Lynn, 1989, 1992) and Snyder and Fromkin's desire for uniqueness model (Snyder & Fromkin, 1977), to analyse the impact of scarcity on consumer behaviour. Their findings indicate that perceived scarcity significantly influences purchase intention through perceived sacrifice and perceived value. Furthermore, Robinson et al. (2016) demonstrated that scarcity cues impact consumer willingness-to-pay and product selection in real-world settings. Park et al. (2020) observed that even in the absence of actual scarcity, certain natural settings can create a perceived shortage, prompting consumers to panic buy and stockpile goods unnecessarily.

According to Zhang and Liu (2020), the uncertainty surrounding COVID-19, coupled with the lack of a definitive cure, intensified a reactive behaviour in consumers. The fear of scarcity significantly altered purchasing intentions due to panic and uncertainty. The urgency to purchase essential goods was driven not only by personal needs but also by others' behaviour. As people observed increased demand and dwindling supplies, they felt compelled to stockpile, fearing an unpredictable future. As noted in the social impact theory (Latane, 1981), an individual undergoes psychological change due to the real or perceived presence of others. Hence, their beliefs, emotions, and actions are shaped by social influences. Consumer purchasing decisions in crises are found to be more externally driven than by intrinsic needs. During the pandemic, media coverage and collective consumer behaviour fostered fear, panic, and a heightened perception of scarcity. This influenced consumers' intention to purchase in bulk to minimise uncertainty and feel secure.

> ***H6:*** *Consumer uncertainty significantly impacts consumers' intention to purchase in bulk.*
> ***H7:*** *Consumer uncertainty significantly mediates the relationship between perceived scarcity and consumers' intention to make bulk purchases.*

Methodology

This study employed a structured approach to data collection and analysis to examine the impact of perceived scarcity on consumer behaviour, particularly in bulk purchasing and panic buying during the COVID-19 pandemic. A quantitative research design was adopted, utilising an online survey to reach a broad sample while adhering to COVID-19 safety protocols.

Sampling Procedure and Data Collection

To minimise physical contact, data was collected through an online survey conducted between April and June 2020. The three-month data collection window was intentional, as it captured the most volatile phase of the lockdown in Ghana. This period witnessed initial panic buying, adjustment behaviours, and the stabilisation of supply chains. Collecting data across this timeframe ensured the study captured both immediate and sustained behavioural responses, offering a more representative snapshot of consumer decision-making under crisis conditions.

Google Forms was used to host the questionnaire, and the survey link was distributed via WhatsApp groups associated with the University of

Ghana Business School, including faculty, staff, and students. Additionally, the survey was shared on popular Ghanaian Facebook communities, such as Tell It Mums and Tell It Dads, to ensure a diverse sample. A total of 501 responses were collected; however, after a thorough data-cleaning process that removed incomplete responses, duplicate entries, and inconsistencies, 402 valid responses were retained for analysis. This process ensured data accuracy and reliability, strengthening the study's findings.

Data Collection Instrument

The questionnaire was structured into two main sections. The first section captured demographic information and consumer purchasing behaviour before and after the COVID-19 lockdown announcement. The second section introduced key study variables and their indicators, using a five-point Likert scale ranging from 'Strongly Disagree' to 'Strongly Agree.' To enhance validity, survey items were not created in isolation but adapted from established scales. Adaptation involved contextualising items to reflect Covid-19 experiences in Ghana, and the items were reviewed by three academic experts in consumer behaviour. A pilot study further refined wording, ensuring cultural relevance and comprehension. These steps strengthened both content validity and reliability of the instruments used. The perceived scarcity and purchase intention survey items were derived from Wu et al. (2012), and their reliability was affirmed by Chen and Sun (2014). Panic-buying items were adapted from Lins and Aquino (2020), while consumer uncertainty scales were based on Bollen et al. (2010). Items with factor loadings below 0.70 (Hair et al., 2016) were removed, leaving 18 final indicators for the main study.

Assessment of Common Method Bias

To address potential common method bias, both procedural and statistical remedies were implemented, following the recommendations of Podsakoff et al. (2003). Measurement items were sourced from multiple studies to reduce bias, and respondents were assured of confidentiality and anonymity to minimise response distortions. The study also refined the measurement items to ensure they were relevant to the research context. Additionally, Harman's single-factor test was conducted using an exploratory factor analysis, which indicated that a single factor accounted for only 43.25% of the variance, confirming that common method bias was not a significant concern. In conclusion, this methodology ensured a rigorous and reliable data collection process, enabling the study to effectively analyse the relationship between perceived scarcity, panic buying, consumer uncertainty, and bulk purchasing behaviour during a pandemic. By employing validated measurement scales, a structured sampling process, and robust bias mitigation techniques, the study provides a strong foundation for understanding consumer responses in times of crisis.

Findings and Analysis

This section presents an in-depth analysis of the study's findings, focusing on demographic characteristics, purchasing behaviour during the lockdown, and structural equation modelling (PLS-SEM) results. The demographic profile of respondents provides a foundation for understanding their purchasing decisions, while the analysis of product categories highlights consumer behaviour in response to perceived scarcity. The study further examines the reliability and validity of the measurement model before evaluating the structural relationships between key variables.

The mediation analysis explores the indirect effects of perceived scarcity on purchase intention through consumer uncertainty and panic buying. The mediation analysis was designed to test whether panic buying and consumer uncertainty acted as amplifiers or attenuators of the main effect of perceived scarcity on purchase intention. Panic buying was hypothesised to amplify the effect by heightening emotional urgency, while uncertainty was hypothesised to attenuate rational decision-making, both indirectly reinforcing bulk purchase intentions. This design enabled the study to disentangle direct from indirect pathways, clarifying the psychological mechanisms underpinning crisis-driven purchasing.

The reported findings show that the effects stem specifically from mediation, not moderation. Panic buying and consumer uncertainty partially mediated the relationship between perceived scarcity and purchase intention. In other words, scarcity directly influenced purchase intentions, but its impact was significantly strengthened through these mediating variables. No moderating effects (e.g. demographic differences altering the strength of relationships) were detected. This distinction underscores the centrality of emotional and psychological responses as mediators rather than contextual moderators in shaping consumer behaviour under crisis conditions.

Justification of Hypotheses

H1: Perceived scarcity has a significant impact on consumer intention to make bulk purchases. When consumers perceive that a product is scarce, they are more likely to purchase in larger quantities to avoid missing out. Psychological theories like loss aversion (Prospect Theory) suggest that people act to prevent perceived future losses, leading them to buy in bulk when they anticipate shortages.
H2: Perceived scarcity significantly influences consumers to panic buy. Scarcity triggers fear of unavailability, prompting impulsive buying behaviours known as panic buying. Studies during crises (e.g. Covid-19) show that perceived scarcity leads consumers to hoard essential goods irrationally.
H3: Perceived scarcity significantly influences consumer uncertainty during a crisis. Scarcity creates a lack of confidence in future product availability, heightening consumer uncertainty. This uncertainty forces consumers to rethink their purchasing patterns to mitigate perceived risks.
H4: Panic buying significantly affects consumers, leading them to make bulk purchases during a pandemic. Panic buying escalates bulk purchasing behaviour, especially during uncertainty. Psychological stress and the bandwagon effect lead consumers to follow the crowd, reinforcing bulk-buying tendencies.
H5: Panic buying significantly mediates the relationship between perceived scarcity and consumers' intention to make bulk purchases during a pandemic. Scarcity leads to panic buying, which, in turn, reinforces bulk purchasing behaviours. The emotional response to scarcity (panic) serves as a bridge between perceived shortage and bulk buying intention.
H6: Consumer uncertainty significantly impacts consumers' intention to purchase in bulk. When consumers are uncertain about product availability, they opt for bulk purchasing as a coping mechanism to secure their needs in advance, thereby reducing risk.
H7: Consumer uncertainty significantly mediates the relationship between perceived scarcity and consumers' intention to make bulk

purchases. Perceived scarcity creates uncertainty about future availability, which motivates consumers to buy in bulk. Uncertainty acts as a psychological trigger, strengthening the perceived need for bulk purchasing.

Demographics

Table 5.1 presents the demographic characteristics of the participants. Of 401 respondents, 50.1% were male, and the dominant age group (26–35 years) accounted for 44.6% of the sample. The majority (52.4%) had completed a degree programme, while 27.4% held a postgraduate degree. Regarding occupation, 46.6% were employed in the private sector. Regarding marital status, 75.8% of respondents were married, while 22.9% were single.

Regarding monthly income, 47.6% of participants earned between 2,000 and 4,900, while only a few reported earnings above 10,000. The demographic profile suggests that the sample represents an appropriate target audience for the study, as the majority were educated, married, and fell within the affluent worker category, as defined by the National Employment Report by the Ghana Statistical Service (2015). This group was likely to understand the impact of the pandemic and the consequences of a lockdown. The study further examined the types of goods and services respondents purchased following the lockdown announcement. Table 5.2 outlines the results, showing that 61.1% of respondents purchased and stockpiled food, 21.7% hoarded groceries, and 9.7% prioritised toiletries.

Surprisingly, pharmaceutical products accounted for only 6.7% of purchases, despite the pandemic's health-related nature. Given the circumstances, a higher percentage of medical purchases would have been expected.

PLS-Structural Equation Modelling

Data analysis was conducted using PLS-SEM 2.0. This method was chosen to avoid parameter-estimation biases common in regression analysis, accommodate non-normal data, and impose minimal constraints on variable measurement (Hair et al., 2019). A two-stage approach

Table 5.1 Demographics

Demographic variables	*Frequency (402)*	*Percentages (100)*
Gender		
Male	201	50.1
Female	200	49.9
Age		
18–25 years	143	35.7
26–35 years	179	44.6
36-45 years	60	15.0
46–55 years	17	4.2
56 and above	2	.5
Level of education		
Certificate	1	.2
Diploma	78	19.5
Degree	210	52.4
Postgraduate	110	27.4
Occupation		
Government employee	88	21.9
Self-employed	70	17.5
Unemployed	9	2.2
Private sector employed	187	46.6
Student	47	11.7
Marital status		
Married	304	75.8
Single	92	22.9
Divorced/Separated	4	1.0
Widow	1	.2
Level of Income(cedi)		
250–1,990	84	20.9
2,000–4,990	191	47.6
5,000–9,000	82	20.4
10,000 and above	44	11.0

Table 5.2 Product category purchased

Products purchased	*Frequency (401)*	*Percentages (100) (%)*
Food stuff	245	61.1
Groceries	87	21.7
Toiletries	39	9.7
Pharmaceutical	27	6.7
Mothercare	2	0.5

was employed, comprising measurement model assessment and structural model evaluation.

Measurement Model Assessment

Before testing the hypothesised relationships, the data's validity and reliability were assessed. The reflective indicator loadings were examined, with a recommended threshold of 0.70 (Hair et al., 2019). Table 5.3 shows that all factor loadings exceeded this threshold, confirming their significance in measuring the latent variables. However, two indicators (PB5 and CU5) did not meet the minimum requirement and were removed (Gefen & Straub, 2005). This indicates that the retained indicators effectively captured the latent variables. Next, the internal consistency of the constructs was evaluated using Cronbach's alpha (CrA), with all values exceeding the 0.7 reliability threshold. Composite reliability (CR), a stronger measure of internal consistency, also demonstrated high reliability, with all values above 0.8 (Chin, 1998). Convergent validity was assessed using the average variance extracted (AVE), which should be above 0.5 (Fornell & Larcker, 1981; Hair et al., 2019). Table 5.3 confirms that all AVE values exceeded this benchmark, indicating strong convergent validity.

Discriminant validity was tested using Fornell and Larcker's (1981) criteria, which require that the square root of AVE values (italicised) exceed the off-diagonal correlation values. Table 5.4 displays the results, confirming discriminant validity.

Structural Model Assessment

Structural equation modelling (SEM) was used to examine the hypothesised relationships. Following Hair et al. (2019), bootstrapping with 5,000 resamples was applied. Table 5.4 presents the model's path coefficients, t-values, p-values, and the coefficient of determination (R^2). The independent variable accounted for 57% of the model's total variance ($R^2 = 0.570$). All hypotheses (H1–H5) were statistically significant. Perceived scarcity had a notable effect on purchase intention ($\beta = 0.136$, $p = 0.011$) and was a strong predictor of panic buying ($\beta = 0.411$, $p = 0.000$) and consumer uncertainty ($\beta = 0.363$, $p = 0.000$). The model demonstrated good fit metrics (SRMR = 0.74, NFI = 0.806), aligning with the criteria set by Hu and Beanntler (1999) (Fig. 5.1).

Table 5.3 Reliability and validity analysis

Variables	*Items*	*Loading*	*CrA*	*CR*	*AVE*
Perceived scarcity	PS1	0.797	0.879	0.917	0.735
	PS2	0.895			
	PS3	0.861			
	PS4	0.873			
Customer uncertainty	CU	0.724	0.807	0.863	0.559
	CU2	0.701			
	CU3	0.741			
	CU4	0.778			
	CU6	0.79			
Panic buy	PB1	0.864	0.904	0.933	0.777
	PB2	0.883			
	PB3	0.886			
	PB4	0.892			
Purchase intention	PI1	0.872	0.829	0.898	0.746
	PI2	0.899			
	PI3	0.818			

Perceived Scarcity (PS), Customer uncertainty (CU), Panic buy (PB), Purchase intention (PI), Also, CR—Composite reliability, CrA—Cronbach alpha, AVE—Average variance extracted

Table 5.4 Path analysis

Hypothesis	*Path description*	*β*	*t-value*	*p-value*	*Results*
H1	Perceived scarcity - > Purchase intention	0.136	2.56	0.011	Supported
H2	Perceived scarcity - > Panic buy	0.411	7.679	0.000	Supported
H3	Panic buy - > Purchase intention	0.086	2.101	0.036	Supported
H4	Perceived scarcity - > Customer uncertainty	0.363	4.964	0.000	Supported
H5	Customer uncertainty - > Purchase intention	0.654	15.047	0.000	Supported

Notes $*p \leqslant 0.05$; $***p \leqslant 0.001$

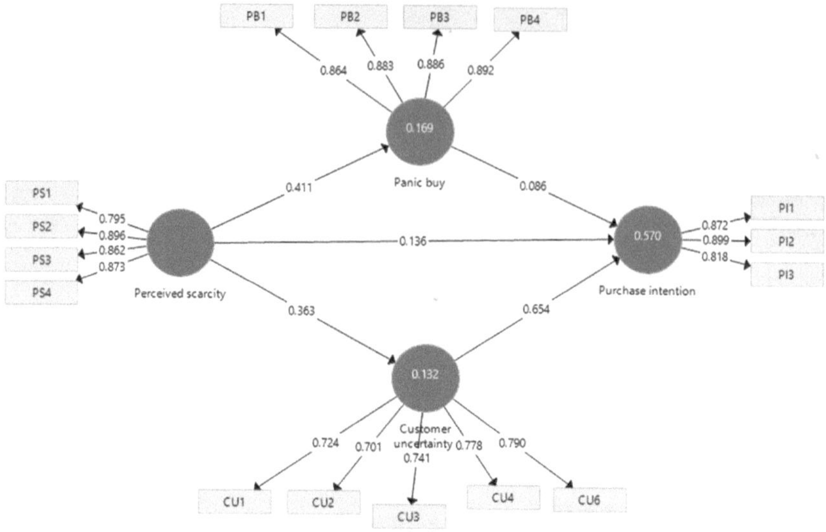

Fig. 5.1 Structural model results

Mediation Analysis

To evaluate mediation effects, a bootstrapping analysis with 5,000 resamples was conducted. Table 5.5 summarises the findings, indicating that both panic buying and consumer uncertainty partially mediated the relationship between perceived scarcity and purchase intention. This confirms the hypothesised mediation effects (H6, H7). These findings align with prior research. Adams et al. (2015) identified panic buying as a transitional phase leading to stockpiling, while Ghaderi et al. (2020) found that consumer-perceived ambiguity (uncertainty) partially mediated the relationship between consumer satisfaction and purchase intention.

The findings provide strong empirical support for the proposed hypotheses, demonstrating the significant role of perceived scarcity in influencing panic buying, consumer uncertainty, and bulk purchasing behaviour during a pandemic. The study also highlights the mediating effects of panic buying and consumer uncertainty in shaping purchase intentions. These insights contribute to a better understanding of consumer behaviour under crisis conditions and offer valuable implications for businesses and policymakers.

Table 5.5 Mediation analysis

Hypothesis	*Relationship*	*p-value*	*Mediation*
H6	Perceived scarcity - > Customer uncertainty - > Purchase intention	0	Partial mediation
H7	Perceived scarcity - > Panic buy - > Purchase intention	0.04	Partial mediation

Notes $^{*}p \leqslant 0.05$; $^{***}p \leqslant 0.001$

The results of this study confirm that perceived scarcity significantly influences consumers' intention to make bulk purchases during a global pandemic. A strong, positive relationship was observed between perceived scarcity, panic buying, and consumer intention to stockpile goods. Additionally, the study examined the relationship between perceived scarcity, consumer uncertainty, and bulk purchasing intentions, revealing significant positive associations among these variables.

Robinson et al. (2016) found that perceived scarcity strongly affects consumer preferences during crises, shaping their purchasing decisions. This supports the argument that, during emergencies, consumers prioritise product availability over brand preference, opting for alternative products that fulfil the same needs. For instance, during the early stages of the Covid-19 pandemic, essential goods such as sanitisers, disinfectants, and groceries quickly became scarce, leading to price surges. Consumers, driven by urgency, purchased available products irrespective of brand preferences. Similarly, Park et al. (2020) assert that even when products remain available, consumers may perceive scarcity and increase their purchasing volume. This aligns with the current study's hypothesis that perceived scarcity positively influences consumer intentions to buy in larger-than-usual quantities. Hamilton (2021) further emphasises that scarcity during a pandemic significantly affects consumer behaviour. The findings of this study validate this claim, showing that panic buying emerges as a direct response to perceived scarcity. As a result, consumers not only deviate from conventional purchasing behaviours but also make impulsive stockpiling decisions to minimise perceived risks.

The Role of Uncertainty and Panic Buying

The behavioural changes observed during the pandemic were primarily driven by the fear of scarcity, prompting consumers to anticipate and prepare for potential shortages. Yuen et al. (2020) argue that when consumers experience high levels of product scarcity, they are more likely to resort to panic buying. Additionally, perceived scarcity was found to significantly affect consumer uncertainty and bulk purchasing behaviour. This aligns with the findings of Schvaneveld et al. (2016) and Yuen et al. (2020), who reported that in times of crisis, consumers tend to increase spending on essential goods while deprioritising luxury purchases. This indicates that heightened uncertainty compels consumers to take drastic measures to prevent stockouts.

The study also explored the mediating role of panic buying and consumer uncertainty, revealing partial mediation effects for both variables. This suggests that while perceived scarcity directly influences consumers' intention to stockpile, uncertainty and panic buying further amplify this effect. These findings corroborate previous studies that demonstrated the mediating role of panic buying in consumer responses to scarcity (Wu et al., 2020; Wu et al., 2021). Similarly, consumer uncertainty partially mediated the relationship between perceived scarcity and stockpiling intentions. This suggests that uncertainty exacerbates consumers' inclination to hoard goods when scarcity is perceived, reinforcing the direct impact of perceived scarcity on purchasing decisions. Studies in related disciplines have supported this conclusion (Ghaderi et al., 2020; Li et al., 2020a, 2020b). Sharif (2017) asserts that uncertainty during crises influences consumer behaviour by altering psychological responses, social interactions, and purchasing patterns. Similarly, Hamilton (2018) conclude that natural disasters, including health crises, trigger consumer distress, shaping their buying decisions.

Discussion and Conclusions

The COVID-19 pandemic heightened consumers' panic and uncertainty, leading to an unprecedented shift in their purchasing behaviour. This change was primarily influenced by perceptions of product scarcity and the desire to mitigate regret. The present study examined the direct impact of perceived scarcity on consumers' intention to stockpile during a global pandemic and explored the mediating role of panic buying and consumer uncertainty in this relationship. All hypotheses tested were found to be significant.

Using the Social Impact Theory as a framework, this study suggests that in times of crisis, the traditional consumer decision-making process, originally proposed by Dewey (1910) and later expanded by Engel et al. (1968), witnesses a shift, in line with previous study findings of changes in consumer behaviour, as noted in the theory of social impact and the review of the literature (Tsao et al., 2019; Loxton et al., 2020; Kulemeka, 2010; Latane & Wolf, 1981; Latane & Nida, 1981; Sharma & Sonwalka, 2013). The typical five-stage process of need recognition, information search, evaluation of alternatives, purchase, and post-purchase behaviour is shortened to four stages: need recognition, purchase, ownership, and satisfaction. Information search and alternative evaluation are muted, while ownership is introduced as a critical component. According to Social Impact Theory, consumer need recognition during crises is not necessarily driven by an urgent personal requirement for a product. Instead, it is often influenced by the real or perceived actions of others who are stockpiling essential goods. Observing increased demand for key products triggers a heightened sense of scarcity, reinforcing consumer uncertainty about future product availability, mobility restrictions, and accessibility. This, in turn, alters purchasing behaviour.

Consumer Behaviour in Times of Crisis

Another perspective holds that perceived scarcity during a pandemic generates fear, prompting consumers to engage in panic buying and stockpiling to address uncertainty. Sedikides and Jackson (1990) argue that the impact of perceived scarcity depends on the number of sources (i.e. other consumers making bulk purchases), their influence strength, and the immediacy of the situation. As more consumers participate in bulk purchasing, the perceived urgency and scarcity intensify. This study aligns with previous research supported by Social Impact Theory, which suggests that the effects of social influence escalate as the number of influencing sources increases (Badgaiyan & Verma, 2015; Cameron & Shah, 2015; Thompson et al., 2017). Latane (1981) posits that Social Impact Theory is particularly relevant in situations requiring rapid responses, such as pandemics. The behavioural shifts observed during the COVID-19 pandemic provide strong evidence supporting this theory. Research also suggests that consumers respond to social impact by making precautionary purchases to avoid future regret (Yangui & Hajtaïeb El Aoud, 2015). Regret Theory explains that consumers faced with uncertainty must choose between making an immediate purchase or risking unavailability in the future. The findings of this study suggest that consumers are more likely to stockpile goods in response to perceived scarcity to alleviate fears of potential shortages.

This study provides valuable insights into the impact of perceived scarcity on consumer stockpiling behaviour during global crises. One of its key contributions is highlighting the significant behavioural shifts that occur during pandemics, particularly in consumer decision-making. The findings confirm that perceived scarcity strongly influences consumer intentions to make bulk purchases.

Moreover, this study underscores the mediating roles of panic buying and consumer uncertainty in the relationship between perceived scarcity and stockpiling behaviour. The Covid-19 pandemic is a strong example of how external disruptions, such as lockdowns and supply chain restrictions, can trigger panic-driven purchasing behaviour. For instance, the closure of Chinese ports, with China being a major supplier of goods to many African countries, including Ghana, instilled fear and panic among consumers across the continent. The lockdown measures imposed further reinforced perceptions of scarcity, leading to a rush for goods. Ghana, among other nations, experienced widespread panic buying, driven by illusions of imminent shortages.

Overall, this study reaffirms the significance of perceived scarcity in shaping consumer behaviour during crises. As pandemics and global disruptions continue, understanding the psychological and social drivers of consumer purchasing decisions will remain crucial for predicting and managing future market behaviour.

Implications, Limitations, and Future Research Directions

This study explores consumer decision-making during crisis periods and notes a four-stage purchasing decision model rather than the conventional five during the Covid-19 pandemic. The four-stage process consists of need recognition, purchase, ownership, and satisfaction. It found that information search and evaluation of alternatives were muted, and a new construct of ownership was introduced. This adjustment reflects the urgency and instinct-driven nature of consumer behaviour during crises. The findings have significant implications for managing the marketing mix during a crisis. It suggests that not all the elements of the marketing mix, the 4Ps of product, price, place, and promotion, are of equal importance during a crisis. While product and place become critical due to perceived scarcity and the threat of one's inability to obtain essential goods, the influences of price and promotion in the decision-making are reduced. However, the promotional mix also has a mixed appeal. Public relations, for example, emerges as critical for reassurance as branding becomes less influential. These insights reshape our understanding of marketing strategies during periods of heightened uncertainty.

Despite its contribution, the study has limitations related to data-collection constraints imposed by the pandemic, which necessitated the use of online surveys and led to incomplete responses, duplicate entries, and inconsistencies, requiring a thorough data-cleaning process to ensure reliability. Future research could examine post-COVID consumer behaviour to provide a comprehensive understanding of purchasing patterns before, during, and after the pandemic. A qualitative approach is also recommended to capture consumer perspectives in greater depth, enriching the literature with insights into how the pandemic influenced buying behaviour. Moreover, while this study focused on consumer behaviour, future research should adopt a firm-centric perspective and use a longitudinal research design to assess how businesses have adapted their strategies in response to crisis-driven shifts in consumer demand.

Acknowledgements This is a revised, revamped, and updated version of a preprint article. Mensah, K., Madichie, N., & Mensah, G. (2023). Consumer Buying Behaviour in Crisis Times: Uncertainty and Panic Buying Mediation Analysis. Preprints. https://doi.org/10.20944/preprints202302.0403.v1

Appendix

Table A.1 Product category purchased

Hypothesis	*Relationship*	*Justification*
H1	Perceived Scarcity → Bulk Purchase Intention	Consumers buy in bulk to avoid missing out due to fear of scarcity
H2	Perceived Scarcity → Panic Buying	Scarcity triggers emotional responses, leading to irrational panic-driven purchases
H3	Panic Buying → Bulk Purchases During Pandemic	Stress and social influence increase bulk buying during uncertain times
H4	Perceived Scarcity → Consumer Uncertainty	Lack of product availability increases uncertainty and anxiety
H5	Consumer Uncertainty → Bulk Purchase Intention	Consumers buy in bulk as a precautionary measure to reduce risk
H6	Perceived Scarcity → Panic Buying → Bulk Purchase Intention	Panic buying bridges the gap between scarcity and bulk purchases
H7	Perceived Scarcity → Consumer Uncertainty → Bulk Purchase Intention	Uncertainty due to scarcity strengthens the tendency to buy in bulk

References

Adair, W. L., & Xiong, T. X. (2018). How Chinese and Caucasian Canadians conceptualize creativity: The mediating role of uncertainty avoidance. *Journal of Cross-Cultural Psychology, 49*(2), 223–238.

Adam, I., Adongo, C. A., & Amuquandoh, F. E. (2019). A structural decompositional analysis of eco-visitors' motivations, satisfaction and post-purchase behaviour. *Journal of Ecotourism, 18*(1), 60–81.

Adams, R., Jones, A., Lefmann, S., & Sheppard, L. (2015). Rationing is a reality in rural physiotherapy: A qualitative exploration of service level decision-making. *BMC Health Services Research, 15*(1), 1–12.

Agu, G. A., Okwara, O. O., Okocha, E. R., & Madichie, N. O. (2022). COVID-19 pandemic and entrepreneurial intention among university students: A contextualisation of the Igbo Traditional Business School. *African Journal of Economic and Management Studies, 13*(1), 89–104.

Amankwah-Amoah, J., Khan, Z., Wood, G., & Knight, G. (2021). COVID-19 and digitalization: The great acceleration. *Journal of Business Research, 136*, 602–611.

Amirani, E., Milajerdi, A., Mirzaei, H., Jamilian, H., Mansournia, M. A., Hallajzadeh, J., & Ghaderi, A. (2020). The effects of probiotic supplementation on mental health, biomarkers of inflammation and oxidative stress in patients with psychiatric disorders: A systematic review and meta-analysis of randomized controlled trials. *Complementary Therapies in Medicine, 49*, Article 102361.

Arafat, S. Y., Kar, S. K., & Kabir, R. (2020). Possible controlling measures of panic buying during COVID-19. *International Journal of Mental Health and Addiction*, 1–3.

Baddeley, M. (2020). Hoarding in the age of COVID-19. *Journal of Behavioral Economics for Policy, 4*(S), 69–75.

Badgaiyan, A. J., & Verma, A. (2015). Does urge to buy impulsively differ from impulsive buying behaviour? Assessing the impact of situational factors. *Journal of Retailing and Consumer Services, 22*, 145–157.

Bassett, R. L., & Latané, B. (1976). Effects of other's presence on children's performance. *Developmental Psychology, 12*(6), 525–526. https://doi.org/10.1037/0012-1649.12.6.525

Banbury, L. K., Shou, Q., Renshaw, D. E., Lambley, E. H., Griesser, H. J., Mon, H., & Wohlmuth, H. (2015). Compounds from Geijera parviflora with prostaglandin E2 inhibitory activity may explain its traditional use for pain relief. *Journal of Ethnopharmacology, 163*, 251–255.

Barnes, S. J., Diaz, M., & Arnaboldi, M. (2021). Understanding panic buying during COVID-19: A text analytics approach. *Expert Systems with Applications, 169*, Article 114360.

Barnett, M. D., Moore, J. M., & Archuleta, W. P. (2019). A loneliness model of hypochondriasis among older adults: The mediating role of intolerance of uncertainty and anxious symptoms. *Archives of Gerontology and Geriatrics, 83*, 86–90.

Billore, S., & Anisimova, T. (2021). Panic buying research: A systematic literature review and future research agenda. *International Journal of Consumer Studies, 45*(4), 777–804.

Bollen, K., Euwema, M., & Müller, P. (2010). Why are subordinates less satisfied with mediation? *The Role of Uncertainty. Negotiation Journal, 26*(4), 417–433.

Bown, C. P. (2020). COVID-19: Demand spikes, export restrictions, and quality concerns imperil poor country access to medical supplies. *COVID-19 and Trade Policy: Why Turning Inward Won't Work*, 31.

Chang, J. H., Zhu, Y. Q., Wang, S. H., & Li, Y. J. (2018). Would you change your mind? An empirical study of social impact theory on Facebook. *Telematics and Informatics, 35*(1), 282–292.

Chen, H. J., & Sun, T. H. (2014). Clarifying the impact of product scarcity and perceived uniqueness in buyers' purchase behavior of games of limited-amount version. *Asia Pacific Journal of Marketing and Logistics, 20*(2), 168–171.

Chen, M. Y., & Teng, C. I. (2013). A comprehensive model of the effects of online store image on purchase intention in an e-commerce environment. *Electronic Commerce Research, 13*(1), 1–23.

Chin, W. W. (1998). The partial least squares approach to structural equation modelling. *Modern Methods for Business Research, 295*(2), 295–336.

Dewey, J. (1910). How we think. D. C. Heath & Co.

Engel, J. F., Blackwell, R. D., & Kollat, D. T. (1968). Consumer behavior, Holt, Rinehart and Winston.

Fornell, C., & Larcker, D. F. (1981). Structural equation models with unobservable variables and measurement error: Algebra and statistics 382–388.

Frank, B., & Schvaneveldt, S. J. (2016). Understanding consumer reactions to product contamination risks after national disasters: The roles of knowledge, experience, and information sources. *Journal of Retailing and Consumer Services, 28*, 199–208.

Gandhi, S., Buragohain, C., Cao, L., Zheng, H., & Suri, S. (2007, April). A general framework for wireless spectrum auctions. In *2007 2nd IEEE International Symposium on New Frontiers in Dynamic Spectrum Access Networks* (pp. 22–33). IEEE.

Gerard, H. B., Wilhelmy, R. A., & Conolley, E. S. (1968). Conformity and group size. *Journal of Personality and Social Psychology, 8*(1p1), 79.

Ghaderi, M., Ahi, Q., Vaziri, S., Mansouri, A., & Shahabizadeh, F. (2020). The mediating role of emotion regulation and intolerance of uncertainty in the relationship between childhood maltreatment and nonsuicidal self-injury in adolescents. *International Archives of Health Sciences, 7*(2), 96.

Ghana Statistical Service. (2015). The National Employment Report, Integrated Business Establishment Survey [see https://statsghana.gov.gh/gssmain/fileUpload/pressrelease+NATIONAL%20EMPLOYMENT%20REPORT_FINAL%20%2024-5-16.pdf, assessed on 20/09/2025]

Grier, S., & Davis, B. (2013). Are all proximity effects created equal? Fast food near schools and body weight among diverse adolescents. *Journal of Public Policy & Marketing, 32*(1), 116–128.

Guo, Y., Zhang, J., Zhang, Y., & Zheng, C. (2018). Examining the relationship between social capital and community residents' perceived resilience in tourism destinations. *Journal of Sustainable Tourism, 26*(6), 973–986.

Gupta, S., & Gentry, J. W. (2016). The behavioural responses to perceived scarcity–the case of fast fashion. *The International Review of Retail, Distribution and Consumer Research, 26*(3), 260–271.

Hair, J. F., Risher, J. J., Sarstedt, M., & Ringle, C. M. (2019). When to use and how to report the results of PLS-SEM. *European Business Review, 21*(2), 5–16.

Hamilton, R., Mittal, C., Shah, D., Thompson, D., & Griskevicius, V. (2018). How scarcity impacts consumer decision making: Insights from the consumer psychology of scarcity. *Journal of the Academy of Marketing Science, 46*(3), 801–824. https://doi.org/10.1007/s11747-017-0564-6

Hamilton, R. (2021). Consumer behaviour in a pandemic: Understanding scarcity, panic buying, and decision heuristics. *Journal of Consumer Behaviour, 20*(3), 567–575.

Harton, H. C., & Bullock, M. (2007). Dynamic social impact: A theory of the origins and evolution of culture. *Social and Personality Psychology Compass, 1*(1), 521–540.

Hashemi, H., Rajabi, R., & Brashear-Alejandro, T. G. (2022). COVID-19 research in management: An updated bibliometric analysis. *Journal of Business Research, 149*, 795–810.

Helsloot, I., & Ruitenberg, A. (2004). Citizen response to disasters: A survey of literature and some practical implications. *Journal of Contingencies and Crisis Management, 12*(3), 98–111.

Jackson, J. M., & Latané, B. (1981). All alone in front of all those people: Stage fright as a function of number and type of co-performers and audience. *Journal of Personality and Social Psychology, 40*(1), 73–85.

Kemp, E., Bui, M.(M)., & Porter, III, M. (2021). Preparing for a crisis: examining the influence of fear and anxiety on consumption and compliance. *Journal of Consumer Marketing, 38*(3), 282–292.

Kinata, E. J. (2016). The effect of market volatility and firm size towards the difference of market reaction around stock-split announcement in Indonesia stock exchange. *Journal of Administrative and Business Studies, 2*(6), 304–313.

Kulemeka, O. (2010). US consumers and disaster: Observing "panic buying" during the winter storm and hurricane seasons. In M. C. Campbell, J. J. Inman & R. Pieters (Eds.), *Advances in Consumer Research. (Proceedings of the ACM; No. 37). Association for Consumer Research.*

Laato, S., Islam, A. N., Farooq, A., & Dhir, A. (2020). Unusual purchasing behavior during the early stages of the COVID-19 pandemic: The stimulus-organism-response approach. *Journal of Retailing and Consumer Services, 57*, Article 102224.

Latané, B. (1981). The psychology of social impact. *American Psychologist, 36*(4), 343–356. https://doi.org/10.1037/0003-066X.36.4.343

Latané, B., & Nida, S. (1981). Ten years of research on group size and helping. *Psychological Bulletin, 89*(2), 308–324. https://doi.org/10.1037/0033-2909.89.2.308

Latané, B., & Wolf, S. (1981). The social impact of majorities and minorities. *Psychological Review, 88*(5), 438–453. https://doi.org/10.1037/0033-295X.88.5.438

Li, C., Yang, Y., & Ren, L. (2020a). Genetic evolution analysis of 2019 novel coronavirus and coronavirus from other species. *Infection, Genetics and Evolution, 82*, Article 104285.

Li, J., Xia, Y., Cheng, X., & Li, S. (2020b). Fear of uncertainty makes you more anxious? Effect of intolerance of uncertainty on college students' social anxiety: A moderated mediation model. *Frontiers in Psychology, 11*, 2301.

Lim, W. M. (2021). Toward an agency and reactance theory of crowding: Insights from COVID-19 and the tourism industry. *Journal of Consumer Behaviour*.

Lindell, M. K. (2024). Where is the panic in "panic buying"? Consumer purchases at the outset of the COVID pandemic. *International Journal of Mass Emergencies & Disasters*, 02807270241239666.

Lins, S., & Aquino, S. (2020). Development and initial psychometric properties of a panic buying scale during COVID-19 pandemic. *Heliyon, 6*(9), Article e04746.

Loomes, G., & Sugden, R. (1982). Regret theory: An alternative theory of rational choice under uncertainty. *The Economic Journal, 92*(368), 805–824.

Loxton, M., Truskett, R., Scarf, B., Sindone, L., Baldry, G., & Zhao, Y. (2020). Consumer behaviour during crises: Preliminary research on how coronavirus has manifested consumer panic buying, herd mentality, changing discretionary spending and the role of the media in influencing behaviour. *Journal of Risk and Financial Management, 13*(8), 166–187.

Lynn, M. (1989). Scarcity effects on desirability: Mediated by assumed expensiveness? *Journal of Economic Psychology, 10*(2), 257–274.

Lynn, M. (1992). The psychology of unavailability: Explaining scarcity and cost effects on value. *Basic and Applied Social Psychology, 13*(1), 3–7.

Madichie, N. O. (2015). The European 'horsemeat scandal': A welcome opportunity for the halal supply chain? *Journal of Customer Behaviour, 14*(1), 63–82.

Madichie, N. O., & Yamoah, F. A. (2017). Revisiting the European horsemeat scandal: The role of power asymmetry in the food supply chain crisis. *Thunderbird International Business Review, 59*(6), 663–675.

Mele, C., Russo-Spena, T., Tregua, M., & Amitrano, C. C. (2021). The millennial customer journey: A Phygital mapping of emotional, behavioural, and social experiences. *Journal of Consumer Marketing, 38*(4), 420–433.

Milgram, S., Bickman, L., & Berkowitz, L. (1969). Note on the drawing power of crowds of different size. *Journal of Personality and Social Psychology, 13*(2), 79–82. https://doi.org/10.1037/h0028070

Naeem, M. (2021). Do social media platforms develop consumer panic buying during the fear of Covid-19 pandemic. *Journal of Retailing and Consumer Services, 58*, Article 102226.

Nettle, D. (1999). Using social impact theory to simulate language change. *Lingua, 108*(2–3), 95–117.

Nistorescu, T. & Puiu, S. (2009). Marketing strategies during the economic crisis. *Annals of the University of Craiova – Economic Sciences Series, 36*(1), 1–11.

Nowak, A., Szamrej, J., & Latané, B. (1990). From private attitude to public opinion: A dynamic theory of social impact. *Psychological Review, 97*(3), 362.

Park, H., Lalwani, A. K., & Silvera, D. H. (2020). The impact of resource scarcity on price-quality judgments. *Journal of Consumer Research, 46*(6), 1110–1124.

Parker, J. R., & Lehmann, D. R. (2011). When shelf-based scarcity impacts consumer preferences. *Journal of Retailing, 87*(2), 142–155.

Podsakoff, P. M., MacKenzie, S. B., Lee, J. Y., & Podsakoff, N. P. (2003). Common method biases in behavioral research: A critical review of the literature and recommended remedies. *Journal of Applied Psychology, 88*(5), 879.

Putri, A., Retsan, A., Andika, H., & Hendriana, E. (2021). Antecedents of panic buying behavior during the COVID-19 pandemic. *Management Science Letters, 11*(6), 1821–1832.

Robinson, S. G., Brady, M. K., Lemon, K. N., & Giebelhausen, M. (2016). Less of this one? I'll take it: New insights on the influence of shelf-based scarcity. *International Journal of Research in Marketing, 33*(4), 961–965.

Sachdeva, S., & Zhao, J. (2021). Distinct impacts of financial scarcity and natural resource scarcity on sustainable choices and motivations. *Journal of Consumer Behaviour, 20*(2), 203–217.

Sedikides, C., & Jackson, J. M. (1990). Social impact theory: A field test of source strength, source immediacy and number of targets. *Basic and Applied Social Psychology, 11*(3), 273–281.

Shanker, S., Barve, A., Muduli, K., Kumar, A., Garza-Reyes, J. A., & Joshi, S. (2021). Enhancing resiliency of perishable product supply chains in the context of the COVID-19 outbreak. *International Journal of Logistics Research and Applications*, 1–25.

Sharma, V., & Sonwalkar, J. (2013). Does consumer buying behavior change during economic crisis? *International Journal of Economics & Business Administration, 1*(2), 33–48.

Shou, B., Xiong, H., & Shen, X. (2013). Consumer panic buying and quota policy under supply disruptions. *Manufacturing and Service Operations Management, 6*(6), 1–9.

Snyder, C. R., & Fromkin, H. L. (1977). Abnormality as a positive characteristic: The development and validation of a scale measuring need for uniqueness. *Journal of Abnormal Psychology, 86*(5), 518.

Tambunan, T. T. (2019). The impact of the economic crisis on micro, small, and medium enterprises and their crisis mitigation measures in Southeast Asia with reference to Indonesia. *Asia & the Pacific Policy Studies, 6*(1), 19–39.

Tsao, Y. C., Raj, P. V. R. P., & Yu, V. (2019). Product substitution in different weights and brands considering customer segmentation and panic buying behavior. *Industrial Marketing Management, 77*, 209–220. https://doi.org/10.1016/j.indmarman.2018.09.004

Ulqinaku, A., Sarial-Abi, G., & Kinsella, E. L. (2020). Benefits of heroes to coping with mortality threats by providing perceptions of personal power and reducing unhealthy compensatory consumption. *Psychology & Marketing, 37*(10), 1433–1445.

Wang, E., An, N., Gao, Z., Kiprop, E., & Geng, X. (2020). Consumer food stockpiling behavior and willingness to pay for food reserves in COVID-19. *Food Security, 12*(4), 739–747.

Wang, H. H., & Na, H. A. O. (2020). Panic buying? Food hoarding during the pandemic period with city lockdown. *Journal of Integrative Agriculture, 19*(12), 2916–2925.

Wen, J., Aston, J., Liu, X., & Ying, T. (2020). Effects of misleading media coverage on public health crisis: A case of the 2019 novel coronavirus outbreak in China. *Anatolia, 31*(2), 331–336.

Wong, I. A., Ou, J., & Wilson, A. (2021). Evolution of hoteliers' organizational crisis communication in the time of mega disruption. *Tourism Management, 84*, Article 104257.

Wood, B., Williams, O., Nagarajan, V., & Sacks, G. (2021). Market strategies used by processed food manufacturers to increase and consolidate their power: A systematic review and document analysis. *Globalization and Health, 17*(1), 1–23.

Wu, W. Y., Lu, H. Y., Wu, Y. Y., & Fu, C. S. (2012). The effects of product scarcity and consumers' need for uniqueness on purchase intention. *International Journal of Consumer Studies, 36*(3), 263–274.

Wu, Y., Xin, L., Li, D., Yu, J., & Guo, J. (2021). How does scarcity promotion lead to impulse purchase in the online market? *A Field Experiments. Information & Management, 58*(1), Article 103283.

Xu, S., Qamruzzaman, M., & Adow, A. H. (2021). Is financial innovation bestowed or a curse for economic sustainably: The mediating role of economic policy uncertainty. *Sustainability, 13*(4), 2391.

Yangui, W., & Hajtaïeb El Aoud, N. (2015). Consumer behaviour and the anticipation of a total stockout for a food product: Proposing and validating a theoretical model. *The International Review of Retail, Distribution and Consumer Research, 25*(2), 181–203.

Yuen, K. F., Wang, X., Ma, F., & Li, K. X. (2020). The psychological causes of panic buying following a health crisis. *International Journal of Environmental Research and Public Health, 17*(10), 3513.

Zaky, A., Mohamed, H., & Saxena, G. (2022). Conceptualising the panic buying phenomenon during COVID-19 as an affective assemblage. *European Journal of Marketing, 56*(12), 3313–3346.

Zhang, L., & Liu, Y. (2020). Potential interventions for novel coronavirus in China: A systematic review. *Journal of Medical Virology, 92*(5), 479–490.

CHAPTER 6

Democracy and Elections as Political Brands in an Emerging African Economy: A Micro, Meso, and Macro-Social Marketing Perspective

Charles Blankson, Julius A. Nukpezah, Esi A. Elliot, and Kobby Mensah

Introduction

This chapter poses the research question: How important is the consumption of democracy in the context of an emerging African economy?

Democracy is based on the idea that the people should shape a nation's future (Kotler, 2016, p. 9, cited in Peterson & Godby, 2020). As Peterson and Godby (2020) explain, this may seem simple, but debate about democracy's form, effectiveness, and the level of citizen participation has

C. Blankson (✉)
Department of Marketing, G. Brint Ryan College of Business, University of North Texas, Denton, USA
e-mail: Charles.Blankson@unt.edu

A. Gbadamosi et al. (eds.), *Contemporary Marketing Practices in Africa, Volume 1*, Palgrave Studies of Marketing in Emerging Economies,
https://doi.org/10.1007/978-3-032-27126-6_6

continued since democracy's origins in the city-state of Athens 2500 years ago (Waldron, 2012, cited in Peterson & Godby, 2020, p. 412).

Although many discussions have focused on different forms of political marketing (e.g., Adel et al., 2023; Ormrod et al., 2013; Si, 2019), most research principally relies on Western-centric models. These models often overlook the socio-political complexities and historical legacies unique to African nations. Emerging African markets have distinct political, cultural, and institutional dynamics that these models do not adequately reflect. There is a need for developing indigenous theories that capture the realities of these regions (see, for example, Francis & Mugabo, 2025).

Additionally, while political ties are known to influence firm performance and voter behavior, their mechanisms and effects in emerging African markets remain poorly understood. Research has yielded mixed results, prompting calls for more detailed and interdisciplinary approaches. These markets are marked by high diversity in income, education, media access, and political involvement, making one-size-fits-all political marketing strategies ineffective. Scholars are therefore encouraged to adopt context-sensitive frameworks and explore micro-level segmentation and localized communication methods.

Political marketing, a subfield of both marketing and political science, has unique traits that distinguish it from its parent disciplines (Ormond et al., 2013). Yet it often fails to address the challenge of reaching

J. A. Nukpezah
Department of Political Science and Public Administration, College of Arts & Sciences, Mississippi State University, Starkville, USA
e-mail: jnukpezah@pspa.msstate.edu

E. A. Elliot
Vackar College of International Business and Entrepreneurship, University of Texas, Austin, USA
e-mail: esi.elliot@utrgv.edu

K. Mensah
Ghana Tourism Development Company Limited (GTDC), Accra, Ghana

Department of Marketing & Entrepreneurship, University of Ghana Business School, University of Ghana, Legon, Ghana

K. Mensah
e-mail: Kobbymensah@ug.edu.gh

consumer groups at the micro, meso, and macro levels. In emerging markets, weak regulatory frameworks and reliance on informal networks and patronage systems further complicate political messaging. These contexts demand a deeper understanding of how political branding is adapted to and received in contexts where formal institutions are evolving.

To address these gaps, this study draws on macro-social marketing, branding theory, social capital theory, and institutional theory to examine how voters perceive and engage with political products in transitioning African economies. These frameworks provide a multi-level lens for analyzing how democratic values are marketed and consumed, and how voter behavior is shaped by individual, community, and systemic factors.

Paradoxically, approval of democracy remains performance-driven, but hinges less on economic delivery than on the guarantee of fundamental political rights. As Bratton and Mattes (2001, p. 452) note, "Africans seek democracy as a matter of survival," emphasizing concrete economic and social rights over abstract political ideals.

Despite interest in Ghana's political and economic transition as a model for Africa's renaissance (Parku, 2014; Whitfield, 2005) and the branding activities by political parties (see Mensah, 2011; Tweneboah-Kodua et al., 2010), limited attention has been paid to empirical assessments of consumers' perceptions of democracy and elections. This chapter aims to identify the factors shaping voters' (i.e., consumers') perceptions of democracy deliberations, general elections, and political brands—offering a deeper understanding of how democratic ideals are internalized and expressed through electoral behavior in African contexts. Our contribution to research is threefold:

First, we offer conceptual innovation: We frame democracy as a product that can be "consumed," introducing a lens that treats democratic values, institutions, and practices as goods or services citizens engage with, demand, or reject. This opens a pathway for integrating political marketing, democratic theory, and consumer behavior.

Second, we provide contextual relevance: We focus on African political economies, addressing a geographic gap in the literature that centers on Western or Asian contexts. In these settings, democratic institutions are often hybrid, contested, or evolving. Our research examines how citizens perceive and assess democracy amid varying state capacity, media freedom, and civil society strength.

Third, we deliver practical implications: Our findings inform political marketing strategies in emerging democracies, helping parties and governments better align their messages with public expectations. This alignment is essential for fostering trust, legitimacy, and sustained democratic engagement among diverse voter segments.

Literature and Theoretical Review

Democracy in Africa

Democracy is a disputed term, in that definitions range from a minimalist concern with election procedures to sweeping requirements for socio-economic equality (Ake, 1996, p. 451). Bratton and Mattes (2001, p. 452) acknowledge that democracy is valued not so much for what it is but for what it can do. The authors explore how the public in new multi-party political regimes in sub-Saharan Africa (e.g., Ghana, Zambia, and South Africa) is oriented toward democracy and question the conventional wisdom that governments in new democracies legitimate themselves through economic performance.

All three countries—Ghana, Zambia, and South Africa—underwent an electoral transition to multi-party democracy during the last decade, but their political trajectories have since diverged (Bratton & Mattes, 2001, p. 449). For its part, Ghana experienced improved electoral quality, with the flawed November 1992 elections followed by a December 1996 poll that drew almost universal praise. Thus, regarding the institution of elections alone, South Africa's democracy has stabilized, Ghana's is gradually consolidating, and Zambia's is slowly dying (Bratton & Mattes, 2001, p. 449).

The dearth of research in this area, given the importance of understanding political dispensation on the continent, leaves a significant gap in our understanding of the African perspective—and more specifically, the highly touted Ghanaian democratic dispensation (Mensah, 2011; Ninsin, 2006; Parku, 2014; Whitfield, 2005). Like other transitioning economies in Africa, research on voting patterns in Ghana suggests a complex mix of factors underpinning political allegiance and voter choice (Anebo, 2001), including family history, party traditions, personality, tribe/ethnicity, and economic basis.

That "African society is a system of mutually benefiting reciprocities" through which exchange within extended families takes place (Francis &

Mugabo, 2025; Khavul et al., 2009) cannot be overemphasized. These extended family networks and loose relationships with tribesmen coalesce with social capital and institutional theories to reveal Ghanaian voters' voting choices. This intersection of informal networks and institutional structures provides a culturally grounded lens for understanding democratic engagement.

The latter underscores the inspiration for this study and justifies our adaptation of social capital theory and institutional theory as a backdrop to explicate the purpose of this study—to identify the factors explaining voters' (i.e., consumers') perceptions of political brands, general elections, and democracy deliberations (Vigsø, 2017; Wald & Shye, 1995).

Social Capital Theory

Existing scholarship reveals that scholars examine social capital at the individual, community, societal, and institutional levels of analysis. The community and societal levels tend to focus on collective resources and the institutions that foster them (Kapucu & Garayev, 2016; Rivera & Nickels, 2014). The individual-level analysis emphasizes how individuals interact with members of their social network to enhance their collective social capital resources (Brehm & Rahn, 1997; Glaeser, 2001; Nukpezah & Soujaa, 2018). The literature also suggests that trust, norms, and networks are foundational resources that underpin social capital theory (Kawachi & Berkman, 2000; Newton, 2001; Putnam, 2001 Sobel, 2002). The theory is inherent in social relations that facilitate links, bonds, shared values, and culture, enabling individuals and groups in a society to trust and relate to one another.

Social capital offers a theoretical explanation for why family relations and communities may collectively share the same ideology due to institutional influence and consequently support a particular political party. In a recent study in the United States, Jha et al. (2018) find that communities with high levels of social capital tend to support a particular political party.

Reviewing the literature on social capital in developing countries, one finds that social capital networks are attracting attention across many social science disciplines through debate and research (Woolcock & Narayan, 2000). Social capital theory enhances understanding of the value of social resources to populations in transitioning economies (Blankson et al., 2018; Bourdieu, 1986; Portes, 1998).

Regarding the deliberations of political parties in transitioning economies in Africa—and specifically in Ghana—social capital theory provides an important backdrop for discussing political networks and the relationships between politicians and their constituents. In addition, social capital plays a significant role in the formulation and implementation of social policy in transitioning countries. As noted by Blankson et al. (2018), social capital theory views people's social networks as capital, aiming to facilitate information flow and serve as a repository of value for future reciprocation of social obligations. Thus, in transitioning economies, the influence of social networks in relationships is pivotal, and outcomes of social networks in day-to-day interactions have been well documented (see Blankson, Cowan, & Darley, 2018; Viswanathan, Rosa, & Ruth, 2010; Woolcock & Narayan, 2000).

Institutional Theory

Institutional theory explores how organizational structures and behaviors are shaped by social norms, values, and external constraints. Selznick (1957) defined institutionalization as an adaptive process where organizations evolve in response to participant commitments and environmental influences and emphasized that "'to institutionalize' is to infuse with value beyond the technical requirements of the task at hand" (p. 17). Institutionalization is rooted in social order, which Berger and Luckmann (1967) describe as a human construct formed through interaction: "Social order is a human product, or an ongoing human production. Social order in essence exists only as a product of human activity" (p. 52). Institutionalization occurs when actions—such as political party activities—are repeated and assigned shared meanings: "Institutionalization occurs whenever there is a reciprocal typification of habitualized actions by types of actors" (Berger & Luckmann, 1967, p. 54).

Political activism and democratic governance are social institutions embedded in enduring systems of beliefs and practices that span societal domains, including religion, work, and family. Hughes (1939, pp. 283–284) noted that institutions are "features of social life which outlast biological generations or survive drastic social changes." Hertzler (1961) added that institutions ensure continuity: "The institutions of a society have a high degree of stability and function as the major mechanisms for social continuity" (p. 81), and are "organized, established, regularized, chartered, endorsed, and enforced" (p. 84). Friedland and Alford

(1987) expanded the theory by arguing that institutional spheres operate under distinct belief systems. For instance, capitalism emphasizes accumulation and commodification, the state focuses on regulation through legal hierarchies, and the family prioritizes loyalty and welfare (p. 36).

Drawing on phenomenology, Berger and Luckmann (1967) identified institutionalization as central to the formation of enduring social groups. Institutions emerge from "reciprocal typification of habitualized action by types of actors" (p. 54; Schutz, 1967, cited in Tolbert & Zucker, 1996). Habitualized actions are empirically developed behaviors used to solve recurring problems with minimal effort. These actions become generalized through shared meanings, a process Zucker (1977) termed "objectification."

In Ghana's democratic context, Ninsin (2006) observed that most voters struggle with abstract ideological debates, which are largely confined to elite circles. Instead, political parties often appeal to ethnic and religious sentiments (Anebo, 2001), and many voters base their decisions on family ties and political interests. Mensah (2011) described this as "electoral hype," where parties gain appeal during campaigns. This complexity reflects what Luskin (1990) termed "behavioral sophistication," which challenges campaign strategies. Luskin (1990) argued that political sophistication depends on exposure to information, the ability to process it, and motivation to engage. Both internal and external stimuli shape voter attitudes, with interest and intelligence playing key roles. However, Luskin (1990) also found that education and media exposure do not guarantee sophistication, meaning voters vary in their understanding and engagement with political products. Voters can thus be categorized by their level of sophistication (Campbell et al., 1960), encompassing ideological and non-ideological belief systems (Converse, 1964; Luskin, 1990). These levels influence voting patterns and decision-making.

Tweneboah-Koduah et al. (2010) explored voter self-image and brand association in Ghana, finding that fewer than half of respondents linked ethnicity with party preference. This suggests a shift in voter behavior, possibly due to evolving political and media systems. Their findings highlight a growing sophistication in voter-party relationships, resembling consumer decision-making processes (Engel et al., 1986). Despite this, marketing scholars often overlook voter behavior in transitioning democracies, such as Ghana (Mensah, 2011; Gyimah-Boadi, 2001; Ayee,

2000). Institutional theory, therefore, provides a valuable lens for understanding how political behaviors are shaped by enduring social structures, informal networks, and evolving norms—especially in contexts where formal institutions are still consolidating.

Macro-Social Marketing

Macro-social marketing is a systems-level approach that promotes societal change for the public good by addressing large-scale issues, such as public health, civic engagement, and social justice (Domegan, 2008; Kennedy, 2016; Truong, 2017). Unlike traditional marketing, it works through policy integration and collaboration with governments and institutions to shift societal norms and behaviors (Kennedy & Parsons, 2012). Its ethical focus on long-term welfare makes it especially relevant in contexts needing systemic transformation. In this chapter, macro-social marketing reframes democracy and elections as strategic interventions, aligning with the idea of electoral brands and democracy as a market product. It complements micromarketing, which targets individual voter segments, by emphasizing how political actors shape civic engagement on a scale. Together, these approaches form a multi-level framework—micro, meso, and macro—that captures both personalized and structural dimensions of political marketing in Ghana (Bratton & Mattes, 2001; Mensah, 2011).

Branding Theory

Branding theory explains how voters engage with political parties and candidates as they would with consumer brands—using emotional cues, perceived benefits, and identity alignment to guide choices (Engel et al., 1986; Tweneboah-Koduah et al., 2010). In Ghana, where ideological clarity is limited, branding simplifies complex decisions and reinforces voter loyalty through symbolic associations like ethnicity and regional ties (Anebo, 2001; Mensah, 2011). This supports the chapter's view of democracy as a market product, with party manifestos functioning as persuasive tools. Branding theory complements micro and meso-marketing by enabling tailored appeals and supports macro-social marketing by fostering systemic democratic engagement and accountability (Kennedy, 2016; Truong, 2017).

Methodology

The Study Context

Ghana has experienced nine presidential and parliamentary election cycles beginning with the 1992 elections, alternating governments between the two dominant parties—the National Democratic Congress (NDC) and the New Patriotic Party (NPP)—every eight years, with shifts in parliamentary seats every four years. Each of these elections produced remarkably close margins of victory, indicating a high level of competitiveness in the country's electoral system. These two political parties have come to represent the ideological divisions in Ghana, where the NDC is of the left and the NPP is on the right of center.

The excitement over the opportunities that elections bring can, in some voters, foster a democratic ethos—a perception of the benefits of making public policy through democratic processes, in which diverse opinions and proposed solutions are heard and decided during elections (DeLeon & DeLeon, 2002; White & Ypi, 2010).

After years of authoritarian military interruptions, these ideological leanings in Ghana have gradually translated into subliminal identifications, such as tribal, religious, and regional divisions. Research on the early elections of the Fourth Republic (see Gyimah-Boadi, 2001; Ninsin, 2006; Nugent, 2001; Tweneboah-Kodua et al., 2010; Youde, 2005) reveals a strong emphasis on regionalization and ethnocentric patterns in voter perceptions and choice-making. A sizeable proportion of voters identify with regional and ethnic associations for partisan purposes.

In a study of voter choice in the 2000 elections, Anebo (2001) notes that citizens had little incentive to evaluate parties and candidates on issues and competence, attributing this to low levels of political knowledge and to the primordial characteristics of Ghana's social structure (Anebo, 2001, p. 85). Tweneboah-Kodua et al. (2010) similarly found a confused state of voter knowledge and perceptions of political "brands." Their study examined whether Ghanaian voters could associate descriptors with the two leading political parties—NDC and NPP—and whether such constructs influenced their political choices. The authors found that voters were unable to recall any relevant functional component of a political brand when the party names were mentioned.

Political parties have been a component of Ghana's democratic dispensation since the 1950s, during the country's transition from colonial rule to independence in 1957.[1] In the more than 30 years since Ghana returned to multi-party democracy, the country has undergone tremendous changes in its political structure, electoral systems, party systems, media systems, and voter sophistication (see Afrobarometer, 2018; 1999).

Ghana voted for constitutional rule in a 1992 referendum, following decades of political instability due to a series of military regimes that began with the overthrow of the first republican constitution in 1966. Often referred to as one of the most democratic countries in Africa, Ghana is known for conducting free and fair general elections (Afrobarometer, 2018; Parku, 2014). Although other smaller political parties are allowed to operate, voter choice has remained stable across the two dominant parties.

Research shows substantial partisan identification in Ghana. About 69% of respondents prefer that local government leaders be elected (Afrobarometer, 2018). Across Africa, 75% of respondents interviewed in 2016 and 2018 preferred open and fair elections, with support reaching 83% across 35 countries in surveys conducted in 2011 and 2013 (Bratton & Bhoojedhur, 2019).

In Ghana, Afrobarometer (1999) reported that 38% of respondents identified with the NDC, while 25% identified with the NPP. However, this lead did not prevent the NDC from losing power in the 2000 elections, eight years after it took office. The NPP then lost power back to the NDC in 2008, and in 2016, the NDC again lost to the NPP. This alternation of governments reflects high electoral volatility, where voter identification is myriad and fragile, potentially swinging each electoral cycle.

The absence of a dominant party in Ghana's multi-party system creates opportunities for party and candidate branding and marketing to capture undecided voters. Despite branding efforts, unstable patterns of voter loyalty and swing voting remain a challenge for party managers and marketing theorists in transitioning economies such as Ghana, which provides the context for this study (see also DeBerry-Spence et al., 2019).

[1] The interested reader is directed to Tweneboah-Kodua et al. (2010, pp. 80) for an extensive discussion of the historical development of political parties in Ghana.

Data Collection

This study began with a pilot study of observations conducted by the first author in southern Ghana during purposeful visits and during faculty responsibilities. Given the qualitative and exploratory nature of the research and to enhance appreciation of the research setting, we followed the good practices suggested by Sekaran & Bougie (2016) by embarking on a pilot study. Sekaran and Bougie (2016) write that in exploratory studies, when little is known about the situation at hand, researchers may need to conduct extensive interviews with many people to gain a deeper understanding of the situation and the phenomenon. Malhotra et al. (2020) believe that qualitative pilot studies improve researchers' ability to probe respondents to uncover underlying motivations, beliefs, attitudes, and feelings.

The main study, involving in-depth, face-to-face, open-ended, and long interviews, was undertaken by six undergraduate and master's students hired from a major business school in Accra. The interview questions were compiled following the pilot study and discussion with two academic scholars in Ghana. The study encompassed a randomly selected residential and business district in the Greater Accra Region of Ghana. The study setting, however, was chosen for convenience. In all, forty-eight members of the public (see Table 6.1) participated in this research. Compensation of GHC 20.00 [US$1 = GHC 5.00 at the time of data collection] was offered to each participant for the long interviews. The interviews lasted between thirty minutes and one hour. The participants were promised anonymity. The student interviewers relied on snowball and foot-in-the-door data collection techniques to increase the number of interviewees.

The interviews were conducted in designated areas close to the participants' premises or workplaces, in non-contrived settings. In a few instances when some participants did not fully understand a question, the student interviewers rephrased it in Ga or Twi, the popular Ghanaian dialects spoken in the Greater Accra Region. However, they continued to note the participants' responses in English to ensure consistent analysis. The student interviewers took notes and audio-taped the interviewees' comments [via cell phones], ensuring their anonymity. While the interviews addressed research questions (see Appendix), the interviewers allowed the discussion to develop naturally (Kirk & Miller, 1986; Maxwell, 2018). Open-ended questions facilitated participants' sharing of stories and experiences. In line with Mishler's (1990) and Nwankwo's (2005) suggestions, we aimed to promote "storytelling" and elicit participants' oral accounts of their perceptions of democracy, political parties, Ghanaian politics, and general elections. Storytelling is important because it validates participants' lived experiences.

Validity and Reliability

Given the subjective nature of the study and following the suggestions of Kirk and Miller (1986) and Nwankwo (2005), we assessed validity through a discussion with three academic scholars in Ghana who have expertise in political marketing, as well as two experts with knowledge about the study setting and Ghanaian democracy and politics. We incorporated the input from academic scholars and experts into the final discussion and conclusions.

Furthermore, another approach was employed to ensure construct validity: multiple sources of evidence. The multiple sources of evidence included participants' verbatim comments, which were used as perspectives in the analysis. Using multiple sources of evidence increases construct validity (Dubois & Gadde, 2002), resulting in convergence of responses. Regarding the study's reliability, the researchers documented all procedures and measures undertaken during data collection and analysis. These were discussed among the researchers several times before reaching consensus (Spiggle, 1994).

Data Analysis

We employed the data analysis protocol suggested by Moustakas (1994) for interpretation. Thus, the process was iterative, examining the individual transcripts and the complete data to organize key informant statements. First, the transcripts were read, and significant statements were highlighted. These were combined to create "meaning units" (Creswell, 1998, p. 150), from which emanated a description with quotes to elaborate on the experiences of each meaning unit. Next, we created an interpretive description of each meaning unit to capture the essence of themes reflecting democracy and general elections in Ghana. From this step, we interpreted how voters perceived democracy, political party activities, and Ghanaian politics in general. We apply the micro, meso, and macro-social marketing lenses to interpret the results (Kennedy, 2019). This lens is multi-level, with a macro-level focus.

The coding and thematic analysis were guided by principles from social capital theory, focusing on how interpersonal relationships and community dynamics influence political perceptions. Simultaneously, institutional theory informed our understanding of how political practices and party behaviors are normalized and internalized by voters. These theoretical lenses enabled us to interpret the data across micro, meso, and macro levels, revealing how individual beliefs, community affiliations, and institutional structures interact to shape electoral decisions.

Findings and Discussion

In this study, we draw from the marketing literature, which emphasizes the importance of understanding consumer behavior and strategic communication across multiple levels of analysis. Specifically, we present our findings through the lenses of micro-, meso-, and macro-level marketing—each offering a distinct yet interconnected perspective on political marketing in emerging democracies.

Micro-level marketing refers to individual-level interactions and behaviors, focusing on how political messages, party manifestos, and branding influence personal attitudes, perceptions, and voting decisions. At this level, political marketing is tailored to the specific needs, motivations, and values of individual voters, often using segmentation and targeting strategies to target diverse demographic groups. Meso-level marketing operates at the community or organizational level, examining how political parties, campaign teams, and local institutions engage with groups of voters. This level emphasizes social networks, cultural affiliations, and regional dynamics, highlighting how collective identities and interpersonal relationships shape political allegiance and participation. Macro-level marketing encompasses the broader societal and institutional context, including national policies, governance structures, and systemic challenges. At this level, political marketing intersects with macro-social marketing, where governments and upstream actors attempt to influence public opinion, foster civic engagement, and address complex societal issues—often referred to as "wicked problems."

At the micro level, social capital theory explains how trust and familial networks influence individual voting decisions. At the meso level, institutional theory helps interpret how party practices and governance norms

Table 6.1 Profile of participants in the survey

Participant	*Gender*	*Age*	*Level of education*	*Profession*
1	F	22	Undergraduate	Student
2	F	31	Ph.D.	Student
3	F	65	Master	Self-employed
4	M	23	Undergraduate	Student
5	M	47	Masters	Civil servant
6	M	61	Professional qualification (i.e., ACCA)	Accountant
7	M	40	Diploma	Security man
8	F	27	Masters	Teaching assistant
9	M	40	Masters	Teacher
10	M	40	Bachelor's in law	Paralegal
11	M	62	Middle school	Driver
12	M	29	Bachelors	Nurse
13.	M	50	Masters	Company staff
14	F	30	Bachelors	Social worker
15	M	40	Master	Civil servant
16	M	34	Bachelors	Parliament office clerk
17	N	32	Student	Entrepreneur
18	M	32	Bachelors	Director
19	F	31	Bachelors	Entrepreneur
20	M	66	High school diploma	Retired
21	F	44	Diploma	Restaurant owner
22	F	35	Diploma	Salon owner
23	M	67	Masters	Retired lecturer
24	F	29	Bachelors	HR personnel
25	M	34	Bachelors	Bank employee
26	M	35	Bachelors	Civil engineer
27	F	38	High school diploma	Beautician
28	M	39	Master	Teacher
29	M	35	Diploma	Chef
30	M	47	Diploma	Building contractor
31	M	55	Diploma	Entrepreneur
32	M	68	Master	Small business owner
33	M	58	High school diploma	Transport business
34	F	44	High school diploma	Caterer
35	F	71	Diploma	Small hotel owner
36	F	22	Undergraduate	Student
37	M	24	Undergraduate	Student
38	M	66	Bachelor	Entrepreneur
39	M	60	Bachelor	Teacher

(continued)

Table 6.1 (continued)

Participant	*Gender*	*Age*	*Level of education*	*Profession*
40	F	23	High school diploma	Store worker
41	M	50	Master	Bank clerk
42	M	45	Bachelor	Civil servant
43	M	28	Bachelor	Laboratory technician
44	F	35	Bachelor	Company staff
45	M	53	Master	Company executive
46	M	55	High school diploma	Entrepreneur
47	M	70	Bachelor	Small business owner
48	F	65	High school diploma	Retired nurse

create systemic divisions or unity. At the macro level, both theories converge to show how institutionalized political structures and social networks affect national political branding and voter engagement. We present our findings in the form of three themes linked to the micro level, the meso level, and the macro level, which are discussed below:

Relationships, Influence, Perceptions, and Support—Micro Level

At the micro level, political marketing involves politicians strategically communicating and promoting their manifestos to influence individual attitudes and behaviors, ultimately aiming to secure the maximum number of votes. Attitude and behavioral change occur when competing, change-inducing products or services are introduced (Kotler & Zaltman, 1971). In this context, political manifestos function as persuasive tools—akin to product marketing—that aim to shape voter perceptions and choices. This change-inducing service is the desired perception that political marketing seeks to obtain at the micro level. The response from Respondent 1 reflects these perceptions:

> When it comes to manifestos, I look at the policies a political party outlines, assess which are more realistic, and evaluate how beneficial they can be to the country. So, I don't just follow a political party because I like it or because I grew up knowing that my parents or my friends are attached to it. No. I look at their policies and how realistic they are. (Respondent 1).

Respondent 1 highlights that the benefits outlined in political manifestos—particularly those that directly impact individuals and families—are central to his decision-making. His focus is on the realistic attainability of these promises, especially as they relate to his family's welfare. This underscores the idea that political marketing at the micro level must resonate with personal and familial concerns and offer tangible, believable solutions.

Thus, political marketing includes elements of social marketing that aim to provide realistic benefits to families and communities. Social institutions, which shape these interactions, are composed of beliefs, practices, codes, values, and behaviors (Layton, 2019). The role of marketers, therefore, is to assess the "social, legal, and political rationality" behind macro-social marketing interventions, as well as any unintended consequences that may arise. Political marketing, in this context, emphasizes dominant ideologies that promote individual welfare at the micro level. Gurrieri, Previte, and Brace-Goven (2013) argue that social marketing serves as a vehicle for transmitting these dominant ideologies, which in turn offer hope and direction to individuals—a sentiment echoed by Respondent 3 below:

> They are important. They give us hope and guide us on what these political parties will do when they come to power. So, they are important to some of us who are educated or who are of a certain level of education; so, it's very important to us. We are not only interested in slogans and talk, but also in the promises they make and what is in the manifesto, so we can hold them accountable. It's important, maybe if I'm a student, I'll be interested in what one party will say, maybe in terms of education. So, for example, if one promises free education and one has a son or daughter in JSS (Junior Secondary School) now going to SS (Senior Secondary School), as a parent, I will vote for that party because I don't want to pay school fees. You see, so if I am also maybe a parent whose ward has completed university and is looking for a job, and another party comes and promises that they are going to provide, say, 1 million jobs every year, I will vote for that party so that my son or daughter will get a job. So, if I am also a student, I will look at the scholarship aspect. who is giving more scholarships in their manifesto? On the other hand, if I am a market woman or a businessperson, I will look at businesses and how a party will make things more flexible for businessmen and women in the country. These things are particularly important. (Respondent 3).

Respondent 3 explains that political marketing should address the entire system within which individuals operate, recognizing the complexity and interconnectedness of their lived experiences. The systems people navigate—marked by social, economic, and political challenges—are multifaceted and complex, spanning micro, meso, and macro levels and involving diverse stakeholders, from citizens to policymakers, across local, national, and global contexts (Lowe & Plimmer, 2019).

In emerging markets, effective political marketing must begin at the micro level, where individual needs and perceptions are shaped, then dovetail into the meso level to address community and organizational dynamics, before culminating at the macro level, where systemic change is pursued. For example, Truong (2017) described four macro-social marketing initiatives implemented in Vietnam that aimed to enact laws and regulations on helmet use, reduce smoking, curb drink-driving, and increase consumption of fortified foods. These initiatives illustrate that rules and policies in political marketing must be tailored to promote the welfare of individuals at the micro level, ensuring that broader interventions remain grounded in personal relevance and impact. Respondent 5, however, offers a cautionary perspective, emphasizing that manifestos must be realistic and achievable. He details:

> Very important as it is the basis on which you select which party you want to vote for especially if you are someone who dreams of a better Ghana, there is no better way than to judge who to give the mandate of the nation to than to look at the manifestos as to in terms of achievable, the manifestos are they achievable, the things listed in there is it achievable within the time frame they have given themselves? We must match the achievements against the time. So that makes it especially important. (Respondent 5).

However, because individuals are inherently complex—often acting in unpredictable and contradictory ways- the perceived achievability of political manifestos is highly subjective. People's beliefs and behaviors shift, making it difficult to design political messaging that is universally effective (Flaherty et al., 2020). This complexity poses a challenge for political marketing at the meso level, which must address the aggregate social welfare of individuals, including their careers, aspirations, and self-actualization.

Multi-Party Democracy—Meso Level

Multi-party democracy becomes important at the meso level because individuals' needs and expectations become more complex, requiring a broader range of choices. A meso-level analysis focuses on population groups that fall between the micro and macro levels—such as communities or organizations—and examines the connections between individual and systemic dynamics. Political marketing at this level must consider these connections to avoid deepening divisions within the population. Respondent 6 cautions:

> Democracy in Ghana de3 [Ghanaian Akan slang meaning "as for democracy in Ghana..."] forget. It divides us. You see, religion and culture have divided us already. Then the political party comes; for example, where I am working, there is one head of department. He was at the head of power, but they demoted him. I know one Director. When the NPP came to power, they demoted him. How do you think he feels? Or those NDCs will feel? Even though we are divided in terms of religion, which is one, we are divided in terms of tribe, and then politics comes and further divides us again. In my case, it's not about "I support this political party," but rather that the head of the department should have been retained. (Respondent 6).

In emerging markets, the social context dominates, shaped by a myriad of connections. Government-led initiatives must focus on shaping this context (Kennedy & Parsons, 2012). "Wicked problems"—such as obesity, environmental degradation, and poor working conditions—are extraordinarily complex, involving multiple stakeholders and interconnecting factors (Kennedy, 2016). Respondent 6's account illustrates how these connections matter in political marketing. Respondent 9 adds:

> As I said, democracy is not perfect; it has its loopholes, but I do not think there is any better-known option than democracy as it stands now. Exactly. So, currently, the best we can have is democracy because, despite all its loopholes, what is the better alternative? There is no other, but as I have said, our problem is the kind of democracy that we practice. We need to tweak it until then; it will cause division. For now, during the election, there is a sharp division between the two major parties, especially among their supporters, because they practice a democracy that fosters winner-takes-all. So, when that party wins, whether they have the men or not, they take everything. Meanwhile there could be other brilliant

> people from other avenues or across the device so if we could have a system where we make use of the best brains available for the job, so every job we look through the country, who has the best brain for that job, and put the person in that job irrespective of the political party or the divide, that would foster our togetherness. But as it stands now, politics can divide us sharply because one, there is the issue of the winner takes all, where the one who comes to power, whether he can do it or he can't do it, whether he has the men who can or he doesn't have the men, the party decides everything and does everything. So that is a problem. We should have a system where... Look, it is obvious. When there is a new President, all state institutions appoint new board members, who serve as the supervisory bodies with the power over the institutions. So, the President or the executive is driving or controlling all these institutions. So, we should change these, and it will minimize the division that politics brings into our communities. (Respondent 9).

Respondent 9 emphasizes that government-led unity is essential in political marketing at the meso level. Wymer (2011) views macro-social marketing as government-led social marketing, while Domegan (2008) defines it as the use of social marketing by those who shape the social context, aiming for societal rather than individual-level change. For this change to be effective at the meso level, it must be systemic (Kennedy & Parsons, 2012). Respondent 7 agrees:

> Yes, democracy provides a platform for people to freely express themselves without intimidation. So, if I am walking with my colleague and I tell my colleague my opinion, my colleague also tells me his or hers and I know what he or she is thinking, we can then build up from there but if I do not know what my colleague is thinking and is harboring maybe some hate in him then I will not be able to know. But once democracy gives us the platform to freely express ourselves, I think it helps us. (Respondent 7).

Respondent 7 highlights that systemic change requires platforms for free expression. Such platforms can lead to social engineering, which involves centralized planning to manage social change and regulate future societal development (Teeple, 2000). However, this can be perceived as manipulation, so political marketing should facilitate free expression without making leaders the architects of engineered outcomes. Marketers must be cautious of macro-social marketing becoming a tool of social engineering (Kennedy & Parsons, 2012).

Multi-party democracy at the meso level must not only exist but be properly implemented, as emphasized by Respondent 1:

> We already have multi-party in the country, but the question is, are we practicing multi-party? That is the question. Even though we had the last election about eight or seven years ago. But we all know that it is the two political parties that are always leading. That is NPP and NDC. Yes, it is good when you have a lot of variety. We already have multiple parties, but we are not practicing them. (Respondent 1).

Respondent 1's sentiments, which are interestingly corroborated by Respondents 17, 18, 20, and 25, explain that the mere existence of a multi-party system does not guarantee democratic practice. For political marketing to be effective at the meso level, it must be supported by genuine democratic structures that foster inclusion, unity, and systemic accountability.

Country Opportunities—Macro Level

At the macro level, political marketing aligns with macro-social marketing, which aims to create systemic change through government-led initiatives. Truong (2017, p. 410) defines macro-social marketing as "the use of social marketing by governments and other upstream actors within a systemic approach to engender social change." These stakeholders are considered best positioned to reshape societal contexts that perpetuate complex problems. While macro-social marketing seeks positive transformation, the branding aspect of political marketing can introduce elements of deception, potentially undermining democratic ideals. Respondent 28 acknowledges this tension but emphasizes the importance of party manifestos as governance roadmaps:

> Political party manifestos are very important because they highlight the various roadmaps or road prints that a government seeks to use in ruling the people and also spells out the policy agenda of that political party and it will also bring out the interest of the various sectors in which they seek to solicit for their votes and also they use it as a means towards solving national problems. So, it's very important because the main idea behind governance is nation-building, and every political party wants to capture governance through elections, and through that, you must bring in policies that are geared towards solving the problems of the people that you are

> seeking to solicit for their votes. So, within that context, I think party manifestos are particularly important for the reasons I mentioned. They are important to me because they are the main strings you use to assess a government, whether it is performing well or not. Because if a government is going to tell you that they are going to deliver ABC, that's the mandate or that's the criteria that you are using to go and measure how they are performing, but immediately you are not privileged to party manifesto and the party loses power, then you don't have any yardstick towards measuring their progress. (Respondent 28).

As respondent 28 indicates, party manifestos serve as tools of accountability, even if democracy is not fully realized. However, macro-social marketing in transition economies often grapples with "wicked problems"—issues marked by multi-level interconnections, interlinked causal pathways, and stakeholder complexity (Huff et al., 2021; Kock, 2017). These problems are dynamic, resistant to intervention, and shaped by entrenched norms, leading to ineffective or inequitable marketing systems (Duffy et al., 2017). Respondent 41 stresses that political marketing should prioritize needs over branding:

> For that one, yes, truly, because I have a lot of people who are in the government sector. Sometimes those with needs call for assistance. I remember when my brother needed a scholarship; we had to guide him through the process, and he got it. Relate them very well. That is, if you qualify and have what it takes. I do not see the reason they will deny you. So, for that, I can say yes, I relate with them very nicely. (Respondent 41).

Respondent 41's views reinforce the need for a paradigm shift in political marketing—one that moves beyond branding to address real needs. Solving wicked problems requires a macro-social marketing perspective grounded in systemic change (Kilbourne et al., 1997; Kennedy, 2016; Ertekin & Atik, 2015).

Conclusion

This study draws on macro-social marketing, branding theory, social capital theory, and institutional theory to examine how voters in transitioning African economies—specifically Ghana—engage with political products during general elections. By conceptualizing elections as electoral brands, we explored how democratic values are marketed and consumed across micro, meso, and macro levels. At the micro level, voter decisions are shaped by personal welfare concerns, trust in political promises, and community influence. At the meso level, political marketing interacts with institutional practices and social dynamics, revealing how party structures can foster unity or deepen divisions. At the macro level, political branding serves as a tool for systemic change, though often constrained by complex governance challenges. These findings highlight the need for context-sensitive, multi-level strategies that reflect the realities of emerging democracies and the social systems within which voters operate.

By integrating social capital theory and institutional theory, this study offers a nuanced understanding of political marketing in Ghana. These frameworks illuminate how interpersonal trust and institutional norms shape voter perceptions, campaign effectiveness, and democratic engagement. The micro-level findings highlight the importance of tailoring political messages to individual needs and values, while meso-level insights emphasize the role of community cohesion and institutional fairness in sustaining democratic participation. At the macro level, the study reveals how political branding and governance structures must align with broader societal goals to foster legitimacy and long-term civic engagement. The findings collectively point to the importance of multi-level, adaptive political marketing approaches that are grounded in both local realities and institutional integrity.

Theoretical Implications

In this study, we introduce a novel conceptualization of general elections in emerging African economies—as electoral brands—shifting the theoretical lens from traditional political science to one grounded in marketing, including consumer behavior and branding theory. This reframing suggests that voters engage in elections in much the same way as consumers engage with products.

Branding theory deepens this understanding by explaining how voters form perceptions of political parties and candidates through symbolic cues, emotional associations, and perceived value—much like consumers evaluating products. Political brands serve as heuristics that simplify complex political choices, especially in transitioning economies where ideological clarity may be limited. These brands influence voter loyalty, trust, and engagement, and their effectiveness depends on consistent messaging, cultural relevance, and emotional resonance. In Ghana's context, branding helps voters navigate political uncertainty by aligning their choices with parties that reflect their identities, needs, and aspirations.

By emphasizing micro, meso, and macro perspectives, the study proposes a micromarketing approach to political marketing. This layered framework enriches existing theory by highlighting individual voter behavior (micro), party and campaign strategies (meso), and broader institutional and societal influences (macro). It encourages scholars to move beyond siloed analyses and consider the interconnectedness of political marketing dynamics.

By positioning political marketing in transition economies as a "wicked problem"—one that is complex, context-dependent, and resistant to simple solutions—we challenge the assumption that branding strategies can be universally applied. Instead, it calls for adaptive, context-sensitive approaches and invites interdisciplinary dialogue with systems theory and complexity science. By proposing a three-pronged model that begins at the micro level and scales up to the macro, the research bridges the gap between individual-level behavior change and societal transformation, offering a scalable framework for understanding how political marketing can influence democratic development. Grounded in the Ghanaian context, the study provides both empirical and theoretical insights relevant to African transition economies.

Managerial and Public Policy Implications

The study offers several practical insights for political campaign managers, strategists, and policymakers operating in transitioning democracies. By conceptualizing elections as brand-driven experiences, political actors can better understand how voters engage with parties, candidates, and manifestos as they would with consumer products. This calls for investment in brand identity development, consistent messaging, and emotional resonance—especially in contexts where party loyalty is fluid and voter expectations are evolving.

Adopting a micro–meso–macro framework enables campaign teams to tailor strategies across levels:

- *At the micro level,* messages should be personalized to address individual voter needs, values, and aspirations.

- *At the meso level,* branding efforts must engage communities and regional networks, fostering unity and trust in political institutions.
- *At the macro level,* campaign narratives should align with national development goals and democratic values, promoting systemic change and civic engagement.

Political marketing in transition economies is inherently complex and context sensitive. Branding alone cannot resolve deep-rooted political challenges. Therefore, campaign strategies must be adaptive, incorporating stakeholder engagement, feedback mechanisms, and cultural relevance. Electoral commissions and political institutions can apply macro-social marketing principles to design campaigns that not only persuade but also educate, empower, and mobilize citizens toward long-term democratic participation.

Finally, political marketers in African contexts must avoid importing Western strategies wholesale. Instead, they should localize campaign approaches, integrating historical narratives, socio-economic realities, and indigenous values. This requires capacity-building for campaign staff in branding, digital marketing, public relations, and voter analytics to ensure effective and ethical political communication.

Limitations and Future Research Directions

This study has several limitations. First, it is a cross-sectional design that captures voter perceptions at a single point in time, limiting insights into changes across election cycles. Second, data were collected primarily from residents in Greater Accra, which may not fully represent the diversity of voter experiences across Ghana. Third, although the sample includes diverse demographics, the findings are not generalizable to the entire Ghanaian population or to other African contexts.

Future research should consider longitudinal designs to track evolving voter behavior and campaign strategies. Expanding the geographic scope to include rural and less urbanized regions would offer a more comprehensive view of political marketing. Comparative studies across multiple African transitioning economies could help validate the micro–meso–macro framework. Additionally, exploring the role of digital media, youth engagement, and diaspora influence would enrich the understanding of voter dynamics. Combining quantitative and qualitative methods could further strengthen the empirical foundation and provide deeper insights into political marketing in emerging democracies.

Appendix: Qualitative Questions Used in the Study

Q1: What do you understand by the term "Democracy"? How important is Democracy to you?

Q2: What are your views about Democracy as practiced in Ghana and in Africa as a whole?

Q3: How important are Political Party Manifestos to you?

Q4: Would you say that Party Political campaigns and rallies are good for the country? Why?

Q5: What do you think about the General Elections in Ghana?

Q6: Do you enjoy discussing politics among your family and friends?

Q7: Please, do you belong to a particular Political Party? What are your reasons for belonging to, or not belonging to, a Political Party?

Q8: Do you usually pay Party dues? Why?

Q9: Do you support Political Parties (or your Party) financially? Why?

Q10: Do you think it is important to support Political Parties financially? Why?

Q11: Do you think it is important that companies support Political Parties financially? Why?

Q12: Please, how old are you?

Q13: Please, what is the highest educational achievement you have obtained?

Q14: Finally, what is your profession? Or what do you do for a living?

References

Adel, T. A., Amankwah-Amoah, J., & Puthusserry, P. (2023). Political ties in emerging markets: A systematic review and research agenda. *International Marketing Review, 40*(6), 1344–1378.

Afrobarometer Survey (1999). *A Pan African series of National Public Attitude Surveys on Democracy, Governance, & Society*. http://www.afrobarometer.org/data/ghana-round-1-data-1999

Afrobarometer Report. (2018). *Ghanaians favour election of Metropolitan, Municipal, and District Chief Executives (MMDCEs)*. Available at http://www.afrobarometer.org/

Ake, C. (1996). *Is Africa democratizing?* (Vol. 5). Malthouse Press.

Anebo, F. K. G. (2001). The Ghana 2000 elections: Voter choice and electoral decisions. *African Journal of Political Science/Revue Africaine de Science Politique, 6*(1), 69–88.

Ayee, J. R. A. (2000). Deepening democracy in Ghana: Politics of the 2000 elections. *Freedom Publication*, 1–11.

Berger, P. L., & Luckmann, T. (1967). *Social construction of reality*. Anchor Books.

Blankson, C., Cowan, K., & Darley, W. K. (2018). Marketing practices of rural micro and small businesses in Ghana: The role of public policy. *Journal of Macromarketing, 38*(1), 29–56.

Bourdieu, P. (1986). The forms of capital. In J. G. Richardson (Ed.), *Handbook of theory and research for the sociology of education* (pp. 241–258). Greenwood Press.

Bratton, M., & Mattes, R. (2001). Support for democracy in Africa: Intrinsic or instrumental? *British Journal of Political Science*, 447–474.

Bratton, M. & Bhoojedhur, S. (2019, June). Africans want Open Elections–Especially if they Bring Change. Afrobarometer Policy Paper No. 58, 1–25.

Brehm, J., & Rahn, W. (1997). Individual-level evidence for the causes and consequences of social capital. *American Journal of Political Science, 41*(3), 999–1023.

Campbell, A., Converse, P. E., Miller, W. E., & Stokes, D. E. (1960). *The American voter*. University of Chicago Press.

Converse, P. E. (1964). The nature of belief Systems in Mass Publics. In D. E. Apter (Ed.), *Ideology and discontent*. Free Press.

Creswell, J. W. (1998). *Qualitative inquiry and research design: Choosing among five traditions*. Sage.

DeBerry-Spence, B., Ekpo, A. E., & Hogan, D. (2019). Mobile phone visual ethnography (MpVE): Bridging transformative photography and Mobile phone ethnography. *Journal of Public Policy & Marketing, 38*(1), 81–95.

DeLeon, L., & DeLeon, P. (2002). The democratic ethos and public management. *Administration & Society, 34*(2), 229–250.

Domegan, C. T. (2008). Social marketing: Implications for contemporary marketing practices classification scheme. *Journal of Business & Industrial Marketing, 23*(2), 135–141.

Dubois, A., & Gadde, L. E. (2002). Systematic combining: An abductive approach to case research. *Journal of Business Research, 55*(7), 553–560.

Duffy, S., Layton, R., & Dwyer, L. (2017). When the commons call 'enough', does marketing have an answer? *Journal of Macromarketing, 37*(3), 268–285.

Engel, J. F., Blackwell, R. D., & Miniard, P. W. (1986). *Consumer behavior* (5th ed.). Dryden.

Ertekin, Z. O., & Atik, D. (2015, June). Aging of youth through fashion: Influential dynamics and societal implications. In *Proceedings of 40° Annual Macromarketing Conference.*

Flaherty, T., Domegan, C., Duane, S., Brychkov, D., & Anand, M. (2020). Systems social marketing and macro-social marketing: A systematic review. *Social Marketing Quarterly, 26*(2), 146–166.

Francis, J. N. P., & Mugabo, L. (2025). A call for Afrocentric Decolonial endogenous marketing and public policy research and practices: Toward sustainable peace and well-being in African societies. *Journal of Public Policy & Marketing, 44*(1), 10–24.

Friedland, R. & Alford, R. R. (1987). *Bringing Society back in: Symbols, structures and institutional contradiction.* Paper presented at Conference on Institutional Change, Centre for Advanced Study in the Behavioral Sciences, Stanford, CA, May 15–16.

Glaeser, E. L. (2001). The formation of social capital. *Canadian Journal of Policy Research, 2*(1), 34–40.

Gyimah-Boadi, E. (2001). A peaceful turnover in Ghana. *Journal of Democracy, 12*(2), 103–117.

Hertzler, J. O. (1961). *American social institutions: A sociological analysis.* Allyn and Bacon.

Hughes, E. C. (1939). Institutions. In R. E. Park (Ed.), *An outline of the principles of sociology* (pp. 283–346). Barnes & Noble.

Huff, A. D., Humphreys, A., & Wilner, S. J. (2021). The politicization of objects: Meaning and materiality in the US cannabis market. *Journal of Consumer Research, 48*(1), 22–50.

Jha, A., Boudreaux, C. J., & Banerjee, V. (2018). Political leanings and social capital. *Journal of Behavioral and Experimental Economics, 72*, 95–105.

Kapucu, N., & Garayev, V. (2016). Structure and network performance: Horizontal and vertical networks in emergency management. *Administration & Society, 48*(8), 931–961.

Kawachi, I., & Berkman, L. (2000). Social cohesion, social capital, and health. *Social Epidemiology, 174*(7).

Kennedy, A. M. (2019). *Macro-social marketing insights: Systems thinking for wicked problems*. Routledge.
Kennedy, A. M. (2016). Macro-social marketing. *Journal of Macromarketing, 36*(3), 354–365.
Kennedy, A. M., & Parsons, A. (2012). Macro-social marketing and social engineering: A systems approach. *Journal of Social Marketing, 2*(1), 37–51.
Khavul, S., Bruton, G. D., & Wood, E. (2009). *Informal family business in Africa* (pp. 1219–1238). Entrepreneurship Theory and Practice.
Kilbourne, W., McDonagh, P., & Prothero, A. (1997). Sustainable consumption and the quality of life: A macromarketing challenge to the dominant social paradigm. *Journal of Macromarketing, 17*(1), 4–24.
Kirk, J., & Miller, M. L. (1986). *Reliability and validity in qualitative research* (Vol. 1). Sage.
Kock, C. (2017). *Deliberative rhetoric: Arguing about doing* (Vol. 5). University of Windsor.
Kotler, P., & Zaltman, G. (1971). Social marketing: An approach to planned social change. *Journal of Marketing, 35*, 3–12.
Kotler, P. (2016). *Democracy in decline: Rebuilding its future*. SAGE Publications.
Layton, R. (2019). Marketing systems–looking backward, sizing up and thinking ahead. *Journal of Macromarketing, 39*(2), 208–224.
Lowe, T., & Plimmer, D. (2019). Exploring the New World: Practical insights for funding, commissioning, and managing in complexity. *Newcastle Business School and Collaborate.*. http://wordpress.collaboratei.com/wp-content/uploads/Exploring-the-New-World-Report_DigitalReport.pdf
Luskin, R. C. (1990). Explaining political sophistication. *Political. Behaviour, 12*(4), 331–361.
Malhotra, N. K., Nunan, D., & Birks, D. F. (2020). *Marketing research*. Pearson.
Maxwell, J. A. (2018). *Collecting qualitative data: A realist approach* (pp. 19–32). The SAGE Handbook of Qualitative Data Collection.
Mensah, K. (2011). *Political Brand Management: Forms and strategies in modern party politics*. Unpublished Ph.D. Thesis. The University of Sheffield.
Mishler, E. (1990). Validation in inquiry-guided research: The role of exemplars in narrative studies. *Harvard Educational Review, 4*, 415–443.
Moustakas, C. (1994, July 27). *Phenomenological research methods*. Sage.
Newton, K. (2001). Trust, social capital, civil society, and democracy. *International Political Science Review, 22*(2), 201–214.
Ninsin, K. A. (2006). *Political parties and political participation in Ghana*. Konrad Adenauer Stiftung.
Nugent, P. (2001). Ethnicity and recent democratic experiments in Africa. *African Issues, 29*(1/2), 2–7.

Nukpezah, J. A., & Soujaa, I. (2018). Creating emergency prepared households—What really are the determinants of household emergency preparedness? *Risk, Hazards, & Crisis in Public Policy, 9*(4), 480–504.

Nwankwo, S. (2005). Characterization of black African entrepreneurship in the UK: A pilot study. *Journal of Small Business and Enterprise Development, 12*(1), 120–136.

Ormrod, R. P., Henneberg, S. C. & O'Shaughnessy, N. J. (2013). *Theoretical and conceptual issues in political marketing*. 7th International Political Marketing Conference, Stockholm, Sweden, September 19–21.

Parku, S. (2014 November). Who says elections in Ghana are free and fair? *Afrobarometer Policy Paper, 15*, 1–9.

Peterson, M., & Godby, R. W. (2020). Citizen participation in political markets: Extending service-dominant logic to public policy. *Journal of Public Policy & Marketing, 39*(4), 412–429.

Portes, A. (1998). Social capital: Its origins and applications in modern sociology. *Annual Review of Sociology, 24*, 1–24.

Putnam, R. (2001). Social Capital: Measurement and Consequences. *Canadian Journal of Policy Research, 2*(1), 41–51.

Rivera, J. D., & Nickels, A. E. (2014). Social capital, community resilience, and faith-based organizations in disaster recovery: A case study of Mary queen of Vietnam Catholic Church. *Risk, Hazards & Crisis in Public Policy, 5*(2), 178–211.

Schutz, A. (1967). *The phenomenology of the social world*. Northwestern Press.

Sekaran, U., & Bougie, R. (2016). *Research methods for business: A skill-building approach*. John Wiley & Sons.

Selznick, P. (1957). *Leadership in administration*. Harper & Row.

Si, S. (2019). Political marketing: An emerging theory. *Business Analyst*, *40*(1), 103–113 & *GSJ*, *11*(2).

Sobel, J. (2002). Can we trust social capital? *Journal of Economic Literature, 40*(1), 139–154.

Spiggle, S. (1994). Analysis and interpretation of qualitative data in consumer research. *Journal of Consumer Research, 21*(3), 491–503.

Teeple, G. (2000). *Globalization and the decline of social reform: Into the twenty-first century*. Simon Fraser University.

Tolbert, P. S., & Zucker, L. G. (1996). The institutionalization of institutional theory. In S. Clegg, C. Hardy, & W. Nord (Eds.), *Handbook of organization studies* (pp. 175–190). SAGE.

Truong, V. D. (2017). Government-led macro-social marketing programs in Vietnam: Outcomes, challenges, and implications. *Journal of Macromarketing, 37*(4), 409–425.

Tweneboah-Koduah, E. Y., Akotia, M., Akotia, C. S., & Hinson, R. E. (2010). Political party brand and consumer choice in Ghana. *Journal of Management Policy and Practice, 11*(5), 79–88.

Vigsø, O. (2017). The visual construction of personal ethos in election posters. *The Poster, 4*(1–2), 31–57.

Viswanathan, M., Rosa, J. A., & Ruth, J. A. (2010, May). Exchanges in marketing systems: The case of subsistence consumer-merchants in Chennai, India. *Journal of Marketing, 74*, 1–17.

Wald, K. D., & Shye, S. (1995). Religious influence in electoral behavior: The role of institutional and social forces in Israel. *The Journal of Politics, 57*(2), 495–507.

Waldron, J. (2012). Democracy. In D. Estlund (Ed.), *The Oxford handbook of political philosophy* (pp. 187–203). Oxford University Press.

White, J., & Ypi, L. (2010). Rethinking the modern prince: Partisanship and the democratic ethos. *Political Studies, 58*(4), 809–828.

Whitfield, L. (2005). Trustees of development from conditionality to governance: Poverty reduction strategy papers in Ghana. *Journal of Modern African Studies, 43*(4), 641–664.

Woolcock, M., & Narayan, D. (2000). Social capital: Implications for development theory, research, and policy. *World Bank Research Observer, 15*(2), 225–249.

Wymer, W. (2011). Developing more effective social marketing strategies. *Journal of Social Marketing, 1*(1), 17–31.

Youde, J. (2005). Economics and government popularity in Ghana. *Electoral Studies, 24*(1), 1–16.

Zucker, L. G. (1977). The role of institutionalization in cultural persistence. *American Sociological Review, 42*, 726–743.

CHAPTER 7

Decolonizing Consumer Research: A Neocolonial and Critical Social Theory Examination of Marginalized African Communities

Robert A. Opoku, Louicius Michel, Kwame Adom, and Chloe Weir

R. A. Opoku (✉)
Donald School of Business, Red Deer Polytechnic, Red Deer, AB, Canada
e-mail: Robert.Opoku@rdpolytech.ca

L. Michel · K. Adom
School of Business, Burman University, Lacombe, AB, Canada
e-mail: lmichel@burmanu.ca

K. Adom
e-mail: kwameadom@burmanu.ca

C. Weir
School of Education, Burman University, Lacombe, AB, Canada
e-mail: chloeweir@burmanu.ca

A. Gbadamosi et al. (eds.), *Contemporary Marketing Practices in Africa, Volume 1*, Palgrave Studies of Marketing in Emerging Economies,
https://doi.org/10.1007/978-3-032-27126-6_7

Introduction

Marginalization constitutes a structural phenomenon anchored in systemic power asymmetries that reinforce exclusionary societal norms (Henderson, 2022; Koehler et al., 2020). This process arises when specific population segments, typically disadvantaged by unequal resource distribution or political representation, are systematically excluded from mainstream economic and social participation. The mechanics of marginalization operate through what Jahn et al. (2012) term a "dual rejection mechanism," where dominant groups simultaneously establish normative standards while excluding those who deviate from these constructed ideals. Key socioeconomic indicators, including wealth concentration (Shavitt et al., 2016; Grusky, 2019), educational access (Burrows & Marsh, 1992; Fluit et al., 2024), and employment patterns, serve as measurable manifestations of these exclusionary boundaries (Di Pasquale & Parazzi, 2024; Palgrave Macmillan, 2023).

The phenomenon of marginalization operates across nested socio-spatial scales, each exhibiting distinct yet interrelated dynamics. Micro-level marginalization occurs within bounded institutional or geographic contexts (Ferguson, 2003; Sarmento et al., 2025) where localized power structures determine access to opportunities. Macro-level marginalization reflects the enduring legacy of colonial economic architectures, particularly through what Stiglitz (2017) describes as "enforced non-market participation" in global trade regimes. This structural positioning compels many African nations to function primarily as raw material suppliers within international value chains (Giddens, 1991; Razak et al., 2024), thereby perpetuating what Lightfoot & Wisniewski (2014) characterize as "asymmetric market entanglement."

The African context presents particularly salient manifestations of consumer marginalization when analyzed through neocolonial and critical social theory frameworks. Post-colonial economic structures continue to shape consumption patterns (Chidozie et al., 2025) through what recent scholarship terms "legacy market distortions" (Ndlovu-Gatsheni, 2021), while rapid urbanization introduces new forms of peripheralization. This dual dynamic—the persistence of historical exclusion mechanisms alongside emerging marginalization vectors—creates what Mbembe (2016) identifies as "hybrid consumption peripheries." The continent's socioeconomic diversity further enables comparative analysis of marginalization across multiple axes, including rural-urban divides, formal and informal economic sectors, and intergenerational wealth transfers.

To fully understand this exclusion, it is essential to define our core concepts. Decolonisation refers to the intellectual and practical project of dismantling the enduring political, economic, and cultural legacies of colonialism, centering marginalized knowledge systems and challenging Western epistemic dominance (Ndlovu-Gatsheni, 2021). Within this context, consumer research is the study of how individuals, groups, and organizations select, secure, use, and dispose of products and services. A decolonial approach to consumer research actively critiques the field's Eurocentric biases. This leads directly to the concept of epistemic injustice (Bhakuni & Abimbola, 2021; Fricker, 2007; Francis & Mugabo, 2025), which occurs when a person's knowledge and capacity as a knower are systematically discredited on the basis of their social identity, thereby erasing their experiences from academic and market theory.

The academic and practical imperative for examining African consumer marginalization stems from several critical considerations. First, prevailing market theories rooted in Western consumption models (Gibson, 2011; Lewis & Crabbe, 2024) fundamentally misrepresent the experiences of marginalized African consumers (McEwan et al., 2015; Sandikci, 2022). Besides, less attention has been paid to colonialism's enduring everyday impact and visible continuities, including in consumption (Parashar & Schulz, 2021). Second, structural analysis of consumption barriers provides actionable insights for developing inclusive market policies. Third, centering African consumer experiences challenges the universalist assumptions embedded in mainstream marketing theory, creating space for what Holland et al. (2008) term "contextualized consumption epistemologies."

This paper is structured to first deconstruct the existing paradigms before building a new, more inclusive framework. Following this introduction, the section on neocolonialism and the marketing research paradigm examines how colonial logics persist in mainstream research. Next, critical social theory, marketing, and marginalized societies explore how theories of power and identity provide essential complementary tools for analysis. The paper then presents a novel conceptual model that integrates these perspectives. After detailing the methodological approach, we introduce the Intersectional Consumer Ethnography (ICE) framework as a practical tool for decolonial research, demonstrating its application through an illustrative scenario. Finally, the conclusion presents future research directions and stakeholder implications, charting a path for a more equitable and epistemologically just consumer research agenda in African contexts.

Deconstructing the Dominant Paradigm: A Neocolonial Critique of Marketing Research

The Hegemony of Western Research Methods

Marketing research has traditionally relied on methodologies heavily influenced by Western developed nations (Anning-Dorson et al., 2025; Burgess & Steenkamp, 2006). This dominance disregards other jurisdictions' unique cultural, social, and economic realities (Steenkamp, 2019), often perpetuating a neocolonial dynamic in research practices. The term "neocolonialism" refers to the situation in which former colonies remain dependent on the metropolises and institutions of the West even after they achieved formal independence from the old European empires (von Hirschhausen & Kreienbaum, 2019).

Conceptual Foundations of Neocolonialism

The coinage of the term "neo-colonialism" has been attributed to the first president of Ghana, Kwame Nkrumah (Ashcroft et al., 2013, p.134), who used it in his 1963 preamble to the Organization of African States Charter and the title of his 1965 book Neo-colonialism: The Last Stage of Imperialism. The term assigns descriptive value to policies, infrastructures, and agents within post-colonial African societies that sustain colonial practices (Nkrumah, 1965, p. 7). Overall, the core of neocolonialism is that, despite the state appearing independent and exercising complete control over its affairs, it is subject to external economic and political pressures (Hallen, 2002; Nkrumah, 1965).

As a powerful intellectual tool in the service of the struggle for decolonization, the concept (neocolonialism) was also backed by debates and theoretical developments in academia, especially in the field of dependency and world system theories (Alaye & Fakoya, 2024; Tegegne, 2024). In the 1960s and 1970s, the concept provided an essential intellectual framework for anti-colonial movements in the South and solidarity movements in the North to understand global dynamics and imagine alternative world orders (Degli Esposti, 2024).

Methodological Mismatches and Epistemic Exclusion

This paper contends that neocolonialism, the persistent economic and intellectual dependence of former colonies on the Global North, fundamentally distorts marketing research paradigms. Current methodologies disproportionately privilege Western frameworks while systematically excluding local knowledge systems (Das et al., 2024; Greeff, 2025; Gilani, 2024; Konadu-Osei et al., 2023; Weaver, 2023), resulting in significant gaps in contextual consumer understanding. The overreliance on quantitative surveys and focus groups, mainstays of conventional marketing research, proves particularly problematic in non-Western contexts. Collectivistic cultures, for instance, often struggle with individualistic survey questions, yielding artificially skewed responses (Sun et al., 2024; Shavitt et al., 2016). Likewise, focus groups predicated on open debate frequently misfire in cultures valuing hierarchical communication and indirect expression (McGregor, 2004). These methodological mismatches compound when studying societies where communal values and shared resource systems inherently conflict with Western consumerist assumptions central to mainstream marketing theory.

Toward Decolonial Research Practices

To address these issues, consumer behavior research must adopt decolonial approaches to overcome these systemic biases (Das et al., 2024; Konadu-Osei et al., 2023). This transformation requires both recognizing the power imbalances embedded in traditional research practices and actively engaging local researchers and participants as equal partners in knowledge production (Fredericks et al., 2024; Ohajunwa & Mji, 2021). The decolonization process should incorporate Indigenous methodologies, such as storytelling and community-based participatory research, which offer more culturally attuned ways to understand consumer behavior across diverse markets (Smith et al., 2012). Positive examples are emerging, such as research that privileges local languages and epistemologies (Dadze-Arthur & Mangai, 2024; Seltzer et al., 2024) or projects co-designed with community elders to ensure cultural protocols are respected (Kovach, 2021). Such paradigm shifts in marketing research can cultivate more inclusive practices that not only enhance cultural understanding but also develop marketing strategies better suited for our interconnected global marketplace.

While the neocolonial critique effectively exposes the structural and external forces of marginalization, a complete framework requires a lens to analyze the internal, social, and lived experiences of power within these structures. The macro-level analysis of neocolonialism must be complemented with a micro-level understanding of how power is enacted and experienced daily. This leads us to the critical insights offered by critical social theory.

A Complementary Lens: Critical Social Theory for Understanding Marginalized Societies

Theoretical Foundations and Cross-Disciplinary Relevance

Critical social theory is grounded in the belief that humans primarily associate with others because of shared ideas (Wendt, 2023). Although it is a highly complex phenomenon to define (Lemert, 2024), it helps us understand human behavior and the factors that contribute to it. The framework of critical social theory is used to evaluate the actions of a social system or an organization (McCall et al., 2023). These systems play out in various ways depending on the ecosystem that provides their well-being. The argument for social theory includes the actors at the social level and the clients (Coleman, 1986).

Critical social theory provides the basis for understanding a group's social reality, including their interests, power relations, structures, and social influence (Celikates, 2006; Fenzl & Pelzman, 2012). As advocated by the Frankfurt School, critical social theory offers a more nuanced and radical approach than that proposed by Horkheimer (Kellner, 1990). It is challenging to define critical social theory, as critical conditions will change and evolve, and specificity should be avoided, as situations differ (Kincheloe & McLaren, 2011). While critical theory has been a theory by the oppressed and for the oppressed, it provides a framework for understanding how individuals manage their lives using their knowledge and historical context (Ahmed, 2022).

The Gap in Marketing Literature.

Despite being widely debated in a range of disciplines, including sociology (Collins et al., 2021; Elliott, 2021), criminology (Groves & Sampson, 1986; Yar, 2012), education (Brown & Lloyd, 2024; Carrington & Selva, 2010; Giroux, 2024), socio-legal studies (Buckel et al., 2024), public administration and policy research (Box, 2015;

Young et al., 2024; Van Hulst et al., 2025;), religious studies (Delaney, 2024; Sutterlüty, 2016), archaeology (Agbe-Davies, 2024), medicine (Annandale, 2025), security studies (Bilgin, 2023), nursing (Bell, 2024; Browne, 2000; Hopton, 1997), critical social theory has not attracted a great deal of attention in marketing (Burton, 2001; Bradshaw & First, 2012; Möller, 2025; Williams, 2024;). Since critical theory has been widely discussed in areas outside of marketing, this paper also contributes to the burgeoning literature in the critical marketing research (Bertilsson & Egan-Wyer, 2025; Galalae, & Licsandru, 2025; Helm et al., 2024; Rémy et al., 2024) and critical social theory discourse (Brown & Lloyd, 2024; Burton, 2001; Gordon, 2011) by evaluating the relevance of critical social theory in the marketing context.

Application to Marginalized Consumer Contexts

The business and market landscape is dynamic and ambiguous, leading to consumer behaviors that are unique to each environment (Möller et al., 2020). Thus, this paper also explores how such behaviors impact consumerism in marginalized, colonized societies. Power inequalities created over time by colonialism result in exclusionary processes for the marginalized (Brevini et al., 2024; Dangschat, 2009). Market research in Western societies may be incongruent with some marginalized societies, where commonality, shared inequalities, and the sense of community negate exclusionary practices. Critical social theory, with its multiple factors, provides a lens that privileges the marginalized in market research. This theoretical approach finds practical application in studies that examine how resistance to dominant market narratives can form through collective consumer action in marginalized communities (Daskalaki et al., 2023), or how marketplace exclusion can spur the creation of alternative, community-owned market infrastructures (Gonzalez-Arcos et al., 2021).

Having established these two powerful but distinct theoretical critiques—one focused on macro-level global structures (neocolonialism) and the other on micro-level social power dynamics (critical social theory)—the necessary next step is to integrate them. A comprehensive understanding of consumer marginalization in Africa requires a framework that accounts for both the enduring legacies of colonial economic architectures and the nuanced, intersectional realities of everyday life. The following section presents a novel conceptual model that synthesizes these perspectives into a unified analytical framework.

Synthesizing the Framework: A Conceptual Model for Decolonial Consumer Research

While conventional market theories offer limited explanatory power regarding systemic exclusion, the synthesis of neocolonial critique and critical social theory proposed in this paper provides a robust analytical framework. This approach builds on three foundational premises: first, that colonial economic structures continue to shape contemporary consumption patterns (Bhambra, 2020; Rodney, 2018); second, that power asymmetries manifest distinctly in African market contexts (Mkandawire, 2015); and third, that meaningful market inclusion requires addressing both material and symbolic dimensions of marginalization (Comaroff & Comaroff, 2012).

The conceptual model (see Figure 7.1) developed in this paper consequently advances consumer theory by integrating these critical perspectives while proposing actionable pathways for equitable market transformation. The model positions neocolonialism and critical social theory as foundational frameworks for understanding systemic marginalization, while identifying information asymmetry as the operational mechanism through which exclusion manifests. This mediation occurs because unequal access to market knowledge replicates colonial-era power imbalances in contemporary consumer contexts (Chen & Wang, 2025; Stiglitz, 2017). The model further specifies that the expression of marginalization depends on contextual factors, including geographic (urban/rural divides), economic (formal/informal sectors), and institutional (policy frameworks) factors that shape its intensity and form. Crucially, these processes are socially constructed through perceptual filters: dominant groups naturalize exclusionary norms, while marginalized consumers internalize or resist them (Jahn et al., 2012). This dynamic construction means that marginalization operates simultaneously as an objective market condition and a subjective lived experience, requiring methodologies such as intersectional ethnography to fully capture its dimensions.

This conceptual model is not merely theoretical; it was developed through a rigorous scholarly process and, more importantly, it demands a methodological approach capable of capturing the complex, multi-layered reality it describes. The model's emphasis on lived experience, social construction, and contextual factors underscores the need for immersive, ethical, and participatory methods. The following section outlines the methodological approach used to construct this model.

Methodological Approach

This paper employs a critical conceptual synthesis to develop its theoretical framework. This approach involves systematically analyzing and integrating concepts from diverse critical traditions, including critical social theory and decolonial thought, to help construct a novel theoretical perspective on marketing research in marginalized African contexts. The selection of sources was guided by their relevance to understanding power asymmetries, epistemic injustice, and methodological decolonization in consumer research. Both seminal theoretical works and contemporary empirical studies were included to ensure both historical depth and contemporary relevance. The discussion is structured to first deconstruct the neocolonial biases in prevailing marketing research paradigms, then to synthesize a positive alternative framework centered on decolonial principles and critical social theory. This methodological transparency aims to make the scholarly rigor of our conceptual development explicit and enhance reader trust in our analytical process.

Having established our conceptual model through this synthesis, we now turn to its practical application. The model's call for methodologies that can navigate objective conditions and subjective experiences necessitates an innovative toolkit. The following section introduces a concrete methodological framework—Intersectional Consumer Ethnography (ICE)—designed to operationalize our model for ethical and effective empirical research.

Operationalizing the Model: The Intersectional Consumer Ethnography (ICE) Framework

Neocolonialism provides a vital analytical framework for examining consumer behavior in marginalized African communities, revealing how global economic structures and Western cultural hegemony maintain dominance. This approach moves beyond history to show how contemporary market forces, like multinational corporations controlling seed patents or algorithms promoting global brands, systematically shape local consumption and create dependency. Rather than focusing solely on individual choice, this lens exposes the structural constraints that privilege external powers and marginalize local communities.

Critical social theory offers a necessary complement to intersectional analysis. To illustrate the necessity of an integrated methodology, consider the case of Serwaa, a young professional and primary shopper for her family in Accra, Ghana. Her in-law, who lives with them, scrutinizes her purchasing decisions. The in-law expects traditional, homemade meals, requiring Serwaa to buy specific local ingredients, while her own aspirations and demanding career push her toward convenient, pre-packaged foods often produced by multinational corporations. This creates a "double burden" where her time poverty, a consequence of gendered professional and domestic roles, is exploited by the market.

Feminist theory, a type of critical social theory, reveals how Serwaa's consumption is an act of navigating complex gendered expectations. A neocolonial analysis further shows that the premium prices of imported convenience foods constitute economic extraction, while the devaluation of local, time-saving alternatives undermines indigenous food systems. This integrated view captures how Serwaa's choices are not expressions of pure preference but are constrained at the intersection of patriarchal social structures and global market forces.

Thus, based on the above scenario, integrating these theories (critical social theory and neocolonialism) can transform critical marketing research (Galalae & Licsandru, 2025) by moving it from abstract theory to grounded, impactful practice in marginalized African communities. The integration further reveals how power operates at the intersection of the global and the local, shaping everything from resource access to cultural identity. To help understand such phenomena, this study proposes the Intersectional Consumer Ethnography (ICE) framework (See Fig. 7.2).

The ICE framework situates African consumer realities at its center. Surrounding it are three interrelated methodological branches—Decolonial Approaches, Participatory Action Research, and Digital Tools—each connected by dynamic, bidirectional arrows that reflect their mutual influence. An outer context ring captures structural forces, such as neocolonial policies and social divides, while a top banner signals practical outputs, such as inclusive strategies and ethical AI. This framework is vital to consumer behavior research in Africa, as it centers local epistemologies, challenges Western biases, and promotes culturally grounded, community-driven insights in both academic inquiry and policy application.

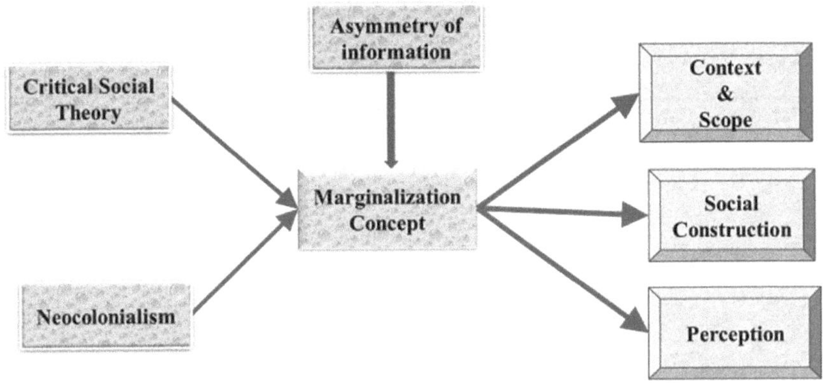

Fig. 7.1 Marginalization: A conceptual model. Authors' Construction (2025)

Core Components of the ICE Framework

Figure 7.2 illustrates multiple methodologies and tools for applying neocolonialism and social theory to marketing research. For instance, conducting in-depth ethnographic studies within marginalized communities can yield rich, contextually grounded data on consumption practices and their underlying meanings (Green et al., 2024; Johnston et al., 2011). Through community immersion, researchers reveal how historical and contemporary power structures influence African consumers' choices and behaviors.

In-depth ethnographic studies of marginalized African communities face challenges in gaining trust and access due to historical power imbalances and research mistrust. Researchers must prioritize building rapport and establishing long-term relationships with community members to overcome this. Transparency about research goals and benefits is crucial, as is involving the community in research design and decision-making through community-based participant observation (CBPO) (Roque et al., 2024). Respecting cultural norms and practices and ensuring participants' safety and anonymity are essential. Marketing researchers can build trust and conduct meaningful ethnographic studies by demonstrating a genuine commitment to understanding and empowering the community.

Additionally, critical discourse analysis (CDA) is a powerful lens that exposes how media and advertising perpetuate damaging stereotypes, actively shaping consumer perceptions and aspirations toward

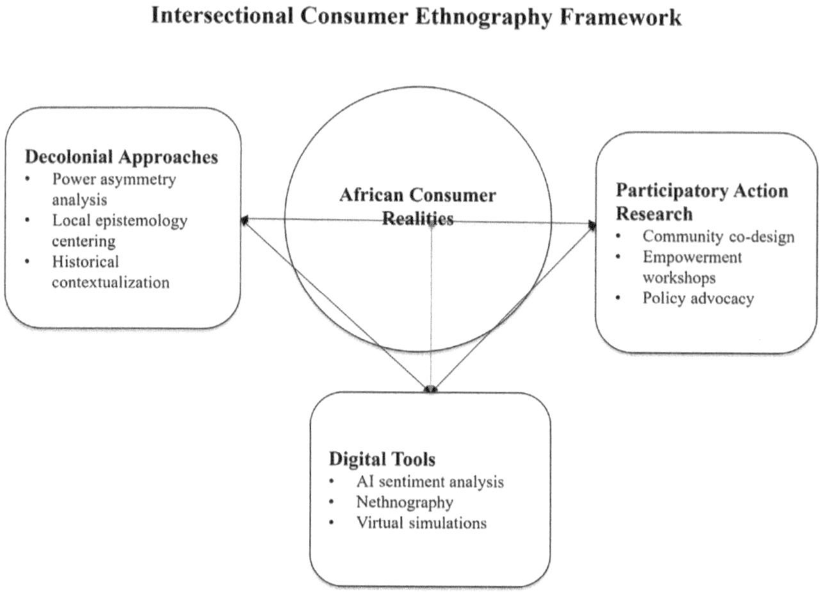

Fig. 7.2 Intersectional consumer ethnography (ICE) Framework *Authors' construction (2025)*

marginalized communities. This methodology deconstructs the dominant narratives that reinforce systemic inequities, revealing the insidious link between language and bias. A growing body of compelling research demonstrates its critical value: from Lu et al. (2024) dissecting Australian disability workforce policies to Friedline et al. (2024) unpacking decades of financial marketing rhetoric. Sepehr et al. (2025) employed CDA to scrutinize the portrayal of migrant workers during crises, while Rad and Melendez-Torres (2025) revealed how social media advertising on platforms such as *Facebook* and *Instagram* manipulates public perception. This work, championed early by Elliott (1996) and advanced by marketing scholars like Ellis et al. (2005), Hackley (2003), and Cross & Ekpo (2025), provides an undeniable evidence base. By deconstructing these messages, CDA empowers us not only to challenge stereotypes but also to actively identify and create opportunities for authentic, equitable representation (Crane, 2025), making it an indispensable tool for ethical and effective communication in marketing research.

Moreover, participatory action research (PAR) can empower marginalized community members to actively participate in the research process. According to De Oliveira (2023), PAR is a qualitative research approach in which researchers and participants work together to investigate social issues and take action to bring about social change. Cahill (2007) argued that PAR practice challenges the normative production of knowledge by including excluded perspectives and involving those most affected by the research. Researchers can foster a sense of ownership and agency while generating valuable consumer insights by involving community members in research design, data collection, and analysis. This approach can also lead to community-based initiatives to address identified consumer needs and challenges.

That notwithstanding, PAR, as an approach, can be a problematic tool for facilitators and communities to apply, given power dynamics within the consumer research process in Africa. Therefore, overcoming power imbalances within participatory action research in Africa requires a deliberate and ongoing commitment to equity. This can be achieved through transparent and inclusive processes that prioritize community ownership. Building strong relationships based on trust and respect is essential. Empowering community members with research skills and knowledge can help to level the playing field. Researchers must also be reflexive about their biases and power positions, actively challenging and dismantling them (Ademolu, 2024; Galalae & Licsandru, 2025; Ide & Beddoe, 2024). By centering the voices and experiences of marginalized communities and ensuring that benefits are shared equitably, it is possible to mitigate power imbalances and create a more just and participatory research process.

When informed by neocolonialism and critical social theory, triangulation can provide a robust approach to studying marginalized African consumers. By combining multiple data sources and methods (De Chernatony et al., 2005; Hamilton, 2024; Nielsen et al., 2020), critical consumer researchers can deepen their understanding of how historical and contemporary power structures shape consumption patterns. For instance, triangulating qualitative data from in-depth interviews with quantitative data from surveys can reveal how economic disparities linked to colonial legacies influence access to goods and services. Incorporating archival research to examine historical policies and their contemporary impacts can further strengthen the analysis. This multifaceted approach enables a more comprehensive exploration of the complex interplay among individual experiences, structural inequalities, and cultural factors that contribute to African consumer marginalization.

Applying qualitative software analytical tools in African market research also offers a unique opportunity to delve deeper into the experiences of marginalized communities. Researchers can uncover the complex interplay between historical, cultural, and economic factors shaping consumption patterns by combining technological advancements with a nuanced understanding of neocolonialism and social theory. One critical application lies in discourse analysis. Researchers can identify how dominant narratives perpetuate stereotypes and inequalities by utilizing software to examine media representations, advertising, and policy documents. For instance, analyzing how African women are portrayed in beauty advertisements can reveal the impact of Western beauty standards on self-perception and consumption choices within marginalized communities. Additionally, thematic analysis can be employed to explore marginalized consumers' underlying meanings and experiences. The software can help identify recurring themes related to poverty, access to essential goods, and social exclusion, providing insights into the challenges these communities face. WhatsApp, a widely used messaging platform in Africa (Aidoo-Frimpong et al., 2024; Pindayi, 2017), provides a rich data source for understanding the experiences of marginalized consumers. Thematic analysis can be applied to WhatsApp conversations (Mbada et al., 2023; Neo et al., 2022) to explore how individuals discuss consumption practices, challenges, and aspirations within their social networks. For instance, researchers can analyze how users discuss access to essential goods, financial products, or healthcare services, revealing the impact of marginalization on their daily lives. By identifying recurring themes and patterns in WhatsApp conversations, consumer culture researchers can gain insights into the social and cultural factors shaping consumer behavior and the role of digital technologies in mediating consumption experiences.

Moreover, narrative analysis and storytelling data can offer powerful tools for understanding the lived experiences of marginalized individuals. Examining how individuals frame their consumption narratives can reveal critical insights into cultural influences, identity formation, and social contexts. For e.g., rural women's narratives about financial service access demonstrate how gender and socioeconomic factors shape consumption behaviors. Further, grounded theory methodology can complement this approach by systematically coding and analyzing qualitative data, enabling researchers to identify emerging patterns in marginalized communities' consumption practices (Clarke, 2021). For instance, exploring the consumption practices of urban youth in relation to social media can reveal the impact of digital technologies on identity formation and consumer culture.

Researchers can contribute to a more nuanced and equitable understanding of marginalized African communities by effectively utilizing qualitative software analytical tools. However, it is essential to approach this work with a critical lens by recognizing the limitations of technology and the importance of human interpretation (Leech & Onwuegbuzie, 2007). When technological advancements combine with a firm commitment to social justice, consumer researchers can produce knowledge that empowers marginalized groups while challenging entrenched power structures.

Artificial Intelligence (AI) can also be a potent tool for understanding marginalized African communities when grounded in neocolonialism and social theory. One potential application is in natural language processing (NLP) to analyze social media content and other textual data generated by these communities. Researchers can uncover hidden narratives, power dynamics, and consumer behaviors that might go unnoticed by applying critical discourse analysis frameworks informed by neocolonialism and social theory. AI can also be used to develop predictive models that identify consumption patterns and behavior within marginalized groups, helping to uncover disparities and inequalities (Cillo & Rubera, 2025; Ma & Sun, 2020). However, ensuring that AI algorithms are trained on diverse, representative datasets is crucial to avoid perpetuating bias (Nazer et al., 2023).

Moreover, AI technologies can offer innovative ways to study marginalized African consumers through virtual environments and simulations. Researchers can create digital replicas of local marketplaces, complete with culturally specific products and pricing structures, to observe authentic shopping behaviors and identify access barriers. These simulations can reveal nuanced consumer preferences often missed in conventional studies. AI-powered sentiment analysis tools further complement this approach by tracking brand perceptions and product attitudes within marginalized communities. When integrated with traditional research methods, these AI applications can provide a multidimensional understanding of the socioeconomic and cultural factors shaping consumption patterns in underserved African markets.

That notwithstanding, AI can also pose a significant risk of exacerbating marginalization among African consumers (Hao, 2022). By amplifying existing biases in data, AI algorithms can reinforce discriminatory practices (Paul et al., 2023) in areas such as credit scoring, insurance, and employment. This can further exclude marginalized groups from economic opportunities and essential services. Additionally, the concentration of AI development and control in the Global North can lead to the exploitation of African data without equitable benefits, creating a new form of digital colonialism. As AI systems increasingly shape consumer experiences, it is crucial to address these issues to prevent the technology from deepening existing inequalities and hindering the potential of marginalized African consumers.

By leveraging neocolonialism and social theory, consumer culture researchers can also employ a multifaceted approach to studying marginalized African consumer communities. Combining ethnography for immersive observation (Mariampolski, 2006), nethnography to analyze online interactions (Asname & Berrada, 2025; Delli Paoli & D'Auria, 2025), discourse analysis to examine language and power dynamics (Fitchett & Caruana, 2015; Moufahim et al., 2007), content and thematic analysis to identify patterns, and narrative analysis (Neuendorf, 2018) to understand lived experiences can provide a comprehensive understanding of consumer behavior. Triangulation can be used to validate findings across these methods (Papavasileiou & Dimou, 2025; Turner et al., 2017). For instance, researchers might conduct ethnographic fieldwork in a rural community by analyzing social media discussions (netnography) to under stand aspirations and by conducting discourse analysis of advertising to reveal underlying power structures. This combined approach, termed "Intersectional Consumer Ethnography (ICE)" in this paper, can offer a more nuanced and holistic perspective on the experiences of marginalized African consumers.

The following scenario demonstrates how the ICE framework can be applied in practice to generate rich, ethical, and actionable insights, moving from theoretical proposition to empirical application.

Empirical Application: An Illustrative Scenario of the ICE Framework in Makoko

Illustrative Scenario: Applying the ICE Framework to "Wellness" in Makoko, Lagos, Nigeria

A research team aims to understand the consumption of "wellness" products (e.g., vitamins, supplements, energy drinks) among residents of Makoko, a community primarily composed of people from West Africa living in a unique stilt community over the water in Lagos, Nigeria.

Vignette: Amina's Choice

Amina, a young mother and call center agent, feels constant fatigue. She sees ads on Facebook for imported vitamins promising "instant energy," but her grandmother advises her to see a local Afa Allah (traditional healer) for a holistic assessment. Amina is caught between the modern, branded promise of a quick fix and a culturally grounded, holistic approach to health. Her dilemma is not a simple choice but a site where global marketing, cultural identity, and economic pressure collide.

Applying the ICE Framework:

Decolonial Approaches: The study begins by challenging the Western biomedical definition of "wellness." Researchers engage local Afa Allah and community elders to co-define physical, spiritual, and communal health. This centers local epistemology from the outset.

Participatory Action Research (PAR): Local youth are trained as co-researchers. They conduct interviews in local wellness and run focus groups, uncovering nuances an outsider would miss. They further discover that energy drink consumption is high among men working night shifts, not for "wellness" but as a necessity to meet labor demands. This finding reframes the research question.

Culturally Attuned Digital Tools: The co-researchers use a private WhatsApp group to share short voice notes and images documenting their own and their peers' consumption journeys, creating a rich, contextual digital diary. This method is chosen because it is low-data, familiar, and allows for storytelling in their native language.

Structural Analysis (The Outer Ring): The data is analyzed through the dual lenses of neocolonialism and social theory. The team finds that aggressive digital marketing by foreign corporations (neocolonial economic power) leverages aspirations shaped by racialized and classed beauty standards (critical race theory). The lack of affordable healthcare (structural inequality) drives people toward seemingly accessible solutions.

Output (The Top Banner): The research outputs are practical and co-created. They include: (a) an academic paper challenging Western conceptions of wellness; (b) a community-led digital literacy workshop on critically evaluating health marketing; and (c) a policy brief advocating for stricter regulation of foreign supplement imports and support for local, traditional health practitioners.

This scenario demonstrates how the ICE framework ensures research is not merely on but for and with communities. It transforms Amina's personal dilemma into actionable knowledge, centering local voices to challenge power structures and propose equitable alternatives.

Future Research Directions, Research Questions, and Stakeholder Implications

The African continent offers a rich yet complex terrain for analyzing marginalized communities through neocolonial and critical social theory frameworks. Historical and contemporary power structures continue to shape distinctive consumption patterns, revealing persistent systemic inequalities that demand scholarly attention. This paper identifies critical research directions with corresponding investigative questions, emphasizing how interdisciplinary approaches grounded in social justice principles can generate transformative insights. Centering the lived experiences of marginalized African consumers remains essential for developing both ethically informed marketing practices and equitable economic policies. This paper, therefore, outlines potential research directions and corresponding research questions, highlighting the need for interdisciplinary collaboration and a commitment to social justice as follows:

Digital Financial Exclusion and Neocolonial Structures

Neocolonialism has exacerbated the digital divide, impacting marginalized communities' access to financial services and e-commerce. Research could explore how digital financial exclusion shapes African communities' consumption patterns and financial behaviors. Potential research questions include: How do digital payment systems reinforce or challenge existing power structures within marginalized communities? What are the implications of financial exclusion for adopting sustainable consumption practices among marginalized consumers?

Food Sovereignty and Decolonial Consumption

Food systems are intricately linked to colonial legacies (Malli et al., 2023; Tilzey & Sudgen, 2024). Research could investigate how food sovereignty movements reshape consumption patterns and consumer agency within marginalized communities (McMichael, 2014). Potential research questions include: How do cultural food practices and traditional ecological knowledge influence marginalized consumers' adoption of sustainable food choices? What are the barriers and opportunities for marginalized communities to participate in local food economies?

Health Equity and Consumer Well-Being

Health disparities and psychological well-being among marginalized communities are often rooted in historical and ongoing inequalities (Machin et al., 2024). Researchers of consumer culture could examine how consumption patterns contribute to or mitigate health inequities and consumer well-being. Potential research questions include: How do advertising and marketing practices influence the health-related consumption behaviors of marginalized communities? What role do social networks and cultural norms play in shaping health-seeking behaviors and access to healthcare among marginalized consumers?

Environmental Justice and Sustainable Consumption

Environmental issues disproportionately affect marginalized communities (Brehm & Pellow, 2002). Research could examine how consumer behavior contributes to social and environmental justice. Potential research questions include: How can marketing strategies promote sustainable consumption practices among marginalized consumers without reinforcing existing inequalities? What are the trade-offs between affordability, accessibility, and sustainability in the consumption choices of marginalized communities?

Intersectional Approaches to Consumer Research

To fully understand the experiences of marginalized communities, research should adopt intersectional approaches that consider multiple dimensions of identity, such as race, gender, class, and sexuality. Potential research questions include: How do intersecting social identities shape marginalized consumers' consumption experiences and aspirations? What are the implications of intersectionality for developing inclusive and effective marketing strategies?

Technology and Digital Marginalization

Technologies can simultaneously be tools of inclusion and marginalization for African consumers. Future research should examine how digital platforms and devices shape marginalized communities' access to information, resources, and markets. Research questions could include: How do mobile payment systems impact financial inclusion and exclusion among low-income consumers? How do social media platforms shape perceptions of beauty, body image, and consumer aspirations among marginalized youth? What are the ethical implications of data collection and use by technology companies operating in Africa? Investigating these technology-marginalization dynamics will enable researchers to develop frameworks that leverage technological innovations for meaningful socioeconomic empowerment while mitigating potential harms.

Artificial Intelligence and Algorithmic Justice

The advancement of artificial intelligence (AI) technology and its applications has significantly transformed consumer behavior (CB) (Jain et al., 2024; Stephen, 2024), and this transformation will continue. Future research should explore the intersection of AI, neocolonialism, and social theory to understand how these factors worsen marginalization among African consumers. Some key research questions include: How is data from African consumers used to train AI models that perpetuate existing inequalities? What are the implications of data privacy and ownership in this context? How can we create AI systems that are fair, accountable, and transparent for marginalized African consumers? How can AI promote financial inclusion while reducing risks of over-indebtedness and exploitation? What are the ethical implications of using AI for credit scoring and insurance underwriting in marginalized communities? How can AI protect the rights of marginalized African consumers? What are the challenges and opportunities for developing AI-powered consumer protection tools? What governance frameworks are needed to regulate AI in Africa and protect the rights of marginalized consumers? How can AI strengthen democratic processes and promote social justice in Africa? By addressing these questions, researchers can help develop AI systems that benefit all segments of African society and reduce the risks of further marginalization.

Concrete Implications for Stakeholders

To translate these research directions into meaningful change, specific actions must be undertaken by key stakeholders:

Academic researchers should adopt community-based participatory research (CBPR) methods that position community members as co-researchers rather than research subjects. This includes implementing participatory budgeting for research funds and establishing community advisory boards to guide research design and dissemination.

Journal editors and reviewers can revise publication criteria to value methodological diversity, explicitly welcoming submissions that employ decolonial, feminist, and Indigenous methodologies. Journals could establish special issues dedicated to Southern epistemologies and mandate ethical oversight committees with Global South representation for studies conducted in African contexts.

University institutions need to reframe marketing and consumer research curricula to incorporate critical race theory, post-colonial studies, and African philosophical perspectives. This should include establishing partnerships with African universities for faculty and student exchanges, creating funding lines specifically for decolonial research, and recognizing community-engaged scholarship in promotion and tenure criteria.

Further, it is recommended that marketing practitioners and corporations conduct ethical impact assessments for all marketing initiatives in marginalized communities, establish diverse hiring practices that prioritize local talent, and develop co-creation frameworks that involve community members in product development and marketing strategy from inception.

Policy makers and regulatory bodies also need to consider developing data sovereignty frameworks that protect African consumers' digital rights, establishing ethical guidelines for AI deployment in consumer markets, and creating funding mechanisms for community-owned market infrastructure that challenge neocolonial economic patterns.

Conclusion

In conclusion, this paper has argued that studying marginalized communities in Africa through integrated neocolonial and critical social theory frameworks offers a profound opportunity to advance both theoretical understanding and practical social change. By exploring the intersection of history, culture, and economic structures, researchers can develop more nuanced understandings of the complex challenges and aspirations that shape consumption experiences in these contexts.

While this paper has established a foundational theoretical framework, it is important to acknowledge certain limitations that also represent opportunities for future research. Our focus has primarily centered on Anglophone African contexts, potentially overlooking important nuances in *Francophone*, *Lusophone*, and *Arabophone* regions of the continent. Additionally, while we have emphasized community-engaged methodologies, further empirical work is needed to develop specific protocols for implementing these approaches across diverse African contexts. The theoretical synthesis presented here, while comprehensive, would benefit from deeper engagement with Indigenous African philosophical traditions and knowledge systems.

Nonetheless, these limitations simultaneously chart a clear course for transformative action. By addressing the research priorities and implementing the practical steps suggested in this conceptual paper, particularly through the development of context-specific methodological protocols and deeper engagement with Indigenous knowledge systems, critical marketing and consumer researchers can contribute to more ethically informed practices and policies. Such work must not only seek to understand but must actively support the aspirations of marginalized African communities. The ultimate goal remains the generation of knowledge that challenges existing power structures and contributes to a more equitable and just marketplace—one that fully recognizes the agency, dignity, and diverse consumption realities of all African consumers.

References

Ademolu, E. (2024). Birds of a feather (don't always) flock together: Critical reflexivity of 'Outsiderness' as an 'Insider'doing qualitative research with one's 'Own People'. *Qualitative Research, 24*(2), 344–366.

Agbe-Davies, A. S. (2024). Intersectional thinking in archaeological analysis. In M. Moen & U. Pedersen (Eds.), *The Routledge Handbook of Gender Archaeology* (pp. 73–86). Routledge.

Ahmed, S. (2022). The marginalized and critical theory: Dialectics of universalism. *International Critical Thought, 12*(2), 305–326.

Aidoo-Frimpong, G., Turner, D., Collins, R. L., Ajiboye, W., Agbemenu, K., & Nelson, L. E. (2024). WhatsApp-propriate? Exploring "WhatsApp" as a tool for research among Ghanaian immigrants in the United States. *Journal of Racial and Ethnic Health Disparities, 11*(4), 1956–1963.

Alaye, A., & Fakoya, V. (2024). Neocolonialism and imperial dominance of the Post-Colonial African states. *NIU Journal of Social Sciences, 10*(1), 7–17.

Alvesson, M. (1994). Critical theory and consumer marketing. *Scandinavian Journal of Management, 10*(3), 291–313.

Annandale, E. (2025). *The Sociology of Health and Medicine: A Critical Introduction* (2nd ed.). Cambridge.

Anning-Dorson, T., Baba, F., Zulu, M., & Acheampong, G. (2025). Data-driven dynamic capabilities in emerging markets: A grounded theory approach to digital transformation in African retail banking. *International Journal of Information Management, 84*, 102914.

Ashcroft, B., Griffiths, G., & Tiffin, H. (2013). *Post-Colonial Studies: The Key Concepts*. Routledge.

Asname, F., & Berrada, A. (2025). Netnography: An innovative approach to qualitative research in the digital age. In D. Elomari (Ed.), *Qualitative Approaches to Pedagogical Engineering* (pp. 1–22). IGI Global Scientific Publishing. https://doi.org/10.4018/979-8-3693-6021-7.ch001

Bell, B. V. (2024). "We'd really love to but we're really busy": Silence, precarity and resistance as structural barriers to anti-racism in nursing education. *Journal of Advanced Nursing, 80*(1), 214–225.

Bertilsson, J., & Egan-Wyer, C. (2025). Envisioning post-growth marketing: A dystopian-optimist's guide. *Marketing Theory, 14705931251313777*.

Bhakuni, H., & Abimbola, S. (2021). Epistemic injustice in academic global health. *The Lancet Global Health, 9*(10), e1465–e1470. https://doi.org/10.1016/S2214-109X(21)00301-6

Bhambra, G. K. (2020). Colonial global economy: towards a theoretical reorientation of political economy. *Review of International Political Economy, 28*(2), 307–322.
Bilgin, P. (2023). Critical Theory. In *Security Studies* (pp. 67–81). Routledge.
Box, R. C. (2015). *Critical Social Theory in Public Administration*. Routledge.
Bradshaw, A., & Firat, A. F. (2012). Rethinking critical marketing. In P. Maclaran, M. Saren, P. Maclaran, C. Goulding, R. Elliott, & M. Caterall (Eds.), *Critical Marketing* (pp. 50–63). Routledge.
Brehm, H. N., & Pellow, D. N. (2022). Environmental justice: Pollution, poverty and marginalized communities. In *Routledge Handbook of Global Environmental Politics* (pp. 348–361). Routledge.
Brevini, B., Fubara-Manuel, I., Le Ludec, C., Jensen, J. L., Jiménez, A., & Bates, J. (2024). Critiques of data colonialism. In J. Jarke & J. Bates (Eds.), *Dialogues in Data Power Shifting Response- abilities in a Datafied World* (pp. 120–137). Bristol University Press.
Bronner, S. E., & Kellner, D. M. (1989). *Critical Theory and Society*. Routledge.
Brown, D. H., & Lloyd, R. G. (2024). Using critical social theory as professional learning to develop scholar—practitioners in Physical Education: The example of Bourdieu's theory of practice. *Education Sciences, 14*(2), 160.
Browne, A. J. (2000). The potential contributions of critical social theory to nursing science. *Canadian Journal of Nursing Research, 32*(2), 35–55.
Buckel, S., Pichl, M., & Vestena, C. A. (2024). Legal struggles: A social theory perspective on strategic litigation and legal mobilisation. *Social & Legal Studies, 33*(1), 21–41.
Burgess, S. M., & Steenkamp, J. B. E. (2006). Marketing renaissance: How research in emerging markets advances marketing science and practice. *International Journal of Research in Marketing, 23*(4), 337–356.
Burrows, R., & Marsh, C. (1992). *Consumption and Class: Divisions and Change*. Palgrave Macmillan.
Burton, D. (2001). Critical marketing theory: the blueprint? *European Journal of Marketing, 35*(5/6), 722–743.
Cahill, C. (2007). Including excluded perspectives in participatory action research. *Design Studies, 28*(3), 325–340.
Carrington, S., & Selva, G. (2010). Critical social theory and transformative learning: Evidence in pre-service teachers' service-learning reflection logs. *Higher Education Research & Development, 29*(1), 45–57.
Catterall, M., & Maclaran, P. (2002). Researching consumers in virtual worlds: A cyberspace odyssey. *Journal of Consumer Behaviour, 1*(3), 228–238.
Celikates, R. (2006). From critical social theory to a social theory of critique: On the critique of ideology after the pragmatic turn. *Constellations: An International Journal of Critical & Democratic Theory, 13*(1).

Chen, W., & Wang, Y. (2025). Dynamic market making with asymmetric information and market power. *The Review of Financial Studies, 38*(1), 235–293.

Chidozie, F., Osimen, G. U., Bhadmus, J., & Newo, O. (2025). Sustainable development goals implementation in a post-colonial African State: Any future for the African Continental Free Trade Area? *Sustainable Development, 33*(1), 1479–1490.

Cillo, P., & Rubera, G. (2025). Generative AI in innovation and marketing processes: A roadmap of research opportunities. *Journal of the Academy of Marketing Science, 53*(3), 684–701.

Clarke, A. E. (2021). From grounded theory to situational analysis: What's new? In *Why? How? In Developing grounded theory* (pp. 223–266). Routledge.

Coleman, J. S. (1986). Social theory, social research, and a theory of action. *American Journal of Sociology, 91*(6), 1309–1335.

Collins, P. H., da Silva, E. C. G., Ergun, E., Furseth, I., Bond, K. D., & Martínez-Palacios, J. (2021). Intersectionality as critical social theory: Intersectionality as critical social theory. *Contemporary Political Theory, 20*(3), 690–725. https://doi.org/10.1057/s41296-021-00490-0

Comaroff, J., & Comaroff, J. L. (2012). Theory from the South: Or, how Euro-America is evolving toward Africa. *Anthropological Forum, 22*(2), 113–131.

Cooke, M. (2025). Decentring critical theory with the help of critical theory: Ecocide and the challenge of anthropocentrism. *Philosophy & Social Criticism, 51*(7), 1029–1043.

Cross, S. N., & Ekpo, A. E. (2025). When marketplaces fail: How market-challenged consumers navigate the marketplace. *Journal of the Academy of Marketing Science, 53*(2), 513–532.

Dadze-Arthur, A., & Mangai, M. S. (2024). The journal and the quest for epistemic justice. *Public Administration and Development, 44*(4), 326–341.

Dangschat, J. S. (2009). Space matters—marginalization and its places. *International Journal of Urban and Regional Research, 33*(3), 835–840.

Das, A., Chaudhuri, H. R., & Turkdogan, O. S. (Eds.). (2024). *Postcolonial Marketing Communication*. Springer Nature.

De Chernatony, L., Drury, S., & Segal-Horn, S. (2005). Using triangulation to assess and identify successful service brands. *The Service Industries Journal, 25*(1), 5–21.

De Oliveira, B. (2023). Participatory action research as a research approach: advantages, limitations and criticisms. *Qualitative Research Journal, 23*(3), 287–297.

Degli Esposti, N. (2024). What happened to neocolonialism? The rise and fall of a critical concept. *Journal of Political Ideologies*, 1–21.

Delaney, T. (2024). *Classical and Contemporary Social Theory: Investigation and Application* (2nd ed.). Routledge.

Delli Paoli, A., & D'Auria, V. (2025). The Digitalization of Ethnography: A Scoping Review of Methods in Netnography. *Journal of Contemporary Ethnography, 08912416251342795*. https://doi.org/10.1177/08912416251342795

Di Pasquale, G., & Parazzi, E. (2024). Shifts in the Boot: understanding inequality's impact on interregional migration patterns in Italy. *Economies, 12*(12), 317.

Dular, N., & Ward, W. (2025). The harms of the internalized oppression worry. *Journal of Social Philosophy, 56*(2), 320–339.

Elliott, A. (2021). *Contemporary Social Theory: An Introduction*. Routledge.

Elliott, R. (1996). Discourse analysis: exploring action, function and conflict in social texts. *Marketing Intelligence & Planning, 14*(6), 65–68.

Ellis, N., Jack, G., & Higgins, M. (2005). (De)constructing the market for animal feeds: A discursive study. *Journal of Marketing Management, 21*(1/2), 117–146.

Fairclough, N. (1990). *Discourse Analysis*. Polity Press.

Fenzl, T., & Pelzmann, L. (2012). Psychological and social forces behind aggregate financial market behavior. *Journal of Behavioral Finance, 13*(1), 56–65.

Ferguson, G. (2003). Classroom code-switching in post-colonial contexts: Functions, attitudes and policies. *AILA Review, 16*(1), 38–51.

Fitchett, J., & Caruana, R. (2015). Exploring the role of discourse in marketing and consumer research. *Journal of Consumer Behaviour, 14*(1), 1–12.

Fluit, S., Cortés-García, L., & von Soest, T. (2024). Social marginalization: A scoping review of 50 years of research. *Humanities and Social Sciences Communications, 11*(1), 1–9.

Francis, J. N., & Mugabo, L. (2025). A Call for Afrocentric Decolonial Endogenous Marketing and Public Policy Research and Practice: Toward Sustainable Peace and Well-Being in African Societies. *Journal of Public Policy & Marketing, 44*(1), 10–24.

Fredericks, J. P., Visagie, S., van Niekerk, L., & Pharaoh, H. G. (2024). Empowering marginalised groups through co-operative inquiry: Illustrated by a practical example. *African Journal of Disability, 13*, 1205.

Fricker, M. (2007). *Epistemic Injustice: Power and the Ethics of Knowing*. Oxford University Press.

Friedline, T., Stewart, K., Bolinger, C., & Wood, A. K. (2024). Fintech as invasive infrastructure: a critical discourse analysis of corporate newswires and press releases, 1995–2021. *Socio-Economic Review, 22*(4), 1891–1920.

Galalae, C., & Licsandru, T. C. (2025). Researching with discomfort: using affective research methodologies to construct knowledge about marginalised groups. *Journal of Marketing Management, 1–28*. https://doi.org/10.1080/0267257X.2025.2540878

Gibson, N. (2011). *Fanonian Practices in South Africa. From Steve Biko to Abahlali base Mjondolo*. University of KwaZulu-Natal Press.
Giddens, A. (1991). *Modernity and Self-Identity: Self and Society in the Late Modern Age*. Stanford University Press.
Gilani, H. (Ed.). (2024). *Decolonizing Marketing Theory and Practice: Beyond Inclusivity and Sustainability Debates*. Routledge.
Giroux, H. A. (2024). *Theory and Resistance in Education: Towards A Pedagogy for the Opposition*. Bloomsbury Publishing.
Gordon, R. (2011). Critical social marketing: definition, application and domain. *Journal of Social Marketing, 1*(2), 82–99.
Greeff, E. (2025). Decolonizing marketing research. In A. Lawson & C. Hancock (Eds.), *Doing Marketing Research: Alternative Methods for Market Sensing* (2nd ed., pp. 197–207). Routledge.
Green, M., Crutcher, V., Lune, O., Mutmainna, M., Lenoir, R., Schuster, A., Urvina, G., & Brown, C. (2024). Methodologies and inequities: Participatory and narrative approaches to research with marginalized communities. *Rhetoric of Health & Medicine, 7*(2), 225–254.
Groves, W. B., & Sampson, R. J. (1986, October). Critical theory and criminology. *Social Problems, 33*, 58–80.
Grusky, D. (2019). *Social Stratification, Class, Race, and Gender in Sociological Perspective*. Routledge.
Hackley, C. (2003). We are all customers now... Rhetorical strategy and ideological control in marketing management texts. *Journal of Management Studies, 40*(5), 13251353.
Hallen, B. (2002). *A Short History of African Philosophy*. Indian University Press.
Hamilton, R. W. (2024). Leveraging opportunities and managing risks in marketing research. *Journal of Marketing Research, 61*(1), 1–4.
Hao, K. (2022). Artificial intelligence is creating a new colonial world order. *MIT Technology Review*. https://www.technologyreview.com/2022/04/19/1049592/artificial-intelligence-colonialism/
Helm, S. V., Little, V. J., & Frethey-Bentham, C. (2024). "No marketing on a dead planet": rethinking marketing education to support a restoration economy. *Journal of Macromarketing, 44*(2), 307–323.
Henderson, K. (2022). The politics of social inclusion: Bridging knowledge and policies towards Social Change. *Contemporary Sociology, 51*(4), 296–298.
Holland, P. W., Zuberi, T., & Bonilla-Silva, E. (2008). Causation and race. *White logic, white methods: Racism and methodology, 4*, 93–109.
Hopton, J. (1997). Towards a critical theory of mental health nursing. *Journal of Advanced Nursing, 25*(3), 492–500.
Ide, Y., & Beddoe, L. (2024). Challenging perspectives: Reflexivity as a critical approach to qualitative social work research. *Qualitative Social Work, 23*(4), 725–740.

Jahn, T., Bergmann, M., & Keil, F. (2012). Transdisciplinarity: Between mainstreaming and marginalization. *Ecological Economics, 79*, 1–10.

Jain, V., Wadhwani, K., & Eastman, J. K. (2024). Artificial intelligence consumer behavior: A hybrid review and research agenda. *Journal of Consumer Behaviour, 23*(2), 676–697.

Johnston, J., Szabo, M., & Rodney, A. (2011). Good food, good people: Understanding the cultural repertoire of ethical eating. *Journal of Consumer Culture, 11*(3), 293–318.

Kellner, D. (1988). Postmodernism as social theory: some challenges and problems. *Theory, Culture and Society, 5*, 239–269.

Kellner, D. (1990). Critical theory and the crisis of social theory. *Sociological Perspectives, 33*(1), 11–33.

Kim, A. E. (1996). Critical theory and the sociology of religion: A reassessment. *Social Compass: International Review of Sociology of Religion, 43*(2), 267–283.

Kincheloe, J. L., & McLaren, P. (2011). Rethinking critical theory and qualitative research. In *Key works in critical pedagogy* (pp. 285–326). SensePublishers.

Koehler, G., Cimadamore, A. D., Kiwan, F., & Gonzalez, P. M. (2020). The politics of social inclusion: Introduction. In G. Koehler, A. D. Cimadamore, F. Kiwan & P. M. Gonzalez (Eds.), *The Politics of Social Inclusion: Bridging Knowledge and Policies Towards Social Change* (p. 13–40). Ibidem Press.

Konadu-Osei, O. A., Boroş, S., & Bosch, A. (2023). Methodological decolonisation and local epistemologies in business ethics research. *Journal of Business Ethics, 186*(1), 1–12.

Leech, N. L., & Onwuegbuzie, A. J. (2007). An array of qualitative data analysis tools: A call for data analysis triangulation. *School Psychology Quarterly, 22*(4), 557.

Lemert, C. (2024). What is social theory? In *Revisiting Social Theory* (pp. 13–27). Routledge.

Leone, M. P., & Potter Shackel, P. (1987). Towards a critical archaeology. *Current Anthropology, 28*, 283–302.

Lewis, A. C., & Crabbe, R. C. (2024). The entrepreneurship of marginalized groups and compatibility between the market and emancipation. *Journal of Business Venturing, 39*(4), 106408.

Lightfoot, G., & Wisniewski, T. P. (2014). Information asymmetry and power in a surveillance society. *Information and Organization, 24*(4), 214–235.

Lu, S. E., Moyle, B., Yang, E. C. L., & Reid, S. (2024). Inclusion of people with disability (PWD) in the tourism workforce: a critical discourse analysis of policies and plans. *Tourism Review*. https://doi.org/10.1108/TR-12-2023-0887

Ma, L., & Sun, B. (2020). Machine learning and AI in marketing–Connecting computing power to human insights. *International Journal of Research in Marketing, 37*(3), 481–504.

Machin, J. E., Mirabito, A. M., Azzari, C. N., Crosby, E., & Adkins, N. R. (2024). Disadvantaged consumers, market access, and consumer well-being. In *Fostering Consumer Well-Being: Theory, Evidence, and Policy* (pp. 69–90). Springer Nature.

Malli, A., Monteith, H., Hiscock, E. C., Smith, E. V., Fairman, K., Galloway, T., & Mashford-Pringle, A. (2023). Impacts of colonization on Indigenous food systems in Canada and the United States: A scoping review. *BMC Public Health, 23*(1), 2105.

Mariampolski, H. (2006). *Ethnography for Marketers: A Guide to Consumer Immersion*. Sage.

Mbada, C. E., Jeje, O. O., Akande, M., Mbada, K. A., Fatoye, C., Olakorede, D., Awoniyi, O., Okafor, U. A., Falade, O., & Fatoye, F. (2023). Social presence and dynamics of group communication: An analysis of a health professionals WhatsApp group chats. *PLoS One, 18*(7), e0288773.

Mbembe, A. (2016). Decolonizing the university: New directions. *Arts and Humanities in Higher Education, 15*(1), 29–45.

McCall, J., Phillips, J. C., Estefan, A., & Caine, V. (2023). The relationship between critical social theory and interpretive description in nursing research. *Global Qualitative Nursing Research, 10*. https://doi.org/10.1177/23333936231211462

McEwan, C., Hughes, A., & Bek, D. (2015). Theorising middle class consumption from the global South: A study of everyday ethics in South Africa's Western Cape. *Geoforum, 67*, 233–243.

McGregor, A. (2004). Doing groups: Situating knowledge and creating stories. *Australian Geographer, 35*(2), 141–149.

McMichael, P. (2014). Historicizing food sovereignty. *Journal of Peasant Studies, 41*(6), 933–957.

Mitra, S., Kerr, T., Cui, Z., Gilbert, M., Fleury, M., Hayashi, K., Milloy, M. J., & Richardson, L. (2024). Patterns of socioeconomic marginalization among people who use drugs: a gender-stratified repeated measures latent class analysis. *Journal of Urban Health, 101*(2), 402–425.

Mkandawire, T. (2015). Neopatrimonialism and the political economy of economic performance in Africa. *World Politics, 67*(3), 563–612.

Möller, K. (2025). Making marketing discipline more scientific–contesting Christian Grönroos's Toward a Marketing Renaissance. *Australasian Marketing Journal, 33*(3), 259–267.

Möller, K., Nenonen, S., & Storbacka, K. (2020). Networks, ecosystems, fields, market systems? Making sense of the business environment. *Industrial Marketing Management, 90*, 380–399.

Moufahim, M., Humphreys, M., Mitussis, D., & Fitchett, J. (2007). Interpreting discourse: a critical discourse analysis of the marketing of an extreme right party. *Journal of Marketing Management, 23*(5–6), 537–558.

Nazer, L. H., Zatarah, R., Waldrip, S., Ke, J. X. C., Moukheiber, M., Khanna, A. K., Hicklen, R. S., Moukheiber, L., Moukheiber, D., Ma, H., & Mathur, P. (2023). Bias in artificial intelligence algorithms and recommendations for mitigation. *PLOS Digital Health, 2*(6), e0000278.

Ndlovu-Gatsheni, S. J. (2021). The cognitive empire, politics of knowledge and African intellectual productions: Reflections on struggles for epistemic freedom and resurgence of decolonisation in the twenty-first century. *Third World Quarterly, 42*(5), 882–901.

Neo, P. H., Lim, J. M., Tan, R. K., & Ong, S. E. (2022). Using WhatsApp focus group discussions to collect qualitative data collection during a pandemic: Exploring knowledge, attitudes, and perceptions of COVID-19 in Singapore. *International Journal of Qualitative Methods, 21*, 16094069221090355.

Neuendorf, K. A. (2018). Content analysis and thematic analysis. In *Advanced research methods for applied psychology* (pp. 211–223). Routledge.

Nielsen, B. B., Welch, C., Chidlow, A., Miller, S. R., Aguzzoli, R., Gardner, E., Karafyllia, M., & Pegoraro, D. (2020). Fifty years of methodological trends in JIBS: Why future IB research needs more triangulation. *Journal of International Business Studies, 51*(9), 1478–1499.

Nkrumah, K. (1965). *Neo-Colonialism, The Last Stage of Imperialism*. Thomas Nelson & Sons.

Ohajunwa, C., & Mji, G. (2021). Expressing social justice within indigenous research: A reflection on process and affirmation. *AlterNative: An International Journal of Indigenous Peoples, 17*(2), 183–190.

Ozanne, J. L., & Murray, J. B. (1995). Uniting critical theory and public policy to create the reflexively defiant consumer. *American Behavioral Scientist, 38*(4), 516–525.

Palgrave Macmillan. (2023). *The Statesman's Yearbook 2024: The Politics, Cultures and Economies of the World*. Springer Nature.

Papavasileiou, E. F., & Dimou, I. (2025). Evidence of construct validity for work values using triangulation analysis. *EuroMed Journal of Business, 20*(5), 98–115.

Paul, J., Ueno, A., & Dennis, C. (2023). ChatGPT and consumers: Benefits, pitfalls and future research agenda. *International Journal of Consumer Studies, 47*(4), 1213–1225.

Parashar, S., & Schulz, M. (2021). Colonial legacies, postcolonial 'selfhood' and the (un)doing of Africa. *Third World Quarterly, 42*(5), 867–881.

Pindayi, B. (2017). Social media uses and effects: The case of Whatsapp in Africa. In *Impacts of the Media on African Socio-Economic Development* (pp. 34–51). IGI Global.

Proctor, S., Proctor, T., & Papasolomou-Doukakis, I. (2002). A Post-modern perspective on advertisements and their Analysis. *Journal of Marketing Communications, 8*, 31–44.

Razak, G. M., Stevenson, M., & Hendry, L. C. (2024). "I am because we are": The role of sub-Saharan Africa's collectivist culture in achieving traceability and global supply chain resilience. *Journal of Supply Chain Management, 60*(4), 46–74.

Reed, D. (1995). Critical theory and the Catholic Church's ambivalence about capitalism. *International Journal of Social Economics, 22*(2), 19–39.

Rodney, W. (2018). *How Europe Underdeveloped Africa.* Verso Books. (Original work published in 1972).

Roque, A., Wutich, A., Brewis, A., Beresford, M., Landes, L., Morales-Pate, O., Lucero, R., Jepson, W., Tsai, Y., Hanemann, M., & Water Equity Consortium, A. for. (2024). Community-based participant-observation (CBPO): A participatory method for ethnographic research. *Field Methods, 36*(1), 80–90.

Rémy, E., Roux, D., Arnould, E., Askegaard, S., Beudaert, A., Galluzzo, A., & Marion, G. (2024). Look up! Five research proposals for rethinking marketing in a post-growth society. *Recherche et Applications en Marketing* (English Edition), 39(1), 73–93.

Salter, M., & Shaw, J. J. A. (1994). Towards a critical theory of constitutional law: Hegel's contribution. *Journal of Law and Society, 21*(4), 464–486.

Sandikci, O. (2022). The scalar politics of difference: Researching consumption and marketing outside the West. *Marketing Theory, 22*(2), 135–153.

Sarmento, M., Huber, C., & Magalhães, C. (2025). Mapping marginalization: A multilevel exploration of chronic homelessness. *Journal of Community & Applied Social Psychology, 35*(4), e70135.

Sasaki, I., & Baba, S. (2024). Shades of cultural marginalization: Cultural survival and autonomy processes. *Organization Theory, 5*(1). https://doi.org/10.1177/26317877231221552

Scambler, G. (1996). The project of modernity and the parameters for a critical sociology: An argument with illustrations from medical sociology. *Sociology, 30*(3), 567–581.

Seltzer, K., Rajendram, S., & García, O. (2024). Translanguaging theory, pedagogies, and future directions from the Global South. In *The Routledge Handbook of Teaching English as an International Language* (pp. 140–152). Routledge.

Shavitt, S., Jiang, D., & Cho, H. (2016). Stratification and segmentation: Social class in consumer behavior. *Journal of Consumer Psychology, 26*(4), 583–593.

Smith, L. H., Valenzuela, J., & Ludke, R. L. (2012). Engaging rural and urban Appalachians in research using a community-based participatory research approach. *PRISM: A Journal of Regional Engagement, 1*(1) .

Steenkamp, J. B. E. (2019). Global versus local consumer culture: Theory, measurement, and future research directions. *Journal of International Marketing, 27*(1), 1–19.

Stephen, A. T. (2024). Keeping up and staying fresh: Reflections on studying emerging topics in Consumer Research. *Journal of Consumer Research, 51*(1), 114–118.

Stiglitz, J. E. (2017). *The revolution of information economics: The past and the future* (Vol. No. w23780). National Bureau of Economic Research.

Sun, Y., Kinsella, E. L., & Igou, E. R. (2024). On cultural differences of heroes: Evidence from individualistic and collectivistic cultures. *Personality and Social Psychology Bulletin, 50*(6), 841–856.

Sutterlüty, F. (2016). The role of religious ideas: Christian interpretations of social inequalities. *Critical Sociology, 42*(1), 33–48.

Tegegne, Y. D. (2024). Neo-colonialism: a discussion of USA activities in the Horn of Africa. *Cogent Arts & Humanities, 11*(1), 2335755.

Tilzey, M., & Sudgen, F. (2024). *Peasants, Capitalism, and Imperialism in an Age of Politico-Ecological Crisis*. Routledge.

Turner, S. F., Cardinal, L. B., & Burton, R. M. (2017). Research design for mixed methods: A triangulation-based framework and roadmap. *Organizational Research Methods, 20*(2), 243–267.

Van Hulst, M., Metze, T., Dewulf, A., De Vries, J., Van Bommel, S., & Van Ostaijen, M. (2025). Discourse, framing and narrative: three ways of doing critical, interpretive policy analysis. *Critical Policy Studies, 19*(1), 74–96.

von Hirschhausen, U., & Kreienbaum, J. (2019). Neocolonialism revisited: An empirical enquiry into the term's theoretical substance today. *Comparativ: Leipziger Beiträge zur Universalgeschichte und Vergleichenden Gesellschaftsforschung, 29*(3).

Weaver, K. (2023). Bridging Indigenous and Western knowledge-systems in knowledge co-production with Amazonian Indigenous communities: A systematic realist review. *Development Studies Research, 10*(1), 2203842.

Wendt, A. N. (2023, November). Hermann Schmitz und die Psychologie. In *Neue Phänomenologie im Widerstreit* (pp. 201–230). Verlag Karl Alber.

Williams, J. (2024). Greenwashing: Appearance, illusion and the future of 'green' capitalism. *Geography Compass, 18*(1), e12736.

Yar, M. (2012). Critical criminology, critical theory and social harm. In S. Hall & S. Winlow (Eds.), *New Directions in Criminological Theory* (pp. 52–65). Routledge.

Young, M. D., Diem, S., & Sampson, C. (2024). The vital necessity of critical education policy research. *Educational Evaluation and Policy Analysis, 46*(2), 397–405.

CHAPTER 8

Market Orientation, New Product Development, and Organizational Performance in Ghana's Fashion Industry

Sadick Abubakari, Robert E. Hinson, and Mahmoud Abdulai Mahmoud

Introduction

The world of business is undergoing profound change driven by technological innovation, unstoppable globalization, and shifting consumer behavior. In such a dynamic and competitive environment, companies,

S. Abubakari · R. E. Hinson · M. A. Mahmoud (✉)
Department of Marketing and Entrepreneurship, University of Ghana Business School, Madina, Ghana
e-mail: mamahmoud@ug.edu.gh

College of Humanities, University of Ghana, Accra, Ghana

S. Abubakari
e-mail: sabubakari016@st.ug.edu.gh

R. E. Hinson
e-mail: rhinson@ug.edu.gh

A. Gbadamosi et al. (eds.), *Contemporary Marketing Practices in Africa, Volume 1*, Palgrave Studies of Marketing in Emerging Economies,
https://doi.org/10.1007/978-3-032-27126-6_8

especially those in emerging and resource-constrained markets, must continually restructure their strategies to survive. Market orientation is one of the most productive strategic orientations in this aspect, whereby it captures the determination of an organization to identify, understand, and respond to the needs of customers and competitors and create cross-functional coordination (Kohli & Jaworski, 1990; Murillo Oviedo et al., 2021; Narver & Slater, 1990). However, in contemporary markets, firms do not only need to collect and share market intelligence; they need to be able to transform that intelligence into innovation, in other words, into new products and services that will provide customers with unique value and help firms maintain a competitive advantage.

The need for innovation is even greater in the fashion industry. The industry is characterized by short product life cycles, volatile demand trends, and aggressive design competition (Crick, 2021). The successful companies operating in such conditions are those that can continuously refine market knowledge into new products, styles, materials, or methods of production that meet the changing tastes and preferences of consumers. The fashion and footwear subsector is an important part of Ghana's creative economy, as it has created jobs, fostered cultural identity, and enabled entrepreneurship (Anim et al., 2018). However, the industry is experiencing increased competition from imports, low technological capabilities, and fragmented supply chains. These structural limitations have led to a greater need for an innovation-based market orientation, in which novel product development (NPD) is becoming the primary facilitator, enabling market knowledge to be converted into high performance.

Although the positive correlation between market orientation and firm performance has been established among global scholars for a long time (Bamfo & Kraa, 2019; Kirca et al., 2005; Ngo, 2021), how this relationship operates remains under debate. Specifically, the growing awareness is that innovation intermediates the relationship between market orientation and performance (Han et al., 1998; Langerak et al., 2007). However, to a large extent, this evidence has been provided by formal, technology-based sectors in developed economies where the innovation processes are highly organized and funded. On the contrary, informal economies, such as the fashion and footwear industry in Ghana, are known to operate within other institutional logics characterized by informal learning, handicraft production, and improvisation-based creativity. Very little is known about how such firms incorporate market knowledge in new product design and development activities that can make them competitive.

In line with this, this chapter applies marketing and innovation theory to an environment in which informal entrepreneurship and indigenous creativity are subject to contemporary competitive forces. It shows that innovation is not only a preserve of high-tech companies but can also be found in small, resource-constrained companies that innovate through design, craftsmanship, and market learning. This chapter contributes both conceptually and empirically to the overall discussion of innovation-driven growth in the creative sector of African markets by stating how market orientation sparks new product development and, thus, organizational performance.

Theoretical and Conceptual Framework

The study is based on two interrelated theories: the Resource-Based View (RBV) and the Dynamic Capabilities Theory (DCT). Together, these frameworks provide a rigorous basis for explaining how both internal and external orientations influence innovation paths and performance outcomes in competitive environments.

Resource-Based View (RBV)

According to Wernerfelt (1984), a firm's competitive advantage is sustained when it is based on resources that are valuable, rare, inimitable, and non-substitutable (the VRIN criterion). In this regard, market orientation is a strategic resource that enables firms to acquire market intelligence, establish effective customer relationships, and mobilize inter-departmental activities (Hunt & Morgan, 1996). Companies with a market-oriented position can leverage high levels of customer needs and competitive forces to develop innovative products and services (Dobni, 2010; Hult & Ketchen, 2001). In line with this, in Ghana's fashion industry, firms that develop an effective market orientation will be able to translate local craftsmanship and market knowledge into unique product offerings that enhance performance.

Dynamic Capabilities Theory (DCT)

Whereas RBV focuses on the possession of resources, DCT focuses on a firm's ability to integrate, develop, and restructure resources in response to environmental change (Teece et al., 1997). Dynamic capabilities emulate the way firms perceive opportunities, act on them through strategic choices, and revolutionize their operations to become competitive. This process is supported by market orientation, which provides an unending flow of relevant market information that guides product development, innovation, and adaptation (Helfat & Peteraf, 2009). The dynamic capabilities of small-scale producers are needed in Ghana's fast-changing fashion industry, where they must respond promptly to changes in style and taste, as well as market trends.

Conceptual Framework

Combining these theoretical lenses, this paper defines market orientation as having three aspects, including customer orientation, competitor orientation, and inter-functional coordination, which all play a role in determining the performance of firms. The mediating variable between these orientations and performance outcomes is placed on new product development. This model suggests that companies that carefully monitor their rivals, align internal operations, and are ready to develop new products at all times are more likely to achieve long-term success. This theoretical reasoning is especially relevant in emerging markets, where innovation and responsiveness play a key role in overcoming structural constraints, including but not limited to limited resources, poor adoption of technology, and intense competition from imported products. The framework, therefore, positions market orientation not as a mere philosophy of marketing but as a strategic capability that drives adaptive learning, innovation, and performance improvement (Fig. 8.1).

Literature Review

Market Orientation: Concept and Dimension

The concept of market orientation has since been considered one of the cornerstones of contemporary marketing strategy, characterized by an organizational-wide culture that places a premium on the creation, distribution, responsiveness, and utilization of market intelligence (Kohli &

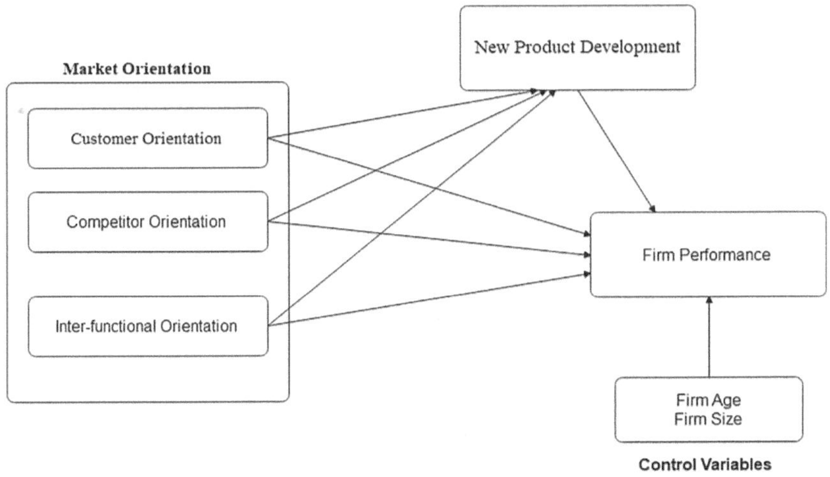

Fig. 8.1 Conceptual framework

Jaworski, 1990; Narver & Slater, 1990). It is an indicator of the extent to which a firm processes and leverages market information to inform its strategic choices and coordinate its internal operations toward value generation for customers. Two conceptualizations dominate the available literature. First, the MKTOR model, which includes customer orientation, competitor orientation, and inter-functional coordination (Narver & Slater, 1990); second, the MARKOR model, which focuses on systematic processes of intelligence generation, dissemination, and responsiveness (Kohli & Jaworski, 1990). Although the two frameworks differ mainly in how they focus on cultural or behavioral aspects, they agree that market orientation increases organizational flexibility and customer satisfaction by aligning internal organizational capabilities with external market factors.

Recent studies support the multidimensionality and context dependence of market orientation. There is general agreement between Crick (2021) and Sahi et al. (2020) that market orientation goes beyond a fixed marketing philosophy and is a dynamic learning process that enables firms to anticipate change and respond strategically. Market orientation in developing economies characterized by prevalent information asymmetry and resource scarcity can help firms identify market gaps, ensure optimal resource allocation, and establish competitive positioning (Bamfo & Kraa, 2019). However, its effect on performance does not entirely depend on it.

The effectiveness of market orientation in delivering concrete financial or non-financial benefits is determined by such variables as industry turbulence, firm size, and internal coordination (Ogbonna & Ogwo, 2013). That is why it is necessary to emphasize the urgency of examining its realization and impact across individual industries and economic contexts.

Firm Performance and Market Orientation

The positive relationship between market orientation and firm performance has been widely observed across industries and economies. Market-based studies have consistently shown that companies that practice market-oriented practices achieve excellent customer satisfaction, improved sales growth, and profitability (Kirca et al., 2005; Ngo, 2021). Systematic acquisition and use of market information enable such firms to be more responsive to consumer demands and environmental changes (Narver & Slater, 1990). Similar patterns are observed in Ghana's formal sectors, such as banking (Hinson et al., 2008), manufacturing (Mahmoud, 2011), and pharmaceuticals (Akomea & Yeboah, 2011).

Although this is the agreed position, various scholars warn that there is no linear, universal relationship between market orientation and performance. According to Han et al. (1998), the relationship is indirect and is regulated by a firm's ability to be innovative. Similarly, Au and Tse (1995) and Taheri et al. (2019) report weaker correlations in high-turbulence areas, suggesting that the performance implications of market orientation depend on how companies realize their market intelligence. Such discrepancies also underscore the need to investigate the mediating mechanisms by which market-oriented firms can use market knowledge to achieve performance benefits, particularly in new product development.

Market Orientation and New Product Development

The nexus between market orientation and new product development (NPD) has become a relevant concern in the current marketing and innovation research. Market-oriented companies have enhanced market knowledge and customer insights, which serve as inputs for idea generation, product design, and market launch (Langerak et al., 2007; Li et al., 2017). Companies that constantly monitor their competition and encourage interdepartmental teamwork are more likely to spot emerging trends and unmet needs, thereby increasing the success rates of new products in the market.

However, the market orientation and NPD correlation are not so simple. According to Lukas and Ferrell (2000), too much customer orientation can trigger me-too-innovations, i.e., those innovations that are merely incremental, i.e., those innovations that just imitate the competition, whereas too high competitor orientation can kill fundamental innovations. In turn, the important point is strategic balance. In new economies, inter-functional coordination is the primary driver of NPD success (Aydin, 2020; Im & Workman, 2004), as formal research and development (R&D) infrastructures tend to be underdeveloped. For Ghanaian shoe manufacturers, effective coordination of design, production, and sales functions fosters creativity and aligns products with changing market expectations, making local products more competitive with imported products.

New Product Development and the Performance of Firms

New product development is a dual-purpose aspect, as it is both an outcome of market orientation and a determinant of firm performance. Effective NPD programs enable companies to launch new products that meet emerging customer demands, build a stronger brand image, and attract new customer segments (Hsu & Fang, 2009; Liu & Atuahene-Gima, 2018). New products are the most important source of competitive advantage in industries like fashion, where differentiation and novelty have been the two key pillars of consumer interest.

In Ghana's fashion industry, the ability to create and commercialize new products is key to competing with inexpensive imports and attracting the attention of young, fashionable consumers. Lee and Tsai (2005) and Najafi-Tavani et al. (2018) affirm that companies that invest strategically in NPD achieve better financial and non-financial performance, especially when these efforts are supported by strong market intelligence and cross-functional teamwork. This highlights NPD as a strategic and operational driver of sustainable performance.

New Product Development: Mediating Role

A market-driven culture promotes interdepartmental learning and knowledge sharing, which in turn drives innovation and the development of new products. This pioneering channel explains why companies convert market acumen into performance results.

This logic is mediating, which is substantiated by empirical evidence in Ghana. Bamfo and Kraa (2019) found that innovation mediated the relationship between market orientation and firm performance among SMEs. However, as several studies view innovation as a collective phenomenon, they do not distinguish the new product development process. The current chapter seeks to address this conceptual shortcoming by focusing on NPD as the channel through which market orientation supplements organizational performance in Ghana's fashion and footwear sector. In this way, it helps better understand how market-based innovation works in informal, creative economies and explains the paths by which market knowledge is transferred into competitive advantage.

Footwear Production in Ghana

Footwear is an essential part of Ghanaian culture. As part of our traditional attire, all tribes wear footwear. For example, the Akans, among other tribes, dress in "Kawkaw" for every significant event. Furthermore, individuals wear shoes, slippers, or heels to work, church, school, and other essential locations. As a result, the footwear sector has tremendous potential. Inadequate knowledge and understanding of consumers' requirements and desires have contributed to a negative "image" of the footwear that manufacturers create for the market. Despite attempts by footwear producers to promote their goods, the bulk of consumers, particularly those in the Kumasi Metropolitan Assembly (KMA), subconsciously retain the impression that Ghanaian footwear is of "bad" quality (Danso et al., 2018). As a result, there is a limited demand for Ghanaian footwear (especially Kumasi). Apart from these reasons, local companies compete with global footwear manufacturers and many prominent international brands, altering the face of competition in the country. Domestic footwear manufacturers are losing market share to international producers as competition intensifies in the country. These producers have the resources and equipment to compete with any producer, and the local market leader has become a minor rival on a global scale. Compared with international companies, most footwear manufacturing firms in Ghana are modest in size; therefore, their competitiveness in the global market is likely to be hampered.

Research Methodology

The study adopted a positivist epistemological approach and used a cross-sectional, quantitative survey design to examine the relationships among market orientation, new product development, and firm performance. It is considered that such a design is especially appropriate for making causal inferences and rigorously testing hypotheses in the context of real-world phenomena. Footwear manufacturing industries located within the Kumasi Metropolis in the Ashanti Region of Ghana, an industrial hub, were surveyed to obtain primary data, as footwear making in Ghana remains vital within the informal sector. The study's target population included owners and managers of small- and medium-sized footwear companies. Given the informal nature of the sector and the absence of a standardized production registry (Anim et al., 2018), a purposive-convenience sampling strategy was used, with 200 respondents being obtained because of it, a sample that is sufficient in Partial Least Squares Structural Equation Modelling (PLS-SEM) terms and provides sufficient statistical power. Data were gathered through a structured questionnaire designed to assess market orientation, product development, and firm performance. The tool was based on previously rigorously validated market orientation scales, namely Narver and Slater's (1990) MKTOR model and the NPD measures of Griffin and Page (1996), all using a five-point Likert scale from 1 (strongly disagree) to 5 (strongly agree).

Measurement of Scale

Market Orientation

Narver and Slater's (1990) and Kohli and Jaworski's (1990) measurement tools are among the most used for determining a company's degree of market orientation. The market orientation scale from Narver and Slater's MKTOR construct (customer, competitor, and inter-functional) was utilized to measure market orientation in this study.

New Product Development

New product development measures by Griffin and Page (1996) indicate how actively footwear producers seek to develop new products to meet market demand across the predevelopment, development, and commercialization stages.

Performance

The performance of footwear producers was measured subjectively. Subjective performance variables include Customer satisfaction, sales growth, and market share. These measures were also used by Zebal and Goodwin (2011) in their study.

Reliability and Validity

It is important to verify the validity and reliability of the study's measurement items to obtain the most accurate result (Mohajan, 2017). Reliability and validity refer to procedures for determining the accuracy of measurements and ensuring that there is no bias or distortion (Read, 2013; Roberts et al., 2006). The reliability was supported by Cronbach's alpha (0.70) and Composite Reliability (CR), both exceeding the traditional value of 0.70, as stated by Hair et al. (2017). Convergent validity was also supported by Average Variance Extracted (AVE) values exceeding 0.50, indicating that the shared variance was well explained by the latent constructs in relation to their manifest indicators. Additionally, all factor loadings ranged from 0.82 to 0.99, further confirming the strength of the measurement indicators.

Analysis and Results

There are two components to the data analysis: The demographic profiles of respondents are the focus of the first phase. Based on the study's objective, the subsequent stage analyzes the main variables under examination and their prevailing relationship. SPSS and Smart PLS were used to analyze the data. As a result, SPSS was employed to obtain the descriptive statistics. Subsequently, Smart PLS was employed to undertake SEM due to its ability to handle highly complex predictive models. Nonetheless, some preliminary data analysis (PDA) was conducted before the main analysis to ensure the dataset was clean and error-free.

The demographic profile of respondents necessary for the study is presented in Table 8.1 above. The respondents were characterized by age, gender, business ownership, academic qualifications, line of business, and nature of business. The results show that most respondents are male (63%), with the remaining 37% female. The study sample was youthful, with about 48% of respondents aged 30 or younger and 21% aged 40 or younger. Regarding the line of business, more respondents are in male footwear production (49%), with 27.5% in both male and female footwear production. 48% of respondents have completed SSCE/WASSCE, and 30.5% have no formal education, indicating that the majority have a basic education. The results show that most (46.5%) of the footwear business is owned by individuals, and 29.5% are partnership businesses.

Table 8.1 Respondents' characteristics

Characteristics	*Frequency (200)*	%
Gender		
Male	126	63.0
Female	74	37
Age (in years)		
Up to 20	8	4.0
21–30	96	48.0
31–40	42	21.0
41–50	30	15.0
50 and above	24	12.0
Line of business		
Male footwear	98	49.0
Female footwear	47	23.5
Both male and female footwear	55	27.5
Education		
SSCE/ WASSCE	93	46.5
HND/diploma	38	19.0
First degree	7	3.5
Postgraduate	1	0.5
No formal education	61	30.5
Nature of business		
Sole proprietor	123	61.5
Partnership	59	29.5
Family business	18	9.0

Constructs under study (Customer orientation, inter-functional orientation, competitor orientation, new product development, and firm performance) are all represented with their means and standard deviation in Table 8.2. The customer orientation mean is 1.54 (SD = 0.737) in the table, suggesting that respondents have a positive understanding of the statements. This suggests that the respondents have a fair knowledge of customer orientation.

The results further show that the respondents have positive perceptions of the items measuring competitor orientation, inter-functional orientation, new product development, and firm performance. These are evident in the total means for competitor orientation (1.485, SD = 0.765), inter-functional orientation (1.31, SD = 0.748), new product development (1.33, SD = 0.759), and firm performance (1.507, SD = 0.783).

Internal Consistency Reliability

To assess the internal consistency of this study, the researcher employed Cronbach's alpha and composite reliability. According to Hair et al. (2017), internal consistency is achieved when the Cronbach's alpha and composite reliability are both above 0.70. For this study, all constructs demonstrated internal consistency, as shown in Table 8.3. The breakdown for the individual constructs is as follows: Customer Orientation had a CA = 0.901 and CR = 0.939; Competitor Orientation had a CA = 0.922 and CR = 0.945; Inter-functional Orientation had a CA = 0.9991 and CR – 0.966; and new product development had a CA = 0.991 and CR = 0.993. This indicates that all the constructs met the criteria for internal consistency.

Indicator Reliability

To calculate indicator loadings, the standard PLS algorithm is employed. As a result, item loadings were utilized to evaluate indicator reliability. Loadings larger than 0.70 may be retained, whereas loadings less than 0.70 are dropped, especially for reflexive contracts. Bootstrapping is used to assess the statistical significance of the loadings. Table 8.3 shows that all loadings are between 0.820 and 0.990, indicating substantial loadings and values above the threshold. As a result, it can be concluded that all the models' indicators have attained appreciable levels of indicator dependability.

Table 8.2 Construct descriptive statistics

Items	*Minimum*	*Maximum*	*Mean*	*Std. deviation*
Customer orientation			**1.54**	**0.73**
Customer information is used to improve the quality of footwear	1.000	5.000	1.490	0.755
Customer comments and complaints are encouraged	1.000	5.000	1.540	0.747
We have a strong commitment to our customers' demands	1.000	5.000	1.590	0.708
Competitor orientation			**1.485**	**0.765**
We regularly monitor our competitors' marketing efforts	1.000	5.000	1.435	0.785
We frequently collect marketing data on our competitors	1.000	5.000	1.530	0.768
We respond rapidly to competitors' actions	1.000	5.000	1.510	0.794
Our employees are instructed to monitor competitor activity	1.000	5.000	1.465	0.713
Inter-functional orientation			**1.31**	**0.748**
Market information is shared inside our organization	1.000	5.000	1.305	0.763
All departments are involved in preparing business plans strategies	1.000	5.000	1.290	0.697
We have inter-department meetings to discuss market trends	1.000	5.000	1.335	0.783
New product development			**1.33**	**0.759**
We always do new products for our customers	1.000	5.000	1.450	0.859
We actively seek ways of coming up with new footwear	1.000	5.000	1.270	0.760
We value customer input in new footwear planning	1.000	5.000	1.345	0.752
We constantly modify and bring new designs to our footwear	1.000	5.000	1.255	0.663
Firm performance			**1.507**	**0.783**
We have been making a profit since we started the business	1.000	5.000	1.510	0.794
There has been revenue growth in our business	1.000	5.000	1.510	0.748
Our customer base increased rapidly	1.000	5.000	1.550	0.798
We constantly attract new customers with our new product	1.000	5.000	1.485	0.781
Our customers are pleased with our product designers	1.000	5.000	1.480	0.793

Table 8.3 Item loadings, AVE, Cronbach's alpha, and CR of constructs

Research constructs	*Cronbach's alpha*	*CR*	*AVE*	*Loadings*
Customer orientation	**0.901**	**0.939**	**0.838**	
CMO1				**0.867**
CMO2				**0.873**
CMO3				**0.965**
CMO4				**0.896**
Competitor orientation	**0.922**	**0.945**	**0.812**	
CO1				**0.821**
CO2				**0.964**
CO3				**0.954**
Inter-functional orientation	**0.939**	**0.961**	**0.892**	
IFO1				**0.919**
IFO2				**0.982**
IFO3				**0.931**
New product development	**0.953**	**0.966**	**0.876**	
NPD1				**0.881**
NPD2				**0.955**
NPD3				**0.959**
NPD4				**0.947**
Firm performance	**0.991**	**0.993**	**0.966**	
FP1				**0.990**
FP2				**0.976**
FP3				**0.979**
FP4				**0.989**
FP5				**0.980**

Convergent Validity

Hair et al. (2017) opined that a latent variable should explain 50% of the variation in the indicator. Also, the concept's variance and its indicator are more than the measurement error variance, and as a result, an indicator's outer loading must be greater than 0.708, because 0.708 squared equals 0.50 for a concept and its indicator. Remove outside loadings of an indicator that are less than 0.70 on or after the scale and are not part of the indicator's internal load (Hair et al., 2017). It's worth noting that, according to the rule of thumb, all the constructions reached an appropriate level of AVE. From Table 5.3, "Customer Orientation" had an AVE = **0.838**, "Competitor Orientation" had an AVE = **0.812**, "Inter-Functional Orientation" had an AVE = 0.892, "New Product

Table 8.4 Variance inflation factor (VIF)

Construct	*Variance inflation factor*
Customer orientation	2.007
Competitor orientation	3.234
Inter-functional orientation	3.186
New product development	2.685

Development" also recorded an AVE = 0.876, and lastly, "Firm Performance" had an AVE = 0.966. This implies the construct AVE is above the threshold of 0.500.

Collinearity Assessment

To establish whether there is a strong association between the constructs, the variance inflation factor was employed. According to Table 8.4, the variance inflation factor (VIF) for all constructs in the model was less than 5.0. As a result, no multicollinearity issues between the constructs can be inferred.

Assessment of a Significant Path

Researchers utilize p-values to assess significance levels, according to Hair et al. (2017). According to the researchers, the p-value must be less than 0.05 to infer that the link under investigation is statistically significant at the 5% level, therefore confirming the hypothesized connection, as shown in Table 8.5. The hypothesized relationships for the constructs Inter-Functional Orientation, Competitors Orientation, New Product Development, and Firm Performance were all supported, but those for Customer Orientation and New Product Development were not. Firm age and Firm size as control variables were also supported (Fig. 8.2).

Mediation Effect

According to the findings, the new product development literature indicates that it can mediate the relationship between market orientation and firm performance. The hypothesis was that if all three correlations

Table 8.5 Path analysis

	Path	*Path coefficient*	T *statistics*	P *value*	*Decision*
H1a	Customer orientation → firm performance	0.182	3.256	**0.001**	Supported
H1b	Competitors orientation → firm performance	0.668	8.259	**0.000**	Supported
H1c	Inter-functional orientation → firm performance	-0.391	3.367	**0.001**	Supported
H2a	Customer orientation → new product development	0.080	1.024	**0.306**	Not supported
H2b	Competitors orientation → new product development	0.166	2.707	**0.007**	Supported
H2c	Inter-functional orientation → new product development	0.756	13.298	**0.000**	Supported
H3	New product development → firm performance	0.597	4.754	**0.000**	Supported
	Firm age	0.052	2.363	**0.000**	Supported
	Firm size	−0.122	2.223	**0.027**	Supported

were significant, the mediation test could be undertaken, based on the assumptions in the Table 8.6.

In ascertaining the type of relationship, New Product Development does not significantly mediate the relationship between customer Orientation and firm performance ($B = 0.048$; $t = 1.031$; $p = 0.303$). Related to the test of New Product Development, relationship between Competitor Orientation and firm performance is significant ($B = 0.099$; $t = 2.527$; $p = 0.012$). Similarly, the test of the New Product Development relationship between inter-functional Orientation and firm performance is also significant ($B = 0.451$; $t = 4.920$; $p = 0.000$).

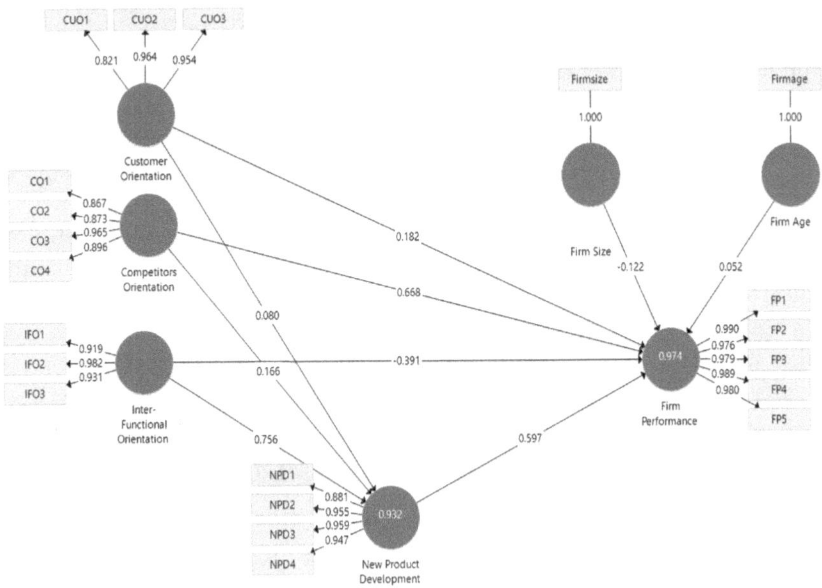

Fig. 8.2 Path diagram

Table 8.6 Testing for the mediating effect of new product development

	Path	*Path coefficient*	T *statistics*	P *values*	*Decision*
H4a	Customer orientation → new product development → firm performance	0.048	1.031	**0.303**	Not supported
H4b	Competitors orientation → new product development → firm performance	0.099	2.527	**0.012**	Supported
H4c	Inter-functional orientation → new product development → firm performance	0.451	4.920	**0.000**	Supported

Discussion of Findings

The degree of market orientation in the fashion sector was assessed using Narver and Slater's (1990) culturally based market orientation model, comprising three components: customer orientation, competitor orientation, and inter-functional orientation. Because the study was interested in the relationship between market orientation and firm performance metrics such as customer satisfaction, market share, and sales growth, subjective performance measures were used. In the fashion industry, the study found a positive, significant association between market orientation and firm performance. The results are consistent with previous studies that suggested that market orientation leads to superior firm performance in the fashion industry (Anim, Agbemabiese, Acheampong et al., 2018).

Firm Performance and Customer Orientation

The data indicate a positive, but insignificant, relationship between customer orientation and firm performance. It means that Ghanaian shoe manufacturers recognize the importance of customer feedback, but their ability to translate this knowledge into new or competitive products is limited. The observation is in consonance with the views of Lukas and Ferrell (2000), and Das et al. (2018), who argue that excessive focus on customer orientation may hamper radical innovation, particularly where businesses do not possess the necessary resources to act on customer information. Besides, the observation highlights the unofficial nature of the shoe industry, in which systematic market research and official customer relationship protocols are often lacking.

Competitor Orientation and Firm Performance

Competitor orientation has the strongest impact on firm performance. This empirical observation supports the findings of Wong and Tong (2012), who found that competitor monitoring leads to product success and market share. For Ghanaian footwear manufacturers, knowledge of competitors' tactics will incentivize small design, pricing, and marketing innovations. However, the evidence also indicates that the performance benefits are mostly due to imitation and adaptation rather than radical innovation, a fact that is especially important in light of the policy intervention aimed at fostering creativity and novelty among local firms.

Inter-functional Co-ordination and Firm Performance

The strategic alignment and innovation resulting from internal collaboration are supported by the positive influence of inter-functional coordination. As emphasized by Aydin (2020), the more departments interact to share and receive market intelligence and collaborate on product development, the more they can respond to environmental changes. In the Ghana footwear manufacturing setting, where artisanal activities are involved, alignment among design, manufacturing, and sales departments fosters product differentiation and uniform quality, leading to improved performance.

Market Orientation and New Product Development

The findings support the claim that competitor and inter-functional orientations are substantial predictors of new product development, and not customer orientation. This observation aligns with the research by Im and Workman (2004), who found that inter-functional teamwork is more effective at generating product novelty than customer feedback. When a producer operates in a resource-constrained environment, formal customer research is unlikely to be used to develop a new product; instead, competitor benchmarking and team-based innovation are commonly used. The trend highlights the significance of organizational learning and knowledge sharing as dynamic capabilities in the Ghanaian footwear industry.

New Product Development and the Performance of the Firm

The strong positive correlation between performance and new product development (NPD) supports the argument that innovation is a source of corporate success. In line with the findings of Liu and Atuahene-Gima (2018) and Najafi-Tavani et al. (2018), the study found that companies that invest in NPD achieve higher sales growth, market share, and customer satisfaction. For Ghanaian fashion SMEs, key strategies for staying competitive in the face of foreign brands' entry include continuous product redesign and product diversification.

The Mediation Role of New Product Development

According to the findings, the new product development literature indicates that it can mediate the relationship between market orientation and firm performance. The hypothesis was that if all three correlations were significant, the mediation test could be undertaken, based on the assumptions in the preceding table. In ascertaining the type of relationship, New Product Development does not significantly mediate the relationship between customer Orientation and firm performance ($B = 0.048$; $t = 1.031$; $p = 0.303$). This indicates that New Product Development does not partially mediate the relationship between customer Orientation and firm performance and does not serve as an important alternative for increasing firm performance. Therefore, this study rejects the hypothesis that if footwear producers focus on being customer-oriented to develop new products, it will not have a significant effect on the firm's performance.

Related to the test of New Product Development, relationship between Competitor Orientation and firm performance is significant ($B = 0.099$; $t = 2.527$; $p = 0.012$). This indicates that New Product Development plays an important role as a mediator in the relationship between Competitor Orientation and firm performance, and as an alternative for increasing firm performance. Therefore, this study accepts the hypothesis, implying that footwear producers can be competitor-oriented in developing new products to enhance the firm's performance.

Similarly, the test of the New Product Development relationship between inter-functional Orientation and firm performance is also significant ($B = 0.451$; $t = 4.920$; $p = 0.000$). This indicates that New Product Development plays a very important role as a mediator in the relationship between inter-functional Orientations and firm performance, and as an important alternative for increasing firm performance. Therefore, this study accepts the hypothesis that the various departments within the firm's activities are properly coordinated in developing new products that will enhance the firm's performance.

Control Variables

The study used respondents' firm age and firm size as control variables. These variables were used to determine the extent of their influence on market orientation and firm performance. After analysis, results revealed that both firm age ($B = 0.052$; $t = 2.363$; $p = 0.018$) and firm size ($B = -0.122$; $t = 2.223$; $p = 0.027$) have a positive and significant impact on the degree to which the fashion industry can employ market orientation to enhance firm performance.

Conclusion

This chapter has discussed the relationships among market orientation, new product development (NPD), and organizational performance in the Ghanaian fashion and footwear industry. The analysis, based on the Resource-Based View (RBV) and the Dynamic Capabilities Theory (DCT), shows that market orientation is a strategic contributor to competitiveness, but its full impact on performance is realized only within innovation-oriented processes such as NPD. Empirical findings indicate that competitor orientation and inter-functional coordination have a significant impact on performance, but customer orientation, although significant, has a relatively low or statistically irrelevant connection in the context of the informal sector. Importantly, NPD is a key mediating process through which market-oriented capabilities are translated into tangible performance outcomes.

These results support the idea that single emphasis on market knowledge cannot suffice; companies need to develop the ability to innovate and, thus, transform market intelligence into new product designs and offerings that meet the changing demands of consumers. In Ghana's informal fashion industry, which is a place of creativity, craftsmanship, and flexibility, innovation is the link between market awareness and sustainable development. This paper, therefore, contributes to the body of knowledge by putting the market orientation-innovation-performance nexus into perspective in a developing economy and how informal firms have used local knowledge to compete in dynamic markets.

Implications

Theoretical Implications

The study advances the field of marketing and innovation by offering empirical evidence that reinforces the mediating effect of NPD in the market orientation-performance relationship. It supports the RBV by showing that intangible, market-oriented capabilities can only perform better when supplemented by innovation-driven operations. In addition, the results support the applicability of the DCT, indicating that informal firms can promote their competitiveness through continuous learning, coordination, and product renewal despite resource-constrained conditions.

Managerial Implications

For practitioners, especially owners and managers of small-scale fashion and footwear businesses, the lessons have shown the necessity of adopting a comprehensive market-oriented approach. The companies should not simply listen to customer comments or monitor their competitors; instead, they need to institutionalize a cross-functional foundation to enable the market to inform their product design and development decisions. Responsiveness to changing consumer preferences can be enhanced through investment in design training, prototype development, and local market research. Moreover, the development of innovation partnerships (i.e., collaborations among artisans, designers, and digital marketers) can accelerate the NPD process and improve market performance.

Policy Implications

Policy-wise, the findings indicate that fostering innovation ecosystems in Ghana's creative industries can create significant socio-economic value. Small manufacturers should be empowered by providing access to design tools, technical training, and micro-financing schemes by the government agencies and industry associations. Enforcement of intellectual property rights and the marketing of local content through trade fairs and the internet would also foster sustained product development and export competitiveness.

Recommendations

Due to the results of the conducted study, the following recommendations are promoted to improve market orientation and innovation potential in the fashion and footwear sector in Ghana:

1. **Encourage Innovation Capability Building**: Companies ought to focus on capacity building in design thinking, product prototyping, and digital marketing to acquire NPD processes.
2. **Support Inter-Functional Cooperation**: Managers ought to create systems like frequent design sessions and common communication platforms that facilitate the flow of information between the production, marketing, and sales units.
3. **Balance Customer and Competitor Orientation**: As much as a firm should respond to their customer preferences, they should also be able to strategically monitor their competitors to find opportunities to be innovative as opposed to copying the current designs.
4. **Institutional Support to SMEs**: Policymakers must provide specific training and funding and incubation services so that small-scale producers can be able to innovate and grow on a sustainable basis.
5. **Enhance Future-Directed Markets Research**: Companies must invest in simple but systematic systems of fashion tracking and customer demands that will allow proactive innovation instead of reactive innovation.

All these suggestions highlight the importance of a market-based innovation culture that connects knowledge generation, innovation, and product differentiation. The development of these capabilities will not only make Ghana's fashion industry more competitive but also advance the overall goals of sustainable industrialisation and creative entrepreneurship in sub-Saharan Africa.

Limitations and Recommendations for Further Research

The empirical study conducted in this case was restricted to footwear producers in Kumasi, and thus, the extent to which the results can be generalized to the Ghanaian fashion industry as a whole is constrained. Further studies should expand the geographical scope or adopt longitudinal designs to shed light on the changing nature of market orientation over time. Moreover, the current analysis favored new product development; future research should consider additional mediators, e.g., digital marketing proficiency, brand equity, or consumer engagement, to provide a more complete picture. A unified approach combining qualitative and quantitative methods would be more likely to yield a better understanding of the causal relationships between market orientation and organizational performance.

References

Akomea, S. Y., & Yeboah, J. K. G. (2011). Market orientation and firm performance in Ghana's pharmaceutical industry. *Journal of Science and Technology (Ghana), 31*(2).

Anim, P. A., Agbemabiese, G. C., Acheampong, G., Adams, M., & Boakye, E. (2018). Market orientation, innovation and business performance: insight from womenpreneurs in the fashion industry in Ghana. *Journal of Creativity and Business Innovation, 4*.

Au, A. K., & Tse, A. C. (1995). The effect of marketing orientation on company performance in the service sector: A comparative study of the hotel industry in Hong Kong and New Zealand. *Journal of International Consumer Marketing, 8*(2), 77–87.

Aydin, H. (2020). Market orientation and product innovation: the mediating role of technological capability. *European Journal of Innovation Management*.

Bamfo, B. A., & Kraa, J. J. (2019). Market orientation and performance of small and medium enterprises in Ghana: The mediating role of innovation. *Cogent Business & Management, 6*(1), 1605703.

Crick, J. M. (2021). The dimensionality of the market orientation construct. *Journal of Strategic Marketing, 29*(4), 281–300.

Danso, D. K., Nuworkpor, A. A., Kuwornu-Adjaottor, J. E., & Aboagyewaa-Ntiri, J. (2018). Challenges facing the marketing of fashion products in Ghana: Case study of fashion businesses in ho municipality. *European Journal of Social Sciences Studies*.

Das, P., Verburg, R., Verbraeck, A., & Bonebakker, L. (2018). Barriers to innovation within large financial services firms: An in-depth study into disruptive and radical innovation projects at a bank. *European Journal of Innovation Management, 21*(1), 96–112.

Dobni, C. B. (2010). The relationship between an innovation orientation and competitive strategy. *International Journal of Innovation Management, 14*(02), 331–357.

Griffin, A., & Page, A. L. (1996). PDMA success measurement project: Recommended measures for product development success and failure. *Journal of Product Innovation Management, 13*(6), 478–496.

Hair, J. F., Hult, G. T. M., Ringle, C. M., Sarstedt, M., & Thiele, K. O. (2017). Mirror, mirror on the wall: A comparative evaluation of composite-based structural equation modeling methods. *Journal of the Academy of Marketing Science, 45*(5), 616–632.

Han, J. K., Kim, N., & Srivastava, R. K. (1998). Market orientation and organizational performance: Is innovation a missing link? *Journal of Marketing, 62*(4), 30–45.

Helfat, C. E., & Peteraf, M. A. (2009). Understanding dynamic capabilities: Progress along a developmental path. *Strategic Organization, 7*(1), 91–102.

Hinson, R., Ofori, D., Kastner, A., & Mohammed, M. (2008). Market orientation and export performance: a Ghanaian study. *African Journal of Business and Economic Research, 3*(2_3), 62–91.

Hult, G. T. M., & Ketchen, D. J., Jr. (2001). Does market orientation matter?: A test of the relationship between positional advantage and performance. *Strategic Management Journal, 22*(9), 899–906.

Hunt, S. D., & Morgan, R. M. (1996). The resource-advantage theory of competition: Dynamics, path dependencies, and evolutionary dimensions. *Journal of Marketing, 60*(4), 107–114.

Hsu, Y. H., & Fang, W. (2009). Intellectual capital and new product development performance: The mediating role of organizational learning capability. *Technological Forecasting and Social Change, 76*(5), 664–677.

Im, S., & Workman, J. P., Jr. (2004). Market orientation, creativity, and new product performance in high-technology firms. *Journal of Marketing, 68*(2), 114–132.

Kirca, A. H., Jayachandran, S., & Bearden, W. O. (2005). Market orientation: A meta-analytic review and assessment of its antecedents and impact on performance. *Journal of Marketing, 69*(2), 24–41.

Kohli, A. K., & Jaworski, B. J. (1990). Market orientation: The construct, research propositions, and managerial implications. *Journal of Marketing, 54*(2), 1–18.

Langerak, F., Hultink, E. J., & Robben, H. S. (2007). The mediating role of new product development in the link between market orientation and organizational performance. *Journal of Strategic Marketing, 15*(4), 281–305.

Lee, T. S., & Tsai, H. J. (2005). The effects of business operation mode on market orientation, learning orientation and innovativeness. *Industrial Management & Data Systems.*

Li, Y., Xie, E., & Cheng, L. (2017). The effect of market orientation on new product development: a literature review *Chinese Management Studies.*

Liu, W., & Atuahene-Gima, K. (2018). Enhancing product innovation performance in a dysfunctional competitive environment: The roles of competitive strategies and market-based assets. *Industrial Marketing Management, 73*, 7–20.

Lukas, B. A., & Ferrell, O. C. (2000). The effect of market orientation on product innovation. *Journal of the Academy of Marketing Science, 28*(2), 239–247.

Mahmoud, M. A. (2011). Market orientation and business performance among SMEs in Ghana. *International Business Research, 4*(1), 241–251.

Mohajan, H. K. (2017). Two criteria for good measurements in research: Validity and reliability. *Annals of Spiru Haret University. Economic Series, 17*(4), 59–82.

Murillo Oviedo, A. B., Pimenta, M. L., Piato, É. L., & Hilletofth, P. (2021). Development of market-oriented strategies through cross-functional integration in the context of the food and beverage industry. *Business Process Management Journal, 27*(3), 901–921.

Najafi-Tavani, S., Najafi-Tavani, Z., Naudé, P., Oghazi, P., & Zeynaloo, E. (2018). How collaborative innovation networks affect new product performance: Product innovation capability, process innovation capability, and absorptive capacity. *Industrial Marketing Management, 73*, 193–205.

Narver, J. C., & Slater, S. F. (1990). The effect of a market orientation on business profitability. *Journal of Marketing, 54*(4), 20–35.

Ngo, Q. H. (2021). The impact of market orientation on small businesses' performance in Vietnam: The mediating effects of the management accounting system. *Entrepreneurial Business and Economics Review, 9*(3), 59–72.

Ogbonna, B. U., & Ogwo, O. E. (2013). Market orientation and corporate performance of insurance firms in Nigeria. *International Journal of Marketing Studies, 5*(3), 104.

Read, J. (2013). Reliability and validity. *Models of madness: Psychological, social and biological approaches to psychosis* (p. 47).

Sahi, G. K., Gupta, M. C., & Cheng, T. C. E. (2020). The effects of strategic orientation on operational ambidexterity: A study of Indian SMEs in the industry 4.0 era. *International Journal of Production Economics, 220*, 107395.

Taheri, B., Bititci, U., Gannon, M. J., & Cordina, R. (2019). Investigating the influence of performance measurement on learning, entrepreneurial orientation and performance in turbulent markets. *International Journal of Contemporary Hospitality Management, 31*(3), 1224–1246.

Teece, D. J., Pisano, G., & Shuen, A. (1997). Dynamic capabilities and strategic management. *Strategic Management Journal, 18*(7), 509–533.

Wernerfelt, B. (1984). A resource-based view of the firm. *Strategic Management Journal, 5*(2), 171–180.

Zebal, M. A., & Goodwin, D. R. (2011). Market orientation in a developing nation—Antecedents, consequences and the moderating effect of environmental factors. *Marketing Bulletin, 22*(1).

CHAPTER 9

Brand Positioning Strategy in a Cross-National Environment: The Case of the USA and Ghana

Charles Blankson, Kwabena G. Boakye, and Jhinuk Chowdhury

Introduction and Study Background

Definitions and Distinctions

Positioning: An offering's position differentiates it in consumers' minds through attributes; firms choose an optimal mix of tangible and intangible product features, price, consumer preferences, and rivals' positions to achieve this (Agyei et al., 2022).

C. Blankson (✉) · J. Chowdhury
Department of Marketing, G. Brint Ryan College of Business, University of North Texas, Denton, TX, USA
e-mail: Charles.Blankson@unt.edu

J. Chowdhury
e-mail: Jhinuk.Chowdhury@unt.edu

A. Gbadamosi et al. (eds.), *Contemporary Marketing Practices in Africa, Volume 1*, Palgrave Studies of Marketing in Emerging Economies,
https://doi.org/10.1007/978-3-032-27126-6_9

Brand versus strategic positioning: Brand (operational) positioning concerns how a target audience perceives a firm's offerings, whereas strategic (market) positioning denotes the firm's competitive stance; intended brand positions typically derive from a firm's strategic positioning (Fuchs & Diamantopoulos, 2010).

Empirical Gaps and Motivation

The literature lacks: (1) an empirically validated, generalizable taxonomy of brand positioning strategies grounded in consumer and executive perceptions; (2) evidence that consumer perceptions align with executives' intended strategies; (3) analysis of how these strategies affect firm performance (Fuchs & Diamantopoulos, 2010).

Researchers have also not clarified which specific strategies to pursue, which are effective, or how selected strategies impact firm performance across different environments, despite concerns raised by Piercy (2005) and Fuchs and Diamantopoulos (2010). There is also scant research on cross-national positioning, despite calls for it in national and international marketing (Batra et al., 2017; Blankson et al., 2019). These gaps persist even as firms become more interdependent globally (Agyei et al., 2022). These combined gaps in theory and practice motivate the present paper.

Study Objectives and Context

The study has three aims: (a) develop and validate a generic typology of positioning strategies relevant to consumers and managers, (b) assess congruence between consumer perceptions and executive intentions across nations, and (c) examine how positioning strategies affect firm performance in cross-national contexts, specifically the USA and Ghana. The two countries were selected for their contrasts in business complexity, culture, and economic development: both have open-market democracies, but Ghana's liberalizing, transitional economy faces new competition, a growing middle class and expatriate population, and an influx of foreign

---

K. G. Boakye
Department of Enterprise Systems and Analytics College of Business Administration, Georgia Southern University, Statesboro, GA, USA
e-mail: kboakye@georgiasouthern.edu

firms and brands. Ghana is among the fastest-growing developing open-market economies in sub-Saharan Africa, has one of the region's more developed financial sectors, and is a leading recipient of foreign direct investment, underscoring the strategic importance of brand positioning for competitive advantage (Asiedu & Lien, 2011).

We next outline the methodologies employed in the four studies that comprise this research, followed by a general discussion, conclusions, managerial implications, limitations, and directions for future research.

Research Design

Study 1a: Generation of Initial Positioning Statements

Study 1 initiates the scale-development sequence to create and validate a consumer- and manager-relevant typology of positioning strategies applicable to both tangible and intangible offerings across various levels of involvement. For this research, brand positioning is used broadly to include brand, product, and service positioning. The objective of Study 1a was to generate a comprehensive pool of consumer-language statements describing product and brand attributes, utility, benefits, and purchase or recommendation reasons. Figure 9.1 summarizes the steps across studies.

Item Generation

We followed established multi-item, multi-study scale procedures (Churchill, 1979; DeVellis, 2017; Mentzer et al., 2001) and considered guidance on multi- and single-item measures (Diamantopoulos et al., 2012). Item sources included a literature review, focus groups with consumers, and in-depth interviews with managers. The aim was to capture natural consumer expressions about attributes, utility, and reasons for purchase or recommendation.

Initial focus groups employed snowball and foot-in-the-door recruitment methods. They were conducted in two US regions: Long Island, New York (Bellport and Bay Shore), and Hackensack, New Jersey. Twenty-four participants (aged 18–54) attended three 30-minute sessions, discussed recent purchases of low- and high-involvement goods and services (e.g., Apple iPhones; Starbucks; BMW; Macy's; Delta), and produced top-of-mind descriptors and statements.

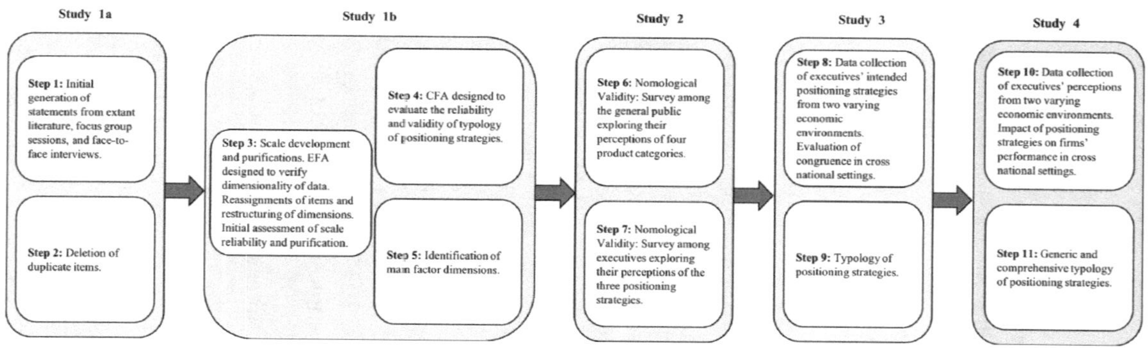

Fig. 9.1 Steps in developing, validating, and applying the concept of positioning

Two additional focus groups ($n = 12$) consisted of university computer technicians, secretaries, and Ph.D. students at a large public university in the southwestern USA. Participants (aged 28–45, balanced by gender) discussed offerings from companies such as T-Mobile, Boeing, Geico, Holiday Inn Express, and ExxonMobil. Responses were comparable across geographic samples.

Following consumer sessions, we conducted 58 in-depth, face-to-face interviews with executives from manufacturing, B2B, logistics, retailing, and services in a major Texas metropolitan area to elicit managerial perspectives on positioning and firm offerings (inspired by Kalafatis et al., 2020). Using inductive coding, we merged consumer and executive inputs, removing duplicates and overlaps to form an initial pool of 75 items.

The 75-item pool was reviewed by four academic scale-development experts and four senior industry practitioners to address ambiguity (Parasuraman et al., 1988). We then pretested the refined list with a convenience sample of 20 university staff and technicians.

To establish face validity, we reviewed the literature (see Table 9.1) and compiled an exhaustive set of 81 items, which were subsequently reduced to 35 due to word repetition. Merging these 35 literature-derived items with interview-derived items produced 110 items. With the assistance of seven doctoral students and two faculty colleagues, we screened for redundancy and clarity, reducing the pool to 48 items while retaining those that reflected divergent thinking (Homburg & Pflesser, 2000).

A final refinement step, involving two additional academic experts and eight doctoral students not previously engaged, removed conceptual overlap and achieved parsimony, yielding 33 items. Content analysis validation among academic experts, doctoral students, and authors reached 98–100% agreement. The resulting 33-item set served as the final questionnaire for subsequent scale validation studies.

Study 1b: Data Collection, Scale Development and Purification, Factor Dimensions, and Validation

The questionnaire was first pretested for readability, relevance, and face validity with 42 respondents (34 members of the public and eight university secretaries and computer technicians). The objective of Study 1b was to synthesize and reduce the items generated in Study 1a into generic constructs that would form the basis of a positioning-strategy typology. Respondents rated the extent to which each statement matched their

Table 9.1 Summary of the extant typology of positioning strategies

Author(s)	*Positioning Constructs*	*Type of scale*
Buskirk (1975)	(1) Features, (2) Price, (3) Advertising, (4) Distribution	Conceptual
Brown and Sims (1976)	(1) Problems solved, (2) Usage situation, (3) Users, (4) Competitors	Conceptual
Berry (1982)	(1) Value (warehouse, off-pricing), (2) Time efficiency (superstores, catalog stores, tele-shopping); (3) High contact (specialty, facilitating, advising, added value, resource usage); (4) Sensory (sounds, smells, visuals)	Conceptual
Wind (1982)	(1) Product features, (2) Benefits, (3) Problem solutions or need, (4) Usage occasions, (5) User, (6) Against another product, (7) Product class dissociation	Conceptual
Aaker and Shansby (1982)	(1) Attributes, (2) Price/quality, (3) Use or application, (4) Product/service user, (5) Product/service class, (6) Competition	Conceptual

(continued)

Table 9.1 (continued)

Author(s)	*Positioning Constructs*	*Type of scale*
Crawford (1985)	(1) Features, (2) Benefits: direct/indirect, (3) Surrogates: nonpareil, parentage (brand, company, person), manufacture (process, ingredients, design), target (end-use, demographic, psychographic, behavioral); rank, endorsements (expert, emulative), experience (other market, bandwagon, years/time); predecessor, competitor	Empirical/content analysis of advertisements
Ries and Trout (1986)	(1) Market leader, (2) Follower, (3) Reposition the competition, (4) Use the name (5) Line extension (use of the house name)	Conceptual based on practical experiences

(continued)

Table 9.1 (continued)

Author(s)	*Positioning Constructs*	*Type of scale*
Easingwood and Mahajan (1989)	(1) Reputation/capabilities of organization: expertise, reliability, innovativeness, performance, (2) Augmentation of product offering: product augmentation, extra service, (3) People advantage, (4) More attractive package offering, (5) A superior product through technology, (6) Accessibility, (7) Extra attention given to individual requirements through customization, (8) Satisfaction of more user needs within the sector; through offering a complete product line	Empirical/content analysis of advertisements
Porter (1996)	(1) Variety positioning, (2) Needs-based positioning, (3) Access-based positioning	Conceptual
Hooley et al. (1998)	(1) Low Price—High Price, (2) Premium Quality—Basic Quality, (3) Innovation—Imitation, (4) Superior Service—Limited Service, (5) Differentiated Benefits—Undifferentiated Features, (6) Tailored Offering—Standard Offering	Conceptual

(continued)

Table 9.1 (continued)

Author(s)	*Positioning Constructs*	*Type of scale*
Kalafatis et al. (2000)	(1) Pricing, (2) Easy to do business, (3) Personal contact, (4) Product performance, (5) Range of offerings, (6) Presence, (7) Safety, (8) Leadership, (9) Distinct identity, (10) Status, (11) Country identity, (12) Differentiation, (13) Attractiveness	Empirical/managerial derived
Blankson and Kalafatis (2004)	(1) Top of the range, (2) Service, (3) Value for money, (4) Reliability, (5) Attractiveness, (6) Country of origin, (7) The Brand Name, (8) Selectivity	Empirical/ consumer-derived
Burton and Easingwood (2006)	(1) Customer productivity, (2) Simplicity, (3) Convenience, (4) Risk (financial and physical/ functional), (5) Environmental friendliness, (6) Hedonic benefit (positive emotional response)	Empirical/analysis of advertising case histories
Fuchs and Diamantopoulos (2010)	(1) Favorability, (2) Differentiation, (3) Credibility, (4) Dissimilarity	Empirical/ consumer-derived/content analysis of advertisements

perceptions of two identified offerings when purchasing, considering purchase, or recommending those offerings, using a 7-point Likert scale (1 = extremely unimportant; 7 = extremely important).

Following Grewal et al., (2004, p. 105), we used a balanced-design approach with eight questionnaire versions to capture responses on sixteen paired offerings: (1) bed and mattress vs. winter coat or jacket; (2) life insurance vs. fast-food restaurant; (3) automobiles vs. cell phones; (4) perfume vs. powdered laundry soap; (5) department store vs. college education; (6) computer laptops vs. wine; (7) Caribbean cruise vs.

hospital care; and (8) airline vs. hairdressing salon or barbershop. These offerings were selected after consultation with two groups of 80 senior undergraduate marketing students and one group of eight MBA students at a southwestern US university. Data collection proceeded in two successive stages (initial and validation) approximately six months apart, with members of the public.

In step three (see Fig. 9.1), we prepared survey packets in university envelopes that contained a cover letter on university letterhead, a self-addressed, stamped envelope, and the three-page questionnaire on benefits, attributes, and likeability. Using a drop-off-and-mail-back mall-intercept procedure, 4000 questionnaires (eight versions, each reflecting a pair of offerings) were distributed in a major Texas metropolitan area. The one-wave effort yielded 2200 responses (a 55% response rate); after excluding incomplete questionnaires, 2,170 surveys remained for analysis. The mall intercept was conducted by 360 senior undergraduate marketing students who participated for extra credit.

Scale Development and Purification (Step 4)

We explored the data structure using principal component analysis (PCA). Initial inspection of the correlation matrices revealed substantial inter-item correlations, with a mean correlation of $r = 0.36$ ($p < 0.001$), indicating the relevance of the model's items. The Bartlett test of sphericity (Approx. $\chi 2 = 27{,}117.653$, df $= 528$, $p < 0.000$) and the Kaiser–Meyer–Olkin measure (KMO $= 0.935$) confirmed suitability for factor analysis. Using an eigenvalue >1 criterion and retaining factors that jointly explained >50% of variance, PCA extracted six factors that accounted for 55% of the variance in survey one. Communalities were high, indicating strong shared variance among variables.

Identification of Main Factor Dimensions (Step 5)

We applied varimax rotation to clarify the factor structure and identify representative reflective indicators. Using a communality cut-off of 0.4, all items met the threshold except for two, which were retained for conceptual coherence pending reliability and CFA. Most items (25 of 33) loaded above 0.50. Internal reliability was assessed using Cronbach's α (cut-off value of 0.70); the 33-item pool yielded an α value greater than 0.90 and split-half reliability greater than 0.80. Item-total correlations prompted the removal of 13 weak items using a 0.40 cut-off, leaving 20 items with high loadings, strong cumulative variance, and high Cronbach's α. All constructs were treated as reflective multi-item scales.

Confirmatory Factor Analysis

Six months after the mall-intercept, we conducted a random-sample survey (Accudata sample frame) across Texas, Oklahoma, New Mexico, Louisiana, and Florida in 2009, using Grewal et al.' (2004) balanced-design method to collect data on the same sixteen offerings. Items were measured on a 7-point Likert scale (1 = extremely unimportant, 7 = extremely important), and respondents were aged 18 years or older. Of 5000 mailed questionnaires, 700 were returned (14% response rate); after excluding incomplete responses, 654 questionnaires were retained for analysis. The two-stage, one-wave data-collection approach mirrored that of Spiro and Weitz (1990); given the sample size and representativeness, non-response bias was deemed minimal. We conducted CFA in STATASE 15. The measurement model fit well: $\chi2 = 224.94$, df = 41; CFI = 0.932; TLI = 0.901; RMSEA = 0.080; SRMR = 0.054. Composite reliability (CR) exceeded the 0.70 threshold for all constructs (see Table 9.2). Convergent validity was evaluated through factor loadings and average variance extracted (AVE); loadings greater than 0.50 were retained, and AVE values ranged from 0.51 to 0.57, indicating that each construct explained more than 50% of the variance of its indicators (Fornell & Larcker, 1981; Hair et al., 2010). Discriminant validity was confirmed using the Fornell–Larcker criterion: each construct's AVE exceeded the squared correlations with other constructs (see Table 9.3).

Three primary factors (strategies) emerged from the measurement model: impressive service, attractiveness, and value. Tables 9.2 and 9.3 summarize the psychometric properties and support that the measurement model meets accepted validity and reliability thresholds. We next evaluate nomological validity, beginning with consumer data and then executive data.

Study 2: Evaluation of Nomological Validity—Consumers and Executives

Consumers' Perceptions of Brand Positioning Strategy (Step 6)

Table 9.2 Study 1b—CFA measurement model, AVE, and composite reliability ($n = 654$)

Construct and items	*Loading*	*AVE*	*CR*
Impressive service			
Consider people important	0.779	0.534	0.821
Friendliness of staff/personnel	0.699		
High principles	0.733		
Personal attention	0.710		
Attractiveness			
Elegant	0.719	0.509	0.806
Posh	0.689		
Status	0.702		
Prestigious	0.743		
Value			
Affordability	0.778	0.574	0.803
Reasonable price	0.819		
Value for money	0.667		

Table 9.3 Study 1b—Descriptive statistics, and discriminant validity—AVE comparison ($n = 654$)

	Mean	*SD*	*1*	*2*	*3*
Impressive service	5.20	0.94	**0.53**		
Attractiveness	4.15	0.88	0.37	**0.51**	
value	5.96	1.16	0.13	0.01	**0.57**

Note SD denotes standard deviation. The values on the diagonals are the average variance extracted (AVE). The off-diagonals are the squared correlations between constructs

Study 2 assessed nomological validity, beginning with a consumer survey conducted in Texas using drop-off-and-mail-back and drop-off-and-pick-up procedures, administered by 150 undergraduate marketing students as part of a course requirement for course credit. Following Grewal et al. (2004), a balanced-design approach with two questionnaire versions was employed to collect data on four product categories (automobiles, wrist-watches, cell phones, and airlines), with offerings borrowed from Fuchs and Diamantopoulos (2012).

Of the 500 questionnaires distributed to a convenience sample in a Texas metropolitan area, 316 usable questionnaires were returned (63.2% one-wave response rate). The first batch yielded 159 complete responses for automobiles and wristwatches (32% one-wave response rate); the second batch yielded 154 completed responses for cell phones and airlines (31.2% one-wave response rate).

Inter-factor correlations were computed between perceptions of the three sub-positioning strategies (impressive service, attractiveness, value) and each product category to test the expected positive relationships (Fuchs & Diamantopoulos, 2012). Internal reliability for the four categories was acceptable: automobiles (α = 0.775), wristwatches (α = 0.796), cell phones (α = 0.734), and airlines (α = 0.778). Corrected item–total correlations for most of the ten items per category ranged from r = 0.334 to 0.681. Results shown in Table 9.4 indicate positive, significant intercorrelations between positioning-dimension scores and consumer perceptions across the four categories, supporting the measure's nomological validity (Fuchs & Diamantopoulos, 2012, pp. 237–238).

Executives' perceptions of brand positioning strategy (Step 7)

We next surveyed executives' perceptions of the 11-item positioning strategies (see Table 9.2) and their fit with firm positioning decisions using drop-off-and-mail-back and drop-off-and-pick-up methods. Questionnaires used a 7-point Likert scale (1 = not a good fit at all; 7 = a very good fit). The executive sample comprised small, medium, and large firms across key industries in a major Texas metropolitan area. A total of 195 marketing undergraduate students conducted data collection as part of their extra-credit assignment. Of the 500 questionnaires distributed to a convenience sample of executives, 155 usable questionnaires were returned (31% one-wave response rate).

Table 9.4 Study 2—nomological validity—correlations with positioning strategies (correlation coefficients) (n = 316)

Product categories	*Positioning strategy*		
	Impressive service	*Attractiveness*	*Value*
Automobiles	0.572**	0.354**	0.516**
Wristwatches	0.681**	0.421**	0.514**
Cell phones	0.307**	0.478**	0.520**
Airlines	0.688**	0.200**	0.642**

Notes Automobiles (n = 159), Wristwatches (n = 159), Cell phones (n = 154), Airlines (n = 154).
** $p < 0.05$; *** $p < 0.01$

CFA was performed in STATASE 15 to assess model fit, reliability, and validity. All factor loadings exceeded 0.50 except "status" (0.484). Despite falling below the 0.50 guideline (Hair et al., 2010), we retained the "status" construct because of its content and face validity in relation to the measured construct. Additionally, the presence of this item did not affect the validity or reliability of the construct. The measurement model demonstrated strong fit: $\chi 2 = 46.49$, df = 32, $\chi 2/df = 1.45$, CFI = 0.979, TLI = 0.971, RMSEA = 0.054, SRMR = 0.064 ($\chi 2/df$ ratios < 2 indicate good fit; Hair et al., 2010). Composite reliability for each positioning strategy exceeded 0.70 (Nunnally, 1978) (see Table 9.5). AVE values exceeded 0.50, indicating convergent validity (Fornell & Larcker, 1981), and the square roots of AVEs exceeded inter-construct correlations, supporting discriminant validity (Fornell & Larcker, 1981). With convergent and discriminant evidence in place and composite reliabilities above thresholds, nomological validity is supported for the executive sample (Bagozzi & Yi, 1988) (Table 9.6).

Study 3: Cross-national Evaluation of Congruence (Steps 8 and 9)

To assess the managerial implications and compare managers' intended strategies with consumers' perceptions, we surveyed practicing executives in the USA and Ghana. Because the typology originated in the USA, we followed Douglas and Craig's (2006) guidance and first assessed content

Table 9.5 Study 2—executives' perceptions of positioning strategy—Nomological validity—Confirmatory factor analysis: measurement model, AVE, and composite reliability ($n = 155$)

Construct and items	*Λ*	*AVE*	*CR*
Impressive service			
Consider people important	0.714	0.518	0.806
Friendliness of staff/personnel	0.753		
High principles	0.629		
Personal attention	0.774		
Attractiveness			
Elegant	0.724	0.560	0.791
Posh	0.961		
Status	0.484		
Value			
Affordability	0.975	0.758	0.914
Reasonable price	0.897		
Value for money	0.719		

Table 9.6 Study 2—executives' perceptions of positioning strategy—nomological validity, descriptive statistics, and discriminant validity—AVE comparison ($n = 155$)

	Mean	*SD*	*1*	*2*	*3*
Impressive service	6.36	0.75	**0.72**		
Attractiveness	4.92	1.36	0.36	**0.75**	
Value	5.99	1.09	0.22	0.03	**0.87**

Note SD denotes standard deviation. The values on the diagonals are the average variance extracted (AVE). The off-diagonals are the squared correlations between constructs

and face validity in Ghana. A validation focus group comprised a convenience sample of 38 EMBA marketing executives from a leading business school in Accra. Participants, who are practicing managers or executives in local and foreign firms, reviewed the strategies identified in Study 1b and then completed a survey on how those strategies are applied in their firms.

The study's rationale was to determine whether consumers' perceived positioning strategies predict executives' intended practices (Walsh & Mitchell, 2005) across contrasting environments, a question central to marketing strategy formulation (Porter, 2001). Statistical significance of intended-practice indicators was used to infer executives' presumed strategies.

Data collection utilized the factors identified in Study 1b (scale development and validation). The identified constructs were included in a one-page, self-completion survey administered concurrently in a large Texas metropolitan area and the Greater Accra Region of Ghana using a one-wave, drop-off-and-collect protocol (Ibeh et al., 2004). For extra credit, undergraduate senior marketing students and MBA marketing students collected responses. A total of 1,000 executives were sampled in the USA and 1,000 in Ghana. Valid executive responses totaled 512 in the USA (51.2% response rate) and 169 in Ghana (16.9% response rate).

Following summated-scaling principles (Slater et al., 2007; Spector, 1992), the questionnaire listed the three factors—impressive service, attractiveness, and value—with their respective items. Executives indicated which factors were "relevant" or "fit" with their firms' positioning strategies; an item was assigned to a factor if an executive deemed it so. Model fit statistics indicated an acceptable fit: USA $\chi2 = 13.109$, df = 2, $p <$

0.001; Ghana $\chi 2 = 26.909$, df $= 2$, $p < 0.001$. Results show that two strategies—impressive service and value—are congruent between executives' intentions and consumers' perceptions and are actively pursued in both the USA (Table 9.7) and Ghana (Table 9.8). The ranking of strategy prevalence in both contexts was identical: impressive service, value, and then attractiveness. These findings support the predictive validity of consumer-perceived strategies, provide external validation, and demonstrate the typology's generalizability across a developed open-market economy (USA) and a liberalizing, developing open-market economy (Ghana).

Table 9.7 Study 3—matching executives' intended positioning strategies and consumers' perceptions (USA) ($n = 512$)

Factors/ strategies	*Frequency (number of times reported as employed)*	*Minimum expected frequency*	*Rank (in order of most popular)*	*Residual*	*Percent*
Impressive service	**113**	**92.0**	1	**21.0**	**40.9**
Attractiveness	65	92.0	4	-27.0	23.6
Value	**98**	**92.0**	2	**6.0**	**35.5**
	Mean = 96.37; Std. Deviation = 18.63				
	Non-parametric $\chi^2 = 13.109$; df = 2; Asymptotic Sig. = 0.001				

Table 9.8 Study 3: Matching executives' intended positioning strategies and consumers' perceptions (Ghana) ($n = 169$)

Factors/ strategies	*Frequency (number of times reported as employed)*	*Minimum expected frequency*	*Rank (in order of most popular)*	*Residual*	*Percent*
Impressive service	**167**	**135.7**	1	**31.3**	**41**
Attractiveness	87	135.7	4	−48.7	21.4
Value	**153**	**135.7**	2	**17.3**	**37.6**
	Mean = 144.64; Std. Deviation = 30.72				
	Non-parametric $\chi^2 = 26.909$; df = 2; Asymptotic Sig. = 0.000				

Study 4: Cross-national Assessment of the Impact of Positioning Strategies on Firm Performance (Steps 10 and 11)

Study 4 had two aims: (1) to evaluate the effectiveness of the identified positioning strategies on firm performance across nations, and (2) to test the applicability of those strategies in differing economies to strengthen the model's generalizability. To meet these aims, we operationalized the measures developed in the USA and applied them in Ghana to produce substantive, empirical, and contextual validation.

Marketing strategies operate within cultural contexts that shape values, beliefs, and normative behavior (Cayla & Arnould, 2008; Nakata & Sivakumar, 2001). Cultural contrasts between the USA and Ghana are well-documented by Hofstede (1980) and others. For example, American culture emphasizes tolerance and individualism, whereas Ghanaian culture stresses respect, collectivism, and distinct power-distance norms (Nakata & Sivakumar, 1996). Accounting for these cultural differences is essential when implementing marketing practices, such as branding, advertising, pricing, positioning, and customer service, especially given the pronounced contrasts between African and Western contexts (Blankson et al., 2019).

Hypotheses Development

Marketing is shifting from distinct product features toward intangible drivers such as reputation, managed consumer perceptions, and strategic positioning. Prior work has linked emphasis on positioning to superior financial and competitive returns (Hooley et al., 2001). Empirical evidence shows that positioning—especially a "high-quality high-price" approach—can raise airline profits (Suzuki, 2000). Despite theoretical claims and recent interest (Iyer et al., 2019), empirical tests remain scarce, prompting calls for more research (Panda et al., 2019).

Independent and Dependent Variables

The three factors—impressive service, attractiveness, and value (see Table 9.2)—derived from Study 1a and validated in Study 1b serve as the independent variables. Dependent variables capture firm performance as reported subjectively by executives and reflect sales, profits, and ROI (Reinartz et al., 2004). We employ a global performance measure due to its cross-contextual relevance (Slater et al., 2007). Although subjective, executive assessments are widely accepted in marketing research and correlate strongly with objective performance data (Morgan et al., 2004; Narver & Slater, 1990; Slater et al., 2007). Consistent with theory, we expect the three positioning dimensions to be mutually inclusive and to exert positive effects on firm performance (sales, profits, ROI) (see Fig. 9.2).

Positioning operates as a higher-order, multidimensional construct enacted through multiple managerial activities (Iyer et al., 2023). While environmental and regulatory factors can blur positioning, it primarily reflects deliberate managerial actions that secure competitive advantage (Doyle & Saunders, 1985; Noseworthy & Trudel, 2011). Consequently, positioning comprises interrelated sub-strategies that complement one another (Kalra & Goodstein, 1998) and, like market orientation, requires sustained investment and evolves over time (Iyer et al., 2019; Narver & Slater, 1990). Treating positioning as a single latent variable risks masking the distinct effects of its dimensions (Kalafatis et al., 2024). Even after identifying prevalent sub-strategies across Studies 1–3, we must still determine which sub-strategies most strongly predict specific outcomes (Batra et al., 2011). The choice and adoption of positioning strategies are not static, and no single strategy suits all firms (Kalafatis et al., 2020, 2024). Firm success depends on skillful design of tangible attributes and management of intangible brand perceptions.

Globalization has homogenized many business practices across open-market economies while local conditions remain distinct (Blankson et al., 2019). Following Fuchs and Diamantopoulos' (2012, p. 241) guidance, our generic measure is thus suitable for cross-national application and for comparing the impact of positioning strategies on performance. We further argue that competition in open and liberalized markets drives firms to pursue competitive positioning strategies (Iyer et al., 2019). Firms in developing open markets may emphasize fewer outcome variables, whereas firms in advanced open markets—facing fiercer competition and greater risk tolerance—pursue multiple concurrent strategies targeting several outcomes. Accordingly, we posit:

> H1: The "impressive service" positioning strategy will have a positive impact on firm performance—(a) sales, (b) profits, and (c) ROI—to a greater extent in developed open-market economies than in developing open-market economies.

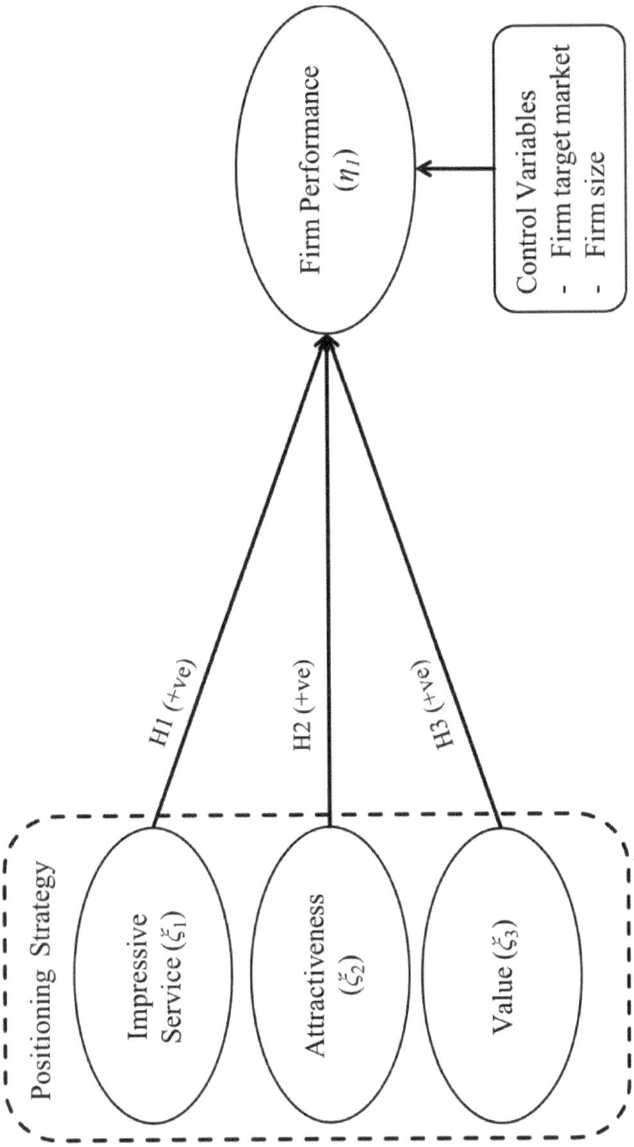

Fig. 9.2 Conceptual framework showing the relationship between brand positioning strategy and firm performance

H2: The "attractiveness" positioning strategy will have a positive impact on firm performance—(a) sales, (b) profits, and (c) ROI—to a greater extent in developed open-market economies than in developing open-market economies.

H3: The "value" positioning strategy will have a positive impact on firm performance—(a) sales, (b) profits, and (c) ROI—to a greater extent in developed open-market economies than in developing open-market economies.

Control Variables

Because firm size and operating scope influence marketing success, we control for firm size (number of employees) and target market (local, national, regional, or international) to account for cross-industry variance across the surveyed national contexts (Verhoef & Leeflang, 2009).

Methodology

Global market integration presents both challenges and opportunities that require managers to refine their positioning strategies to signal value effectively to stakeholders. The USA and Ghana were selected for their contrasts in market complexity, dynamism, culture, and economic development. Because much strategic data is unavailable, managerial judgment plays a central role in strategic decisions (Kalafatis et al., 2020). Selecting appropriate judgmental inputs for tasks such as positioning is particularly crucial at the strategic level (Kalafatis et al., 2024).

Before the main survey, we conducted pilot qualitative work in both countries to confirm the relevance of positioning. In the USA, we conducted 20 in-depth interviews with executives (marketing managers, general managers, logistics and supply chain managers, and CEOs) following Verhoef and Leeflang (2009). In Ghana, we ran four focus groups with 20 EMBA students who are practicing executives, following Larreche and Moinpour (1983). In both settings, participants discussed daily marketing activities and positioning practices (branding, marketing mix, advertising, promotions, sales, customer care) and assessed the perceived effectiveness of these actions on firm performance; discussions focused on managers' own tactics and on antecedents and consequences of positioning in context.

The main study employed a three-page questionnaire reflecting the multidimensional positioning construct (sub-positioning strategies). Page 1 listed the scale constructs and items from Study 1b, rated on a 7-point Likert scale (1 = "very poor fit," 7 = "very good fit"). Page 2 measured firm performance variables on a 7-point scale (1 = below expectations; 7 = above expectations). Page 3 collected nominal demographic and firm characteristics.

Sampling involved simple random draws from frames supplied by Accudata and Dun & Bradstreet in the USA, as well as from the Ghana Club 100 Business Directory (2010). In the USA, 500 questionnaires were mailed to randomly selected respondents in five southern states, followed two weeks later by 500 mailed to eastern and midwestern states; address stickers were supplied without duplicates. The US mailings yielded 236 usable responses (a 24% one-wave response rate). In Ghana, postal administration was impractical, so a drop-off-and-collect protocol was used in the Greater Accra Region. Student data collectors (six recent graduates led by a doctoral student) delivered packets containing a university-letterhead cover letter, questionnaire, and return envelope, with two follow-up collections at one and two weeks. From 1,000 distributed packets, 204 responses were collected (20.4% response rate), of which 161 were usable after excluding incomplete surveys. Fieldwork in the US and Ghana was conducted concurrently.

We assessed non-response bias using Armstrong and Overton's (1977) early-late respondent comparison and found no significant differences for either country cohort, consistent with acceptable representativeness (Steenkamp et al., 1999). Participants were offered a summary of the article as an incentive. Survey administration followed Dillman et al. (2009) best practices: university letterhead for cover letters, user-friendly formats, self-addressed return envelopes where applicable, and an incentive option.

Common Method Bias

Because the independent and dependent variables were collected from a single informant, we tested for common method variance (CMV) using the marker-variable technique (Lindell & Whitney, 2001; Malhotra et al., 2006). The marker-variable method requires an unrelated variable to partial out spurious correlations; lacking a preselected marker, we applied the technique post hoc (Lindell & Whitney, 2001) and used the lowest observed intervariable correlation ($r = 0.0556$) as a proxy marker to compute CMV-adjusted correlations. Differences between CMV-adjusted and unadjusted correlations were minimal.

We then compared the unadjusted and CMV-adjusted correlation matrices via a chi-square difference test (Bollen, 1989) by fitting the hypothesized model to (1) the unadjusted correlations and (2) the CMV-adjusted correlations. The test yielded $\Delta\chi 2 = 3.408$ with $\Delta df = 0$ ($p > 0.1$), indicating no significant difference between models and that CMV does not materially affect the results. To further mitigate common-source concerns and support convergent validity, we collected data from multiple informants within firms where feasible.

Results and Analysis

Respondents in both countries were mainly aged 31–60, with the 31–40 and 41–50 cohorts most prevalent in the USA and Ghana, respectively. Men comprised the majority of respondents in both the USA (67%) and Ghana (62%). Educational levels differed: college graduates accounted for 36.9% in the USA and 53% in Ghana; graduate degree holders or candidates accounted for 13.3% in the USA and 31.9% in Ghana; high school graduates accounted for 29.6% in the USA and 2.5% in Ghana. Most respondents had 1–10 years' tenure at their firms (USA = 70.7%; Ghana = 68.3%). In the USA, firms' primary target markets were local (39.9%), national (21.5%), and global (20.2%); in Ghana, the targets were regional (ECOWAS) at 50.3%, global at 29.0%, and national at 13.2%. Informants included assistant managers, general managers, marketing managers and directors, presidents, CEOs, owners, factory managers, and finance managers.

Testing Hypotheses

We tested hypotheses using a system of three equations because the dependent variables—sales, profits, and ROI—are conceptually and empirically correlated, so their error terms may covary. Ordinary least squares (OLS) treats each equation independently and ignores cross-equation error correlation; therefore, we estimated the system via seemingly unrelated regression (SUR) (Zellner, 1962), which yields more efficient coefficients when equations share similar independent variables or correlated residuals. The structural form estimated was:

Sales = $\beta 0$ + $\beta 1$ Impressive service + $\beta 2$ Attractiveness + $\beta 3$ Value + controls
Profits = $\beta 0$ + $\beta 1$ Impressive service + $\beta 2$ Attractiveness + $\beta 3$ Value + controls
ROI = $\beta 0$ + $\beta 1$ Impressive service + $\beta 2$ Attractiveness + $\beta 3$ Value + controls

To justify SUR, we tested cross-equation error independence with the Breusch–Pagan (1980) test. The null of independent errors was rejected for both samples, confirming correlated residuals and the appropriateness of SUR: US sample $\chi 2 = 267.21$, df = 3, $p < 0.01$; Ghana sample $\chi 2 = 144.95$, df = 3, $p < 0.01$.

We then estimated the three simultaneous equations via SUR for both national samples. For the US sample, "impressive service" was positively and significantly associated with sales ($b = 0.18$, $z = 2.45$, $p < 0.05$), profits ($b = 0.13$, $z = 1.81$, $p < 0.10$), and ROI ($b = 0.13$, $z = 1.67$, $p < 0.10$), providing partial support for H1a–H1c. In the Ghana sample, "impressive service" showed no significant effects on any of the performance variables.

The "attractiveness" strategy in the US sample was positively and strongly related to sales ($b = 0.19$, $z = 3.44$, $p < 0.01$), profits ($b = 0.26$, $z = 4.73$, $p < 0.01$), and ROI ($b = 0.20$, $z = 3.47$, $p < 0.01$); no significant associations were observed in Ghana, yielding partial support for H2a–H2c.

The "value" strategy produced consistent positive effects across both samples. In the US sample, value predicted sales ($b = 0.21$, $z = 4.17$, $p < 0.01$), profits ($b = 0.22$, $z = 4.22$, $p < 0.01$), and ROI ($b = 0.20$, $z = 3.67$, $p < 0.01$). In Ghana, value also predicted sales ($b = 0.27$, $z = 3.04$, $p < 0.01$), profits ($b = 0.35$, $z = 3.73$, $p < 0.01$), and ROI ($b = 0.19$, $z = 1.90$, $p < 0.10$). These results confirm H3a–H3c.

Complete SUR parameter estimates, standard errors, test statistics, and control variable results are presented in Tables 9.9 and 9.10.

Conclusions and Implications

Across four empirical studies, we conceptualized positioning as a multidimensional marketing construct that materially affects firm performance in both developed and developing open-market economies. The 33-item pool developed in Study 1a provides a rigorous item bank for future

Table 9.9 Study 4: seemingly unrelated regression results (USA sample n = 236)

	Sales			*Profits*			*Return on Investment*		
Dependent variable	*Coefficient*	*SE*	*z-statistic*	*Coefficient*	*SE*	*z-statistic*	*Coefficient*	*SE*	*z-statistic*
Explanatory variables									
Impressive service	0.18	0.07	2.45**	0.13	0.07	1.81*	0.13	0.08	1.67*
Attractiveness	0.19	0.05	3.44***	0.26	0.06	4.73***	0.20	0.06	3.47***
Value	0.21	0.05	4.17***	0.22	0.05	4.22***	0.20	0.05	3.67***
Control variables									
Regional market	0.34	0.23	1.50	0.40	0.23	1.74*	0.20	0.24	0.82
National market	-0.04	0.23	−0.17	0.15	0.23	0.66	-0.18	0.24	-0.76
Global market	0.23	0.25	0.94	0.28	0.25	1.13	0.18	0.26	0.71
Medium firm size	-0.13	0.22	−0.61	−0.14	0.22	−0.63	−0.09	0.23	-0.39
Large firm size	0.12	0.22	0.57	0.11	0.22	0.50	0.21	0.23	0.93
χ^2	62.34			73.23			49.60		
R^2	0.21			0.24			0.18		

* $p < 0.1$; ** $p < 0.05$; *** $p < 0.01$; SE = standard errors

academic work, and the diverse brands, goods, services, and firm types sampled in Studies 1b, 2, and 4 increase the positioning model's applicability across industries. The cross-national executive data collected in Study 3 (USA and Ghana) further support the typology's generalizability by demonstrating congruence between executives' intended strategies and consumer perceptions. Study 4 then establishes how the typology relates to firm performance across national contexts.

These findings carry practical implications for brand managers, marketing directors, advertising executives, and business owners operating in international markets (Iyer et al., 2023; Kalafatis et al., 2024). Firms should exploit the complementarity among the three sub-strategies—impressive service, attractiveness, and value—by customizing and combining them to build distinctive, idiosyncratic positioning. The three strategies offer routes to engage customers as partners and

Table 9.10 Study 4—seemingly unrelated regression results (Ghana sample $n = 161$)

	Sales			*Profits*			*Return on investment*		
Dependent variable	*Coefficient*	*SE*	*z-statistic*	*Coefficient*	*SE*	*z-statistic*	*Coefficient*	*SE*	*z-statistic*
Explanatory variables									
Impressive service	0.08	0.09	0.86	0.06	0.10	0.62	0.06	0.10	0.57
Attractiveness	−0.05	0.10	−0.52	−0.06	0.11	−0.56	0.13	0.12	1.13
Value	0.27	0.09	3.04***	0.35	0.09	3.73***	0.19	0.10	1.90*
Control variables									
Regional market	0.75	0.34	2.18**	0.86	0.37	2.34**	0.51	0.38	1.32
National market	0.89	0.40	2.22**	0.65	0.43	1.54	0.08	0.45	0.17
Global market	1.06	0.36	2.95***	1.42	0.39	3.68***	0.51	0.40	1.26
Medium firm size	0.39	0.19	1.99**	0.32	0.21	1.56	0.28	0.22	1.28
Large firm size	−0.01	0.37	−0.02	0.42	0.39	1.06	0.03	0.41	0.06
χ^2	39.06			49.60			24.29		
R^2	0.21			0.25			0.14		

* $p < 0.1$; ** $p < 0.05$; *** $p < 0.01$; SE = standard errors

co-creators of value through targeted attribute changes, image work, and attitude shaping. Although superficially simple, these sub-strategies conceal operational complexity and strategic sophistication comparable to Raynor and Ahmed's (2013) three normative priorities for superior firms:

(1) Compete on differentiators other than price.
(2) Prioritize revenue growth over cost-cutting.
(3) Change anything necessary to sustain the first two principles.

Our measurement rigor also implies that salient positioning concerns—such as product sustainability, safety, reliability, and after-sales service—although not explicitly stated in the final item set (Table 9.2), are implicitly embedded in the comprehensive dimensions and therefore remain actionable levers for managers and advertisers. Marketers targeting consumers in developing, subsistence, or emerging markets—where expectations and purchasing power are rising—can deploy imaginative, culturally congruent brand attributes in advertising and promotions to link the identified strategies with local consumer expectations (The Economist, 2020). Global marketers should therefore craft culturally relevant multi-country brands, as culture-congruent positioning appeals tend to outperform those that are culturally incongruent (Batra et al., 2017).

Limitations and Directions for Future Research

This research has several limitations that suggest opportunities for extension. First, the studies did not employ a uniform sampling strategy: Study 1a and Study 4 relied on convenience samples, and data-collection modes varied across studies (e.g., drop-off/mail-back versus simple random sampling). Although the focal relationships are replicated across contexts, these choices may limit the generalizability of the findings. Future work should harmonize sampling frames and data-collection modes and, where feasible, use probability-based samples to enhance external validity. Second, although the constructs were measured using established scales and model diagnostics were satisfactory, additional tests—such as multi-group measurement invariance across countries and industries—would further support cross-contextual comparisons. Third, our design emphasizes association rather than causal identification; field experiments or quasi-experimental designs (e.g., staggered rollouts, instrumental variables) would help isolate treatment effects. Finally, expanding to more economies and sectors, incorporating behavioral/archival performance data, and examining boundary conditions (e.g., firm size, competitive intensity, channel strategy) would refine the scope of the conclusions and enhance their managerial relevance.

References

Aaker, D. A., & Shansby, J. G. (1982). Positioning your product. *Business Horizons, 25*(3), 56–62.

Agyei, P. M., Manu, F., & Coffie, S. (2022). Positioning strategies for B2B service markets. *Industrial Marketing Management, 106*, 405–419.

Armstrong, J. S., & Overton, T. S. (1977). Estimating nonresponse bias in mail surveys. *Journal of Marketing Research, 14*(3), 396–402.

Asiedu, E., & Lien, D. (2011). Democracy, foreign direct investment and natural resources. *Journal of International Economics, 84*(1), 99–111.

Bagozzi, R. P., & Yi, Y. (1988). On the evaluation of structural equation models. *Journal of the Academy of Marketing Science, 16*(1), 74–94.

Batra, R., Ahuvia, A., & Bagozzi, R. P. (2011). Brand love. *Journal of Marketing, 76*(2), 1–16.

Batra, R., Zhang, C., Aydinoğlu, N. Z., & Feinberg, F. M. (2017). Positioning multicountry brands: The impact of variation in cultural values and competitive set. *Journal of Marketing Research, 54*(6), 914–931.

Berry, L. L. (1982). Retail positioning strategies for the 1980s. *Business Horizons, 25*(6), 45–50.

Blankson, C., & Kalafatis, S. P. (2004). The development and validation of a scale measuring consumer/customer-derived generic typology of positioning strategies. *Journal of Marketing Management, 20*(1–2), 5–43.

Blankson, C., Iyer, P., Owusu-Frimpong, N., Nwankwo, S., & Hinson, R. (2019). Positioning strategies of foreign and indigenous firms in an African cultural milieu. *Journal of Business Research*. https://doi.org/10.1016/j.jbusres.2019.03.001

Bollen, K. A. (1989). *Structural equations with latent variables*. Wiley.

Breusch, T. S., & Pagan, A. R. (1980). The Lagrange multiplier test and its applications to model specification in econometrics. *The Review of Economic Studies, 47*(1), 239–253.

Brown, H. E., & Sims, J. T. (1976). Market segmentation, product differentiation, and market positioning as alternative marketing strategies. In *Educators conference proceedings series No* (Vol. 39, pp. 483–87).

Burton, J., & Easingwood, C. (2006). A positioning typology of consumers' perceptions of the benefits offered by successful service brands. *Journal of Retailing and Consumer Services, 13*, 301–316.

Buskirk, R. K. (1975). *Principles of marketing* (4th ed.). Dryden Press.

Cayla, J., & Arnould, E. J. (2008). A cultural approach to branding in the global marketplace. *Journal of International Marketing, 16*(4), 86–112.

Churchill, G. A., Jr. (1979). A paradigm for developing better measures of marketing constructs. *Journal of Marketing Research, 16*(1), 64–73.

Crawford, C. M. (1985). A new positioning typology. *Journal of Product Innovation Management, 2*(4), 243–253.

DeVellis, R. F. (2017). *Scale development: Theory and applications* (4th ed.). SAGE.

Diamantopoulos, A., Sarstedt, M., Fuchs, C., Wilczynski, P., & Kaiser, S. (2012). Guidelines for choosing between multi-item and single-item scales for construct measurement: A predictive validity perspective. *Journal of the Academy of Marketing Science, 40*(3), 434–449.

Dillman, D. A., Smyth, J. D., & Christian, L. M. (2009). *Internet, mail, and mixed-mode surveys: The tailored design method* (3rd ed.). Wiley.

Douglas, S. P., & Craig, C. S. (2006). On improving the conceptual foundations of international marketing research. *Journal of International Marketing, 14*(1), 1–22.

Doyle, P., & Saunders, J. (1985). Market segmentation and positioning in specialized industrial markets. *Journal of Marketing, 49*(2), 24–32.

Easingwood, C. J., & Mahajan, V. (1989). Positioning of financial services for competitive strategy. *Journal of Product Innovation Management, 6*(September), 207–219.

Fornell, C., & Larcker, D. F. (1981). Structural equation models with unobservable variables and measurement error: Algebra and statistics. *Journal of Marketing Research, 18*(3), 382–388.

Fuchs, C., & Diamantopoulos, A. (2010). Evaluating the effectiveness of brand-positioning strategies from a consumer perspective. *European Journal of Marketing, 44*(11/12), 1763–1786.

Fuchs, C., & Diamantopoulos, A. (2012). Customer-perceived positioning effectiveness: Conceptualization, operationalization, and implications for new product managers. *Journal of Product Innovation Management, 29*(2), 229–244.

Ghana Club 100 Business Directory of Firms. (2010). Enhancing partnership between domestic & foreign investors for sustained economic development. *Ghana Club 100 Magazine – Ghana Investment Promotion Center, 10.*

Grewal, R., Mehta, R., & Kardes, F. R. (2004). The timing of repeat purchases of consumer durable goods: The role of functional bases of consumer attitudes. *Journal of Marketing Research, 41*(1), 101–115.

Hair, J. F., Anderson, R. E., Babin, B. J., & Black, W. C. (2010). *Multivariate data analysis: A global perspective* (7th ed.). Pearson.

Hofstede, G. (1980). *Culture's consequences: International differences in work related values*. Sage Publications.

Homburg, C., & Pflesser, C. (2000). A multiple-layer model of market-oriented organizational culture: Measurement issues and performance outcomes. *Journal of Marketing Research, 37*(4), 449–462.

Hooley, G., Broderick, A., & Möller, K. (1998). Competitive positioning and the resource-based view of the firm. *Journal of Strategic Marketing, 6*(2), 97–116.

Hooley, G., Greenley, G., Fahy, J., & Cadogan, J. (2001, July). Market-focused resources competitive positioning and firm performance. *Journal of Marketing Management, 17*(5–6), 503–520.

Ibeh, K., Brock, J. K. U., & Zhou, Y. J. (2004). The drop and collect survey among industrial populations: Theory and empirical evidence. *Industrial Marketing Management, 33*(2), 155–165.

Iyer, P., Davari, A., Zolfagharian, M., & Paswan, A. (2019). Market orientation, positioning strategy and brand performance. *Industrial Marketing Management, 81*, 16–29.

Iyer, P., Rokonuzzaman, M., Paswan, A., & Alhidari, A. (2023). B2B brand positioning–A capability (exploration x exploitation) based typology: Cases from the Middle East. *Industrial Marketing Management, 108*, 178–189.

Kalafatis, S. P., Tsogas, M. H., & Blankson, C. (2000). Positioning strategies in business markets. *Journal of Business & Industrial Marketing, 15*(6), 416–437.

Kalafatis, S. P., Blankson, C., Boatswain, M. L., & Tsogas, M. H. (2020). Preference for action: Regulatory mode in B2B positioning decision-making. *Journal of Business & Industrial Marketing, 35*(12), 2111–2125.

Kalafatis, S. P., Blankson, C., Boatswain, M. L., & Tsogas, M. H. (2024). Positioning Strategies in B2B Marketing: The Regulatory Focus Orientation. *Journal of Business-to-Business Marketing*, 1–37.

Kalra, A., & Goodstein, R. C. (1998). The impact of advertising positioning strategies on consumer price sensitivity. *Journal of Marketing Research, 35*(2), 210–224.

Larreche, J. C., & Moinpour, R. (1983). Managerial judgment in marketing: The concept of expertise. *Journal of Marketing Research, 20*(2), 110–121.

Lindell, M. K., & Whitney, D. J. (2001). Accounting for common method variance in cross-sectional research designs. *Journal of Applied Psychology, 86*(1), 114–121.

Malhotra, N. K., Peterson, M., & Uslay, C. (2006). Helping marketing research earn a seat at the table for decision-making: An assessment and prescription for the future. *European Business Review, 18*(4), 294–306.

Mentzer, J. T., Flint, D. J., & Hult, G. T. M. (2001). Logistics service quality as a segment-customized process. *Journal of Marketing, 65*(4), 82–104.

Morgan, N. A., Kaleka, A., & Katsikeas, C. S. (2004). Antecedents of export venture performance: A theoretical model and empirical assessment. *Journal of Marketing, 68*(1), 90–108.

Nakata, C., & Sivakumar, K. (1996). National culture and new product development: An integrative review. *Journal of Marketing, 60*(1), 61–72.

Nakata, C., & Sivakumar, K. (2001). Instituting the marketing concept in a multinational setting: The role of national culture. *Journal of the Academy of Marketing Science, 29*(3), 255–276.

Narver, J. C., & Slater, S. F. (1990). The effect of a market orientation on business profitability. *Journal of Marketing, 54*(4), 20–35.

Noseworthy, T. J., & Trudel, R. (2011). Looks interesting, but what does it do? Evaluation of incongruent product form depends on positioning. *Journal of Marketing Research, 48*(6), 1008–1019.

Nunnally, J. C. (1978). *Psychometric theory* (2d ed.). McGraw-Hill.

Panda, S., Paswan, A. K., & Mishra, S. P. (2019). Impact of positioning strategies on franchise fee structure. *Industrial Marketing Management, 81*, 30–39.

Parasuraman, A., Zeithaml, V. A., & Berry, L. L. (1988). SERVQUAL: A multiple-item scale for measuring consumer perceptions of service quality. *Journal of Retailing, 64*(1), 12–40.

Piercy, N. F. (2005). *Market-led strategic change: A guide to transforming the process of going to market*. Elsevier Butterworth Heinemann.

Porter, M. E. (1996). What is strategy? *Harvard Business Review, 74*(6), 61–78.

Porter, M. E. (2001). Strategy and the internet. *Harvard Business Review*, 63–78.

Reinartz, W., Krafft, M., & Hoyer, W. D. (2004). The customer relationship management process: Its measurement and impact on performance. *Journal of Marketing Research, 41*(3), 293–305.

Ries, A., & Trout, J. (1986). *Positioning: The battle for your mind* (1st ed. revised). McGraw-Hill.

Slater, S. F., Hult, G. T. M., & Olson, E. M. (2007). On the importance of matching strategic behavior and target market selection to business strategy in high-tech markets. *Journal of the Academy of Marketing Science, 35*(1), 5–17.

Spector, P. E. (1992). *Summated rating scale construction*. SAGE Publications.

Spiro, R. L., & Weitz, B. A. (1990). Adaptive selling: Conceptualization, measurement, and nomological validity. *Journal of Marketing Research, 27*(1), 61–69.

Steenkamp, J. B. E., Ter Hofstede, F., & Wedel, M. (1999). A cross-national investigation into the individual and national cultural antecedents of consumer innovativeness. *Journal of Marketing, 63*(2), 55–69.

Suzuki, Y. (2000). The effect of airline positioning on profit. *Transportation Journal, 39*(3), 44–54.

The Economist. (2020). Africa goes pop: From Nollywood to Netflix. *September 19th - 25th, Volume 436 (9212)*, 79–80.

Verhoef, P. C., & Leeflang, P. S. H. (2009). Understanding the marketing department's influence within the firm. *Journal of Marketing, 73*(2) (March), 14–37.

Walsh, G., & Mitchell, V. W. (2005). Consumer vulnerability to perceived product similarity problems: Scale development and identification. *Journal of Macromarketing, 25*(2), 140–152.

Wind, Y. J. (1982). *Product policy: Concepts, methods, and strategy* (Vol. 8). Addison-Wesley Publishing Company.

Zellner, A. (1962). An efficient method of estimating seemingly unrelated regressions and test of aggregation bias. *Journal of the American Statistical Association, 57*, 500–509.

CHAPTER 10

Founders' Marketing Activities in the International Market Opportunity Recognition. A Study of Ghanaian Micro Women Entrepreneurs

Fanny Adams Quagrainie, Richard Afriyie Owusu, and Per Servais

Introduction

International market opportunity recognition (IMOR), which involves discovering international market segments, emerging trends, and potential gaps in customer demand, informs the development and implementation of global marketing strategies (Barba-Sánchez et al., 2019). It is one of the pillars of global marketing success (Thompson et al., 2020) as it underlies the survival and growth of small firms in the competitive international business environment (Torkkeli et al., 2019). This identification assumes heightened importance in the context of micro women's

F. A. Quagrainie (✉)
Ghana Institute of Management and Public Administration (GIMPA), Achimota, Ghana
e-mail: fquagrainie@gimpa.edu.gh

A. Gbadamosi et al. (eds.), *Contemporary Marketing Practices in Africa, Volume 1*, Palgrave Studies of Marketing in Emerging Economies,
https://doi.org/10.1007/978-3-032-27126-6_10

entrepreneurship in international business (Jamali, 2009; Kakeesh, 2024). Despite IMOR's central role, research indicates that scholarship on micro women entrepreneurs (MWEs) often overlooks it compared to their larger counterparts. This highlights a distinct divergence in the practical approach to IMOR of MWEs.

Micro businesses are challenged by their size, small number of employees, and low revenue (Boafo et al., 2022; Quagrainie et al., 2023). In their international operations, these businesses often display dynamism, rapidly responding to shifts and changes in the global market, demonstrating adaptability and resilience (Jeong et al., 2023). Their key marketing objectives include increasing visibility through greater customer awareness, finding and retaining customers, and boosting revenue growth (Atarah et al., 2025). These marketing activities are embedded in competencies and the values of the entrepreneurs. Drawing on human capital and social network theories, Mostafiz and Goh (2018) found that founders' international opportunity recognition skills are key success factors for international women entrepreneurs.

As most entrepreneurial activities result in products or services that must be sold through diverse marketing channels, researchers have emphasized the importance of marketing for success (Orth et al., 2007). This suggests that factors underlying successful international business operations include entrepreneurs' ability to identify and address market opportunities. While extensive literature delves into the dynamics of the founder's role in IMOR (Albimani et al., 2025) in women's entrepreneurship, this topic attracted little attention in international entrepreneurship studies until recently.

MWEs are accepted as a key to a society's well-being (Quagrainie, 2020), as entrepreneurship leverages economic and social development. Although some studies have examined MWEs (Mostafiz & Goh, 2018; Albimani et al., 2025), less is known about their IMOR (Swartz et al., 2022). Additionally, most entrepreneurial activities in Africa are deeply

R. A. Owusu · P. Servais
School of Business and Economics, Linnaeus University, Kalmar, Sweden
e-mail: Richard.Owusu@lnu.se

P. Servais
e-mail: per.servais@lnu.se

embedded at the indigenous level (Darley & Blankson, 2020), supporting the claim that the context of entrepreneurship should be considered in scholarship (Ben-Hafaïedh et al., 2024). This signals a gap in the literature regarding the nature of IMOR of African MWEs, their understanding, and their operational mechanisms. This clearly emphasizes the need for further research. Like most economic activities, IMOR is embedded in everyday actions. IMOR can be understood using the lens of practice. Using this lens, IMOR activities are not separate from their everyday performance. This implies that the explanation of IMOR is not possible without considering how these activities are practiced (Gross et al., 2014).

This study focuses on MWEs in developing economies due to the following reasons. First, such economies provide an opportunity to expand and understand the boundaries of theory and its applications (Foo et al., 2020) in a micro-business setting. Second, women's entrepreneurship has been reported to be fundamental for promoting inclusive economic growth in developing economies, according to the Global Entrepreneurship Monitor (GEM) 2023/2024 Report. Consequently, issues surrounding them are of great importance to policymakers and scholars, especially as the internationalization of MWEs is an economic development strategy. For example, the Ghanaian government is enhancing the internationalization of MWEs through the SheTrade Initiative, a tool aimed at reducing poverty and bridging gender inequality. Third, literature on international micro women entrepreneurship in developing economies is scarce. While the Global Entrepreneurship Monitor Report focuses more on women's entrepreneurship as a driver of international growth, there is still a lack of understanding about how women, compared to men, internationalize their business operations (Le Feuvre et al., 2023). Indeed, Yadav and Unni (2016, p. 1) reported that 'the existing theoretical concepts need to be expanded to better explain the uniqueness of women entrepreneurship as a subject of research inquiry.'

This study is influenced by recent calls for research to focus on understanding IMOR in a resource-constrained environment. Franczak et al., (2023 posit that more studies are needed on how international opportunities are recognized among MWEs. Thus, researchers have called for more studies on women entrepreneurs and their intentions and motivations toward international entrepreneurship opportunities in emerging markets (Alon & Rottig, 2013).

Presently, the prevailing IMOR literature predominantly concentrates less on MWEs, especially in developing economies, and therefore often overlooks the specific needs and challenges of these women on the international business journey. Nguyen et al. (2025), in their systematic review of micro and small women entrepreneurs, called for more studies as existing literature may neglect emerging entrepreneurial trends. They argued that a comprehensive understanding would emerge from the primary data and real-time case studies. This study tries to fill this gap. Specifically, the chapter investigates how MWEs engage with IMOR to shape their international marketing activities as they seek to identify and evaluate areas where they can create and deliver value, aiming to earn a return on their investment of personal effort and economic resources. This aim is guided by two research questions (RQs):

> RQ1: What are the international market opportunity recognition activities (IMOR) of Ghanaian micro women entrepreneurs (MWEs) engaged in international business? and
> RQ2: What are the outcomes of these IMOR activities?

This study takes the view that the IMOR processes in which MWEs engage in international markets are embedded in the competencies and resources available to these MWEs. Accordingly, in addition to market opportunity recognition research, the study draws on resource-based theory. Using these frameworks, IMOR is associated with MWE's ability to use and match its resources to recognize unmet demands in the international markets. The study argues that this perspective offers a conceptual framework for understanding the shaping and conditioning of IMOR practices. Given these perspectives and the research objectives, the unit of analysis is MWE IMOR activities. As suggested by the practice turn in entrepreneurship, empirical practice studies should focus on activity as the unit of analysis (Thompson et al., 2020). Accordingly, the study explores the IMOR activities of MWEs engaged in international marketing, employing a qualitative approach. Indeed, an emerging body of research in MWEs in international marketing has demonstrated the depth of understanding that can be achieved through this approach (Nguyen et al., 2025).

This study contributes to the IMOR in micro women entrepreneurship literature. First, it involves an understanding of IMOR as a socially situated, lived, and real experience. It brings the daily experience back into the practice of micro women entrepreneurship discourse and reinforces the emergent understanding of IMOR as a real-time practice. Therefore, there is a need to observe and explain the real-time practices of entrepreneurs in general and MWEs in particular, as advocated by practice theories and scholars. Second, there are few international business studies on the IMOR of MWEs in developing economies. Accordingly, this study sheds light on the call by Le Feuvre et al. (2023) for women to internationalize their business operations.

The remainder of the paper is structured as follows: First, a brief review of the literature on resource-based theory and its relation with IMOR is presented. This is followed by a description of the research methodology and a presentation of the study's findings. The paper concludes with a discussion of the findings and their implications from the perspective of international IMOR theory and practice, and offers avenues for future research.

The Context of the Study: Ghanaian Micro Women Entrepreneurs

It is generally believed that women entrepreneurs do not respond to the dynamic business environment in the same way as other entrepreneurs (Al-Dajani, 2022). This has been attributed to factors such as resource constraints (Franzke et al., 2022), limited entrepreneurial and management styles adopted in their operations (Boohene, 2008), and the types of businesses they operate. This difference can be attributed to both the conditions under which MWEs operate and the actions they undertake, as they are responsible for the operation and management of these businesses.

Research on women's entrepreneurship in Ghana has shown that women entrepreneurs are more risk-averse and conservative (Adom & Anambane, 2020) and are resilient, as they have demonstrated the capacity to overcome challenges (Quagrainie, 2020). They seize opportunities to develop and supply innovative goods and services (Lent, 2022; Quagrainie et al., 2023). In terms of their activities, they value autonomy (Quagrainie, 2020). Ghanaian women entrepreneurs relied on their family social capital as a base for successful business operations. Husbands hold a key position in their wives' lives, serving as a source of financial and emotional support (Islam et al., 2025). It is within these contexts that the entrepreneurial identity of Ghanaian women entrepreneurs is considered for this study.

Resource-Based Theory (RBV)

The RBV posits that valuable, unique, and non-substitutable resources are critical to competitiveness (Barney, 1991; Ngah & Wong, 2020). In line with this theory, MWEs can realize their ideas and opportunities for businesses by mobilizing resources available to them to identify opportunities in international markets. Although RBV is widely regarded as a fundamental that shapes business activities (Agrawal et al., 2025), few studies have examined how it explains IMOR among MWEs in developing economies. Their ability to compete demonstrates the importance of understanding how MWEs participate in IMOR activities. From this perspective, IMOR activities are deeply embedded in the MWE's unique resources.

Identification of Marketing Opportunities

Opportunity recognition is "characterized by being alert to potential business opportunities, actively searching for them, and gathering information about new ideas on products or services" (Kuckertz et al., 2017, p. 92). It involves one's ability to identify and capitalize on trends and new business concepts (Doanh et al., 2021). For many, the decision to engage in entrepreneurship depends on recognizing potential and feasible business opportunities in an environment characterized by high environmental uncertainty (Schmitt et al., 2018). IMOR, relating to international space, involves discovering opportunities in foreign markets and requires a specific set of marketing skills and knowledge (Karra et al., 2008) that span national borders and cultures.

This opportunity is discovered, recognized, created, or imagined according to the Kirzner school of thought, utilizing information on market conditions and developments. Kuckertz et al. (2017) posited that opportunity recognition in entrepreneurship involves being alert to potential business opportunities, actively seeking them, and gathering information about new product or service ideas. From a systems theoretical standpoint, IMOR is seen as a system's response to market inefficiencies.

Research Method

The methodology adopted to accomplish the study's objectives is qualitative, based on a narrative and observational methods. These approaches are considered appropriate for the study for the following reasons. First, the narrative approach was used to achieve the study's primary objective: to gain a better understanding of the marketing strategies micro women entrepreneurs use to identify international marketing opportunities. The approach enables participants in a study to share their stories based on their experiences related to the variables of interest (Haydon & van der Riet, 2017). This researcher hears the day-to-day and real-life practices of women entrepreneurs (Thompson et al., 2020). Third, practice orientation focuses on observational fieldwork, direct involvement at the site where practices occur. Observation was therefore used to address the call of Thompson et al. (2020) for a greater understanding of the diverse realities of entrepreneurs' lived experiences as they unfolded. Secondary data were obtained from the Ghana Export Promotion Council, the Association of Women Entrepreneurs, and organizations supporting women entrepreneurs, such as the United States Agency for International Development.

Sampling and Sample Size

The study's sample was identified through snowball and purposive sampling. Two MWEs engaged in international business known to the researcher were identified, and they, in turn, identified other MWEs. Purposive sampling has been widely applied in both marketing studies and MWEs, as it enables researchers to collect and obtain relevant data. The inclusion criteria used for sample selection were as follows: (1) the women being the owners of the business; (2) having engaged in international business, and (3) having operated for at least 5 years. According to Bvuma and Marnewick (2020), micro businesses that have operated for 5 years are likely to survive for the next 10 to 15 years.

MWEs engaged in the export of various items were invited to share their diverse experiences. Twenty-nine women were identified and contacted. Out of this number, 22 agreed to be interviewed. This number was appropriate as previous studies of women entrepreneurs have sampled comparable numbers. For example, Al-Shami et al. (2020) interviewed 18 entrepreneurs in their study of women who failed to develop their businesses. In exploring the main challenges rural women entrepreneurs in

Bangladesh face in sustaining their family entrepreneurship, Rahman et al. (2022) used data from 7.

Data Collection Instrument and Process

Our interview guide consisted of three sections: personal and business information, IMOR activities, and their outcomes. The questions were designed to elicit narratives of MWEs'international marketing activities and experiences regarding IMOR. We used probing and critical-event questioning to encourage respondents to provide more detailed responses rather than vague or general ones.

The interviews, which lasted approximately 45–60 minutes, were conducted mostly in Twi (a local Ghanaian language spoken fluently by most Ghanaians) and in English (for non-native Twi speakers who preferred English). Some interviewees declined to have their views recorded, even though they were assured of confidentiality. In those cases, one researcher took notes while the other focused on the interview questions. Their common reason was to protect their business secrets. After the interviews, we reviewed our notes with the interviewees. In addition, a follow-up observation was conducted at the offices of entrepreneurs with a physical business presence to gather more information and observe their IMOR activities.

Data Analysis

The data were analyzed using three processes: data condensation, data display, and conclusion. Data condensation involved reducing the collected data to a manageable size by selecting, focusing, abstracting, and transforming it. From the transcribed data, features reflecting IMOR and marketing processes were coded and assigned to themes based on Kuckertz et al. (2017) and the entrepreneurial and marketing literature. Data condensation and display were performed using Microsoft Excel spreadsheets. A content analysis method was used, in which codes, categories, and themes were developed from textual data (Kondracki et al., 2002).

Three steps of content analysis were: Step 1: This stage involves the coding of data by assigning codes to issues raised in responses obtained using the open coding method.

Step 2: It is the development of subcategories. This involves grouping similar codes into a cluster of subcategories.

Table 10.1 Inter-rater reliability estimates of IMOR activities

Types of IMOR activities	*Lowest value*	*Highest value*	*Average value*
Alertness to business opportunities	0.72	0.76	0.74
Searching for business opportunities	0.66	0.81	0.77
Gathering business information	0.65	0.90	0.76
Observing business trends	0.59	0.88	0.73
Engagement with stakeholders	0.61	0.75	0.65

Step 3: This stage involves the formation of categories and a framework, developed by combining subcategories into categories based on the research aim and theoretical insights from the literature review.

Kuckertz et al. (2017) model for business opportunity recognition—alertness to potential business opportunities (alertness), actively searching for business opportunities (searching), and gathering information about new ideas on products or services (gathering), observing changing trends in their environment (observing), and talking to stakeholders about their needs (engagement with stakeholders) —was used to classify the IMOR. Goodwin and Goodwin's (1985) inter-rater reliability estimator was used to determine the reliability of the themes. As shown in Table 10.1, the lowest, highest, and average estimates for each theme are provided. The lowest mean estimate was 0.59 (engagement with stakeholders), with the highest being 0.74 (searching for business opportunities).

Findings

This section discusses the findings from responses across three key themes: respondent profiling, MWE IMOR activities, and the outcomes of these IMOR activities.

Profile of Respondents

A summary of the data on the women's personal and business lives is presented in Table 10.2. The ages of the women range from 35 to 58 years, with a mean age of 47.42 years. This means the age is higher than the mean age at which women typically engage in entrepreneurship. Except for one woman with a basic education, most women had received secondary education, while 31.56 percent had post-secondary education (college or university). The businesses range in size from 2 to 5 employees, with a mean of 3.32 employees. The findings revealed that most of the women traded with European countries, with the United Kingdom making up 47.37 percent. This might be explained by Ghana's colonial link with the United Kingdom.

Table 10.2 Personal and business data of MWEs

MWEs Code	*age*	*Levelof education*	*Type of business*	*Ageof business*	*Locationof foreign business*	*Yearsbefore going inter-national*
M1	34	Secondary	Spices	6	London	3
M2	46	Tertiary	Clothing	7	France	2
M3	50	Secondary	Clothing	10	Holland	3
M4	39	Tertiary	Foodstuff	6	United Kingdom	4
M5	48	Secondary	Arts and Crafts	9	USA	2
M6	49	Basic	Arts and Crafts	12	United Kingdom	4
M7	57	Secondary	Foodstuff	10	USA	4
M8	58	Tertiary	Foodstuff	10	United Kingdom	3
M9	35	Tertiary	Clothing	8	United Kingdom	3
M10	53	Secondary	Paintings	8	USA	3
M11	50	Secondary	Foodstuff	11	Holland	5
M12	51	Secondary	Clothing	7	Holland	3
M13	48	Secondary	Clothing	8	USA	3
M14	39	Secondary	Foodstuff	6	United Kingdom	4
M15	50	Secondary	Foodstuff	12	Germany	5
M16	49	Tertiary	Spices	9	United Kingdom	3
M17	39	Secondary	Beauty products	6	United Kingdom	2
M18	56	Secondary	Foodstuff	11	United Kingdom	4
M19	50	Tertiary	Baskets	9	USA	3
M20	32	Tertiary	Clothing	9	Germany	3
M21	45	Basic	Beads	10	France	4
M22	41	Secondary	Crafts	8	USA	5

Table 10.3 IMOR themes and their behaviors

IMOR themes	*Examples of behaviors*
Alertnesstobusiness opportunities	• Being aware of and anticipating customer needs; • Spotting profitable business opportunities; • Recognizing potential customers • Identifying an unserved niche market
Searchingforbusiness opportunities	• Scanning the market; • Conducting market research • Analyzing government policies discussed on social media • Using business networks
Gatheringbusiness information	• Monitoring activities of other competitors; • Conducting customer surveys to address their needs and complaints; • Seek feedback from customers
Observation of changing business trends	• Attending trade fairs; • Following industry news
Engaging with stakeholders	• involving customers in meaningful exchanges; • personalizing customer experiences; • maintaining open communication channels

IMOR Activities

In all cases, MWEs were able to describe a variety of activities involving IMOR, as suggested by Kuckertz et al. (2017). The three themes that emerged from Kuckertz et al.'s (2017) models were alertness to business opportunities, searching for business opportunities, and gathering business information. From the analysis, two new themes related to IMOR that were not highlighted by Kuckertz et al. (2017) were identified. These are observations on changing business trends and stakeholder engagement, as discussed in the opportunity recognition literature. The sub-themes and their behaviors are presented in Table 10.3.

Alertness to Business Opportunities as IMOR Activity

Based on the data collected, 18 MWEs generally perceived being alert to business opportunities as important for identifying international market opportunities (see Table 10.3). Four items emerged as key indicators of alertness to business opportunities and activities. As highlighted by MWE 22: '. '*to see what is out there, you have to observe, to look for it. This principle is a truism for life, so it is also for entrepreneurship. Go out there and look for it, and you will find it*. This focus is consistent with the findings of Alshaketheep et al. (2025), who argued that a business's ability to anticipate unarticulated consumer needs is a critical frontier in strategic marketing. The finding is also in line with the RBV perspective, which holds that MWEs' internal resources condition their alertness to business opportunities.

Searching for Business Opportunities in IMOR Activity

Searching for business opportunities was found to consist of four IMOR activities by 18 MWEs. Scanning the market was the key activity. Looking for information on international business activities was reported to be achieved by scanning both the international and local business environments. For example, MWE 11 reported: '*it is a policy to spend at least 30 minutes a day on the internet to appreciate emerging issues*' and ' ..... *I call it a seventh sense. Most times, you can read between the lines to separate economic opportunities from not-so-profitable opportunities*. Additionally, MWEs can search for information by '*conducting market research*' (MWE 12), *analyzing government policies being discussed on various social media platforms daily* (MWE 09), and '*using business networks*' (MWE 20). Previous studies have highlighted the importance of business networks for successful operations. Business networks are a key resource for entering the Chinese market in the luxury and fashion industries (Rovai, 2025).

Gathering of Business Information as an IMOR Activity

Three activities were identified among 16 MWEs associated with gathering business information on new product or service ideas. Businesses cannot operate without information. For MWE 18, it is monitoring competitors' activities. She added that: '*The key ingredient for coming up with an opportunity is to gather information. Not any information, but relevant information about the happening in the market*. This underlies the entrepreneur's ability to discover and capture trends (Hassan et al., 2020). For MWE 03, it calls for '*conducting customer surveys to address their needs and complaints that as they engage with the businesses*, while MWE 19 said: *seeking feedback from customers provides businesses with invaluable data.*' These positions are supported by studies from Ferreira et al. (2023) and Bilro et al. (2023). Using the RBV framework, this activity is considered strategic, as MWEs can gather valuable information and present it, thereby identifying unserved market opportunities.

New IMOR Activities: Observation as an IMOR Activity

Using the Oxford Reference Dictionary's definition of observation as a guide, this study defines market observation activity as the systematic monitoring of changing market trends to collect business information. As indicated in Table 10.3, two behaviors—attending trade fairs and following industry news—emerged as associated with observation. The interviews revealed that observing changing trends in their environment is key for IMOR. The argument can be made that this activity is a precursor to IMOR (AlMulhim, 2023), as it equips MWEs with timely knowledge of market occurrences (Shaik et al., 2024). The entrepreneur's ability to make sense of these insights paves the way for detecting gaps and creating value to address them.

Eleven MWEs highlighted the importance of observation as an IMOR activity. According to MWE 09, a trade fair is an opportunity to see and learn about what others have developed. '*There is nothing new under the sun. To me, innovation stems from the known to the unknown. Look at what others have come up with, identify the gaps, and in addressing them, you come up with something new.*' The importance of trade fairs to IMOR has been mentioned in the literature. Kourkouridis et al.'s (2023) study on trade fairs in Greece found that these fairs have economic effects on residents of Thessaloniki.

Following industry news, another behavior reported during the interviews, as aligning with this theme, is a critical antecedent of IMOR. In this sense, observation moves beyond physical settings by including the monitoring and evaluation of signals and insights from industrial news and reports. The ability to interpret such information is a valuable resource, as it helps businesses identify market gaps. Two quotes illustrated this: '*I most times interact with others, especially my customers, to acquire new information on emerging styles. Our business rests entirely on new styles* (MWE 3), and *I engage with my clients for two reasons. One is for them to always remember me when selecting beads for their special occasion, and for me to put myself in their place and understand their needs as well* (MWE 04). With this approach, MWEs are equipped with a resource to sort out and thus prevent the dissemination of fake news (Farhoudinia et al., 2025).

Engagement with Stakeholders as an IMOR Activity

Comments related to the engagement with stakeholders as IMOR activity were also extracted from the interviews. A new IMOR activity was defined to represent these behaviors, with literature on stakeholder theory. This perspective argues that ensuring the business's long-term sustainability calls for deliberate interaction between the business and its stakeholders. This is vital for co-creating value, which, according to Polat (2022), depends on their competencies. In the present study, three behaviors cited by the 15 MWEs relate to this behavior (see Table 10.3). The MWEs trusted and relied on their stakeholders for business support and advice.

As mentioned by MWE 13: '*I do not know it all. So, what I do is constantly seek my customers' views on what is in vogue. It is in addressing their needs that I get money. How better to do this than to engage with them?* Following evidence of a link between customer engagement and understanding market needs, it can be said that the ability to engage with stakeholders is a valuable resource for IMOR. This observation is consistent with the marketing focus on positive engagement for value co-creation or destruction (Nangpiire et al., 2022).

Outcomes of IMOR Activities on Marketing

During interviews, MWEs described their IMOR relationship with the development of the products offered to their international customers, which came across as their IMOR relationship. For example, MWE 04 explained: '*identification of an opportunity on the international market, turning the opportunity into an idea, and successfully implementing the business idea is the beginning of becoming an international entrepreneur.*' Likewise, MWE 16 acknowledged that MOR is important in determining which products to send to the market. '...... *information from my sister gave me the idea of preparing local spices for sale in the United Kingdom.*' These responses reinforce the claim that information is essential for identifying market demands and practices, thereby creating new opportunities for product development (Naeem & Di Maria, 2022).

By using their creativity, analytical skills, and observant nature, some MWEs identified opportunities in the international market, enabling them to address their personal needs. To this group, entrepreneurship is creating value in the market to solve a problem. Two illustrative examples of the value of this relationship are provided. '*I have always loved to be in charge of what I do, and I know I can only do that by finding a problem and solving it (*MWE 17). '*There is going to be a time when I will retire, and I cannot stay at home. What else to do then to get something going until it is time to sign out*' (MWE 18).

These responses support the claim in social marketing theory that calls for applying marketing principles and practices to solve problems. Thus, this study supports the claim that social marketing broadens the boundaries and context of marketing practice by shifting the focus from profit-making to the creation of social value (Domegan, 2008) and the claim that marketing has evolved beyond the sales and marketing eras (Grewal et al., 2025).

Building networks was another marketing practice associated with IMOR that emerged from the analysis. In marketing, networking enables entrepreneurs to build and maintain mutually beneficial relationships. Networking is a business resource for opening doors to collaborations, gaining access to resources, technology, and customers (McGrath & O'Toole, 2021). Some of the phrases used associated with networking are: '*I believe in working with others*' (MWE 03), '*building business alliances*' (MWE 19), '*collaborating with other businesses or entrepreneurs,*' and '*value co-creation*' (MWE 08). These examples demonstrated a key role of IMOR in marketing networking practice. This aligns with relationship marketing theory, which emphasizes the importance of building and maintaining mutually beneficial relationships (Grönroos, 1995).

IMOR was also found to inform MWEs'sales strategies. The way IMOR is developed through engagement and interaction in the market provides the structure and content for how products must be sold. In this way, IMOR delivers a framework for tracking and analyzing why and how customers demand a business's products or services. MWE 08 commented, '*how to sell your products is dependent on what gave birth to the need for the products.*' The ability to link IMOR with marketing practice was seen as a critical practice and resource that MWEs need to deliver their products or services to customers identified in the market.

Discussion of the Findings

The identification of IMOR activities using Kuckertz et al.'s (2017) model reveals commonalities. It offers a reasonable degree of cross-cultural generalizability for the three activities: alertness to business opportunities, searching for business opportunities, and gathering business information. Analysis of the findings reveals that IMOR is embedded in the resources MWEs possess, facilitating an understanding of IMOR through these resources and practices. In Ghana, it is evident that IMOR influences choices and marketing practices, implying the importance of culture in IMOR activities (Darley & Blankson, 2020). The narratives of MWE marketing practice capture the nature of IMOR. Marketing practice is demonstrated in the meanings MWEs attach to their choices and practices made. The data show that marketing practices are generated and maintained when market opportunities are identified. These conditions refer to the practices of MEWs, in which they undertake their marketing activities. Hence, the presence of IMOR is an enabler for marketing practice (Naeem & Di Maria, 2022).

The possible expansion of Kuckertz et al.'s (2017) model, incorporating observation and engagement with stakeholders as potential IMOR activities, supports the dynamic nature of entrepreneurial and marketing activities (Mostafiz et al., 2025). A possible explanation for this observation is the heavy reliance on technology in entrepreneurial and marketing practices (McGrath & O'Toole, 2021). Increasingly, businesses are turning to technology to conduct their marketing operations.

Implications of the Study

Theoretical Implication

In terms of research approach, this chapter demonstrates that complex activities associated with IMOR and marketing practices can be fully understood in the context of and through the belief systems (Darley & Blankson, 2020) of micro women's entrepreneurship, employing qualitative research methods. Thus, by analyzing the activities associated with IMOR and their impact on marketing practices in their context, a deeper understanding of the breadth of marketing practices can be developed. The link between IMOR and marketing practices established in this study makes a unique contribution to understanding the antecedents of marketing practices. The study also provides empirical validation of

Kuckertz et al.'s (2017) work and supports the argument that IMOR is embedded in the resources that entrepreneurs possess. Unlike existing studies that focus on large MNEs, this study examines IMOR practices among small women-owned enterprises. Indeed, the existing literature acknowledges this knowledge scarcity on how international opportunities are recognized (Franczak et al., 2023; Nguyen et al., 2025), and their relationship with marketing (Risitano et al., 2025).) among MWEs and highlights the need for more research (Yadav & Unni, 2016; Xu et al., 2021).

The resource-based theoretical perspective used in this study provides a richer understanding of how marketing practices occur within a complex of IMOR. By elucidating the interplay between IMOR and marketing practices, this study offers a framework that bridges the gap between the two concepts.

Managerial Implication

For practice, the findings support the claim that IMOR is vital to marketing practices. The study therefore shows the importance and need for MWEs to base and relate their marketing practices to their IMOR. Understanding IMOR through the lens of resource-based theory is crucial, as it offers valuable insights for women entrepreneurs in general and MWEs in particular. This leads to better positioning and sustainable competitive advantage within its context (Ben-Hafaïedh et al., 2024).

Understanding marketing practice through the lens of IMOR is important because it provides MWEs with knowledge about how they should operate their businesses. By using the resource-based approach, the study offers MWEs that reflect the realities of marketing practice. This is because the resource-based approach focuses on the actual IMOs and marketing practices of MWEs as they engage in their entrepreneurial activities within their specific entrepreneurial environment (Bullough et al., 2022). By doing so, it addresses the problem of an unclear association between IMOR and marketing practice (Ben-Hafaïedh et al., 2024).

Limitations of the Study and Directions for Future Research

This study was limited to the IMOR experiences of Ghanaian MWEs, a country with a challenging business environment (Quagrainie, 2020). Hence, the situation of MWEs in other developing economies may differ significantly due to the context of entrepreneurship. Future research should investigate MWEs, their IMOR activities, and the relationship between these activities and their marketing practices in various economic contexts. This would allow for a more complete understanding of the relationship.

Conclusion

This study's problem area was founded on three major issues: the importance of women's entrepreneurship for economic development, the necessity of recognizing international market opportunities, and the contributions of research findings in emerging markets to global business theory and practice. Previous research has shown that entrepreneurship in developing countries is characterized by informality, small size, male dominance (Boafo et al., 2022; Quagrainie et al., 2023), a low percentage of international business, and a lack of research on its internationalization (Alon & Rottig, 2013; Franczak et al., 2023; Ben-Hafaïedh et al., 2024).

Therefore, our study aimed to gain a deeper understanding of how MWEs perceive international opportunities and their outcomes, and to contribute to the development of international business theory and practice.

In conclusion, the findings supported and empirically validated three categories of Kuckertz et al.'s (2017) model for IMOR: alertness to business opportunities, searching for business opportunities, and gathering business information. In addition, we found two new categories—observation and engagement with stakeholders as potential IMOR activities. The findings support the dynamic nature of entrepreneurial and marketing activities for market opportunity recognition (Mostafiz et al., 2025). A possible explanation for the new findings is the recent reliance on technology in entrepreneurial and marketing practices (McGrath & O'Toole, 2021). Increasingly, businesses are turning to technology to conduct their marketing operations. The results suggest cross-cultural similarities in these activities, as well as the uniqueness of the model in the context of Ghanaian micro women entrepreneurship, with the identification of two new IMOR activities required for operating within the Ghanaian setting.

References

Adom, K., & Anambane, G. (2020). Understanding the role of culture and gender stereotypes in women's entrepreneurship through the lens of the stereotype threat theory. *Journal of Entrepreneurship in Emerging Economies, 12*(1), 100–124.

Agrawal, R., Samadhiya, A., Banaitis, A., & Kumar, A. (2025). Entrepreneurial barriers in achieving sustainable business and cultivation of innovation: A resource-based view theory perspective. *Management Decision, 63*(4), 1207–1228.

Albimani, N. M., Thottoli, M. M., Almahrouqi, A. T., & Alkhaldi, N. G. (2025). Enhancing entrepreneurial opportunity exploitation through AI: the mediating role of dynamic capabilities. *Journal of Ethics in Entrepreneurship and Technology*. e-ISSN: 2633-7444 p-ISSN: 2633-7436. https://doi.org/10.1108/JEET-03-2025-0013

Al-Dajani, H. (2022). Refugee women's entrepreneurship: Where from and where to next? *International Journal of Gender and Entrepreneurship, 14*(4), 489–498.

AlMulhim, A. F. (2023). Knowledge management capability and organizational performance: A moderated mediation model of environmental dynamism and opportunity recognition. *Business Process Management Journal, 29*(6), 1655–1679.

Al-Shami, S., Mamun, A. A., Sidek, S., & Rashid, N. (2020). Causes of failure among Malaysian female entrepreneurs: A qualitative case study of Malaysian microcredit borrowers. *Qualitative Research in Financial Markets, 12*(1), 43–71.

Alon, I., & Rottig, D. (2013). Entrepreneurship in emerging markets: New insights and directions for future research. *Thunderbird International Business Review, 55*(5), 487–492.

Alshaketheep, K., Al-Ahmed, H., & Mansour, A. (2025). Beyond purchase patterns: Harnessing predictive analytics to anticipate unarticulated consumer needs. *Acta Psychologica, 257*, Article 105089.

Atarah, B. A., Kumasey, A. S., Obeng Ahwireng, P., & Bamfo, B. A. (2025). Relying on what they know: marketing communication tools and female entrepreneurs in developing countries. *Journal of Research in Marketing and Entrepreneurship*.

Barba-Sánchez, V., Arias-Antúnez, E., & Orozco-Barbosa, L. (2019). Smart cities as a source for entrepreneurial opportunities: Evidence for Spain. *Technological Forecasting and Social Change, 148*, Article 119713.

Barney, J. (1991). Firm resources and sustained competitive advantage. *Journal of Management, 17*(1), 99–120.

Ben-Hafaïedh, C., Xheneti, M., Stenholm, P., Blackburn, R., Welter, F., & Urbano, D. (2024). The interplay of context and entrepreneurship: the new frontier for contextualisation research. *Small Business Economics, 62*(2), 571–582.

Bilro, R. G., Loureiro, S. M. C., & Souto, P. (2023). A systematic review of customer behavior in business-to-business markets and an agenda for future research. *Journal of Business & Industrial Marketing, 38*(13), 122–142.

Boafo, C., Owusu, R. A., & Guiderdoni-Jourdain, K. (2022). Understanding internationalization of informal African firms through a network perspective. *International Small Business Journal: Researching Entrepreneurship, 40*(5), 618–649.

Boohene, R. (2009). The relationships among gender, strategic capabilities, and performance of small retail firms in Ghana. *Journal of African Business, 10*(1), 121–138.

Bullough, A., Guelich, U., Manolova, T. S., & Schjoedt, L. (2021). Women's entrepreneurship and culture: gender role expectations and identities, societal culture, and the entrepreneurial environment. *Small business economics, 58*(2), 985.

Bvuma, S., & Marnewick, C. (2020). Sustainable livelihoods of the township's small, medium, and micro enterprises towards growth and development. *Sustainability, 12*(8), 3149.

Darley, W. K., & Blankson, C. (2020). Sub-Saharan African cultural belief system and entrepreneurial activities: A Ghanaian perspective. *Africa Journal of Management, 6*(2), 67–84.

Doanh, D. C., Thang, H. N., Nga, N. T. V., Van, P. T., & Hoa, P. T. (2021). Entrepreneurial behaviour: The effects of the fear and anxiety of COVID-19 and business opportunity recognition. *Entrepreneurial Business and Economics Review, 9*(3), 7–23.

Domegan, C. T. (2008). Social marketing: Implications for contemporary marketing practices classification scheme. *Journal of Business & Industrial Marketing, 23*(2), 135–141.

Farhoudinia, B., Ozturkcan, S., & Kasap, N. (2025). Fake news in business and management literature: A systematic review of definitions, theories, methods, and implications. *Aslib Journal of Information Management, 77*(2), 306–329.

Ferreira, C., Robertson, J., Chohan, R., Pitt, L., & Foster, T. (2023). The writing is on the wall: Predicting customers' evaluation of customer-firm interactions using computerized text analysis. *Journal of Service Theory and Practice, 33*(2), 309–327.

Foo, M. D., Vissa, B., & Wu, B. (2020). Entrepreneurship in emerging economies. *Strategic Entrepreneurship Journal, 14*(3), 289–301.

Franczak, J., Lanivich, S. E., & Adomako, S. (2023). Filling institutional voids: Combinative effects of institutional shortcomings and gender on the alertness–Opportunity recognition relationship. *Journal of Business Research, 155*, Article 113444.

Franzke, S., Wu, J., Froese, F. J., & Chan, Z. X. (2022). Female entrepreneurship in Asia: A critical review and future directions. *Asian Business & Management, 21*(3), 343–372.

Goodwin, L. D., & Goodwin, W. L. (1985). An analysis of statistical techniques used in the Journal of Educational Psychology, 1979–1983. *Educational Psychologist, 20*(1), 13–21.

Grewal, D., Guha, A., Beccacece Satornino, C., & Becker, M. (2025). The future of marketing and marketing education. *Journal of Marketing Education, 47*(1), 61–77.

Gross, N., Carson, D., & Jones, R. (2014). Beyond rhetoric: Re-thinking entrepreneurial marketing from a practice perspective. *Journal of Research in Marketing and Entrepreneurship, 16*(2), 105–127.

Grönroos, C. (1995). Relationship marketing: The strategy continuum. *Journal of the Academy of Marketing Science, 23*(4), 252–254.

Hassan, S. H., Zeqiri, J., Ramadani, V., Zhen, T. S., Azman, N. H. N., & Mahmud, I. (2020). Individual factors, facilitating conditions and career success: Insights from Malaysian female entrepreneurs. *Journal of Enterprising Culture, 28*(04), 375–400.

Haydon, G., & van der Riet, P. (2017). Narrative inquiry: A relational research methodology suitable to explore narratives of health and illness. *Nordic Journal of Nursing Research, 37*(2), 85–89.

Islam, M. S., Azizzadeh, F., Islam, M. S., Adrita, U. W., Mazumder, A. H., & Akhter, R. (2025). Phenomenological insights into socio-psychological and network dynamics of women entrepreneurs. *Journal of Trade Science, 13*(2), 128–146.

Jamali, D. (2009). Constraints and opportunities facing women entrepreneurs in developing countries: A relational perspective. *Gender in Management: An International Journal, 24*(4), 232–251.

Kakeesh, D. F. (2024). Female entrepreneurship and entrepreneurial ecosystems. *Journal of Research in Marketing and Entrepreneurship, 26*(3), 485–526.

Karra, N., Phillips, N., & Tracey, P. (2008). Building the born global firm: Developing entrepreneurial capabilities for international new venture success. *Long Range Planning, 41*(4), 440–458.

Kondracki, N. L., Wellman, N. S., & Amundson, D. R. (2002). Content analysis: Review of methods and their applications in nutrition education. *Journal of Nutrition Education and Behavior, 34*(4), 224–230.

Kourkouridis, D., Frangopoulos, Y., & Kapitsinis, N. (2023). Socio-economic effects of trade fairs on host cities from a citizens' perspective: The case of Thessaloniki, Greece. *International Journal of Event and Festival Management, 14*(1), 113–133.

Kuckertz, A., Kollmann, T., Krell, P., & Stöckmann, C. (2017). Understanding, differentiating, and measuring opportunity recognition and opportunity exploitation. *International Journal of Entrepreneurial Behavior & Research, 23*(1), 78–97.

Le Feuvre, N., Davoine, E., & Cangià, F. (2023). When mobility meets gender in the transnational life-course. In *Withstanding vulnerability throughout adult life: Dynamics of stressors, resources, and reserves* (pp. 67–89). Springer Nature Singapore.

Lent, M. C. (2022). Entrepreneuring in necessity contexts: Effecting change among widow entrepreneurs in Northern Ghana. *Entrepreneurship & Regional Development, 34*(7–8), 630–649.

McGrath, H., & O'Toole, T. (2021). Early-stage network engagement strategies in the network capability development of new ventures. *Journal of Business & Industrial Marketing, 36*(9), 1600–1613.

Mostafiz, I., & Goh, S. K. (2018). International women entrepreneurs and international opportunity recognition skills for start-up ventures. *Journal for International Business and Entrepreneurship Development, 11*(3), 201–220.

Mostafiz, M. I., Ahmed, F. U., & Hughes, P. (2025). Open innovation pathway to firm performance: The role of dynamic marketing capability in Malaysian entrepreneurial firms. *International Journal of Entrepreneurial Behavior & Research, 31*(2/3), 673–701.

Naeem, H. M., & Di Maria, E. (2022). Customer participation in new product development: An Industry 4.0 perspective. *European Journal of Innovation Management*, *25*(6), 637–655.

Nangpiire, C., Silva, J., & Alves, H. (2022). Customer engagement and value co-creation/destruction: The internal fostering and hindering factors and actors in the tourist/hotel experience. *Journal of Research in Interactive Marketing, 16*(2), 173–188.

Ngah, R., & Wong, K. Y. (2020). Linking knowledge management to competitive strategies of knowledge-based SMEs. *The Bottom Line, 33*(1), 42–59.

Nguyen, T. B., Kumar, M., Sahoo, D. K., Nain, N., Yadav, M., & Dadhich, V. (2025). Mapping the landscape of women entrepreneurs in micro and small enterprises: Trends, themes, and insights through systematic review and text mining. *F1000Research, 14*, 422.

Orth, U. R., Lockshin, L., & d'Hauteville, F. (2007). The global wine business as a research field. *International Journal of Wine Business Research, 19*(1), 5–13.

Polat, G. (2022). A dynamic business model for Turkish techno parks: Looking through the lenses of service perspective and stakeholder theory. *Journal of Science and Technology Policy Management, 13*(2), 244–272.

Quagrainie, F. A. (2020). Are small women entrepreneurs resilient? Highlighting the roles of entrepreneurial competencies and motivation. *International Journal of Business and Globalisation, 25*(3), 361–377.

Quagrainie, F. A., Adams, S., Kabalan, A. A. M., & Dankwa, A. D. (2023). Women micro entrepreneurship and social inclusion: The moderating role of individual perceptual factors. *Journal of African Business, 24*(1), 77–94.

Rahman, S. A., Khan, G. M., AlAbri, S., & Taghizadeh, S. K. (2022). The role of intellectual capital on entrepreneurial opportunity recognition among SMEs in the Sultanate of Oman. *Journal of Intellectual Capital, 23*(4), 816–839.

Risitano, M., La Ragione, G., Turi, A., & Ferretti, M. (2025). Analysing the relevance of value creation in the interconnection amongst entrepreneurship, marketing, and innovation: a systematic literature review. *International Journal of Entrepreneurial Behavior & Research, 31*(2/3), 781–809.

Rovai, S. (2025). Building business network relationships in the changing Chinese context: Findings from Italian luxury companies. *Journal of Business & Industrial Marketing, 40*(4), 911–924.

Shaik, A. S., Jain, M., Mendiratta, A., Alarifi, G., & Arrigo, E. (2024). Role of strategic knowledge management practices in enhancing strategic perspectives of an organisation to improve entrepreneurial performance. *Journal of Knowledge Management, 28*(6), 1648–1675.

Schmitt, A., Rosing, K., Zhang, S. X., & Leatherbee, M. (2018). A dynamic model of entrepreneurial uncertainty and business opportunity identification: Exploration as a mediator and entrepreneurial self-efficacy as a moderator. *Entrepreneurship Theory and Practice, 42*(6), 835–859.

Swartz, E. M., Scheepers, C. B., & Toefy, T. (2022). Women entrepreneurs' opportunity identification of digital platform start-ups: emerging evidence from South Africa. *International Journal of Gender and Entrepreneurship, 14*(3), 352–374.

Thompson, N. A., Verduijn, K., & Gartner, W. B. (2020). Entrepreneurship-as-practice: Grounding contemporary theories of practice in to entrepreneurship studies. *Entrepreneurship & Regional Development, 32*(3–4), 247–256.

Torkkeli, L., Kuivalainen, O., Saarenketo, S., & Puumalainen, K. (2019). Institutional environment and network competence in successful SME internationalisation. *International Marketing Review, 36*(1), 31–55.

Xu, F., He, X., & Yang, X. (2021). A multilevel approach linking entrepreneurial contexts to subjective Well-Being: Evidence from rural chinese entrepreneurs: F. Xu et al. *Journal of Happiness Studies, 22*(4), 1537–1561.

Yadav, V., & Unni, J. (2016). Women entrepreneurship: Research review and future directions. *Journal of Global Entrepreneurship Research, 6*, 1–18.

CHAPTER 11

The Intersection of Indigenous Culture and Youth Marketing in Africa

Knowledge Shumba, Ntswaki Matlala, Yvonne Karasi, Chido Shambare, and Richard Shambare

Introduction

Due to its predominantly youthful population, Africa offers virgin ground for studying youth marketing. Globally, Africa has the world's youngest population; approximately 70 per cent of its population is under 30 years

K. Shumba
Stellenbosch University, Stellenbosch, South Africa
e-mail: 30819563@sun.ac.za

N. Matlala
University of Johannesburg, Johannesburg, South Africa
e-mail: ntswaki.matlala@jbs.ac.za

Y. Karasi
Tshwane University of Technology, Pretoria, South Africa
e-mail: Yvonnekarasi42@gmail.com

C. Shambare
University of the Western Cape, Cape Town, South Africa
e-mail: michelleshambare7@gmail.com

A. Gbadamosi et al. (eds.), *Contemporary Marketing Practices in Africa, Volume 1*, Palgrave Studies of Marketing in Emerging Economies,
https://doi.org/10.1007/978-3-032-27126-6_11

old (United Nations, 2025). Latest data reveals that by 2050, African youths will account for over one-third of the world's youth population (Ichikowitz Family Foundation, 2024). Therefore, marketers neglecting the African youth market do so at their own peril. Against this background, surveying the African youth marketing landscape makes a lot of sense from both theoretical and practical perspectives. Marketers ought not only to uncover the salient intricacies of the young consumer market but also to understand the consumer behaviour that results. For instance, the influence of culture on young consumers remains poorly understood (Shavitt & Cho, 2016). In particular, the growing influence of *Ubuntu* among African youths is receiving widespread recognition (Mathebula & Martinez-Vargas, 2023). *Ubuntu* is a highly pervasive African philosophy and cultural posture that affects almost all facets of life among Africans, including consumer behaviour. Even though the latter is gaining popularity in the media and on social media platforms, academic research on the topic remains sparse. For that reason, this chapter is opportune to consider the interconnection between culture, with a special focus on Ubuntu, and young consumer behaviour.

Ubuntu is a cultural belief and a way of life commonly practised in Africa and among African communities that prescribes that to live a rewarding life, one should seek to uphold and pursue communal objectives over personal goals. In other words, in all aspects of life, one's needs and aspirations are subservient to those of the community. *Ubuntu* is central to the African way of life. It influences virtually every dimension of life among the peoples of Africa. *Ubuntu* embodies communalism and heightens consumers' levels of social awareness and social responsibility. The latter is a departure from the Western concept of a consumer. It is not that in Western markets, communities, and society do not exist; they do. But they exert a totally different influence on the individual consumer. In the Western context, consumers are individuals pursuing their personal objectives. Therefore, Western marketing emphasises the needs, wants, and aspirations of individuals. In contrast, marketing in African societies differs. The separation between the individual and

R. Shambare (✉)
University of Fort Hare, Alice, South Africa
e-mail: RShambare@ufh.ac.za

community is much more difficult to discern. Naturally, *Ubuntu* triggers, within consumers, the need to respond to communal needs first before personal ones. As a result, this introduces an additional layer of marketing complexity that marketers need to consider. Naturally, with a growing African youth population, the marketers' urgency to understand *Ubuntu* and its implications on young consumer marketing is all too clear.

To present these arguments, the remainder of the chapter is structured as follows. In the next section, emerging trends in youth consumer behaviour in Africa are discussed. This is followed by a discussion on the foundations of indigenous ethical philosophies. The section is then followed by: Ubuntu and its implications for youth marketing, ethical challenges in marketing to African youth, and opportunities for ethical youth marketing inspired by indigenous Values. These sections are also followed by some case studies on how *Ubuntu* has been incorporated into marketing strategies. Lastly, the chapter concludes by discussing the future directions and implications of ethical considerations related to *Ubuntu* and youth marketing in Africa.

Emerging Trends in Youth Consumer Behaviour in Africa

Young consumers (35 years old or younger) are a distinct consumer segment with unique needs, aspirations, motivations, and behaviours (Ichikowitz Family Foundation, 2024). Beyond just the age factor, youth consumers are distinct in that they are:

a) *Digital natives:* Unlike other consumers, young consumers were born and grew up in a world characterised by the internet, mobile phones, social media, and on-demand access to information, making them not only highly adaptive but also receptive to digital technologies. Social media platforms such as TikTok, Instagram, Snapchat, WhatsApp, and Facebook dominate their digital ecosystems (McKinsey & Company, 2021; Smith, 2019).
b) *Cultural plurality:* Youths are not monolithic. Despite Africa being culturally diverse, spanning more than 3000 ethnic groups and languages, youths in Africa transcend beyond these cultural distinctions. They represent their own culture and identity. For instance, a young consumer in Nairobi may express digital activism through #EndPlasticPollution campaigns, while their counterpart in Johannesburg might connect through Amapiano music, and in Lagos

through Afrobeats culture. This cultural plurality requires brands to adopt nuanced, context-sensitive strategies rather than one-size-fits-all approaches.

c) Brand conscious: African youth value authenticity, inclusivity, and purpose-driven engagement. Surveys reveal that they expect brands to go beyond transactional relationships by demonstrating genuine social responsibility, cultural respect, and transparency (Prasanna & Priyanka, 2024). Ubuntu's philosophy resonates strongly here, as young people increasingly align themselves with brands that prioritise community welfare and fairness over hyper-individualism
d) Digital activists and Social Consciousness: Movements such as #EndSARS in Nigeria and climate activism in Uganda show how youth merge consumption with advocacy, favouring brands that support justice, sustainability, and equity.
e) Cultural hybrids: African youth seamlessly blend global influences with local traditions, creating new cultural products like Afrobeats, Amapiano, and youth-driven streetwear brands. This "global" identity reshapes markets and influences global pop culture.
f) Prone to influencer and peer-to-peer marketing: Young consumers place significant trust in influencers and peer networks. However, they are becoming more critical of inauthentic endorsements, leading to a demand for transparent influencer practices (Shamim & Islam, 2022).

Young consumers in Africa differ from older generations in that their consumption choices are increasingly shaped by digital connectivity and social identity, yet many still draw on the *Ubuntu* philosophy, which emphasises community, shared humanity, and mutual care. Unlike the individualistic tendencies seen in global youth markets, African youth often seek products and brands that reflect collective values and social responsibility. *Ubuntu* encourages them to view consumption not merely as self-expression, but as a means of uplifting others and sustaining communal well-being. This blending of modern digital lifestyles with Ubuntu's communal ethics gives rise to a unique, socially conscious youth consumer culture.

Foundations of Ubuntu Indigenous Ethical Philosophy

The philosophical foundations of *Ubuntu* provide a moral compass deeply rooted in African communal life and ethics. This section explores the core principles that underpin the Ubuntu community, relationality, respect, and mutual care, and contrasts them with Western individualist worldviews to highlight how African thought prioritises interdependence over autonomy. Understanding these ethical underpinnings is essential for situating *Ubuntu* as both a theoretical framework and a practical guide for human relationships, business ethics, and socially responsible marketing within African contexts.

Core Principles of Ubuntu: Community, Relationality, Respect, and Mutual Care

The *Ubuntu* philosophy embodies a communal viewpoint that emphasises shared responsibility, mutual trust, and the interconnectedness of individuals within a community. As such, the philosophy of *"ubuntu"*, which emanated from the phrase "I am, because you are", holds significant power within the African context (Tynan, 2021). *Ubuntu* signifies the foundational concepts of human interconnectedness and compassion, as expressed in the Shona phrase *"munhu munhu, nevanhu"*, which embodies the essence of "*Ubuntu or Hunhu*" (Mbiti, 1990).

Table 11.1 above presents a comparative analysis of Ubuntu, an African philosophy that promotes collectivism, and the Western concept of individualism. Du Toit (2021) elaborates that *Ubuntu,* as an African philosophy, constrains individualism and stresses the significance of social interrelations and responsibilities as prerequisites for human existence, suggesting that individual identity is derived from communal experiences. On the contrary, individualism, independence, and self-expression are promoted in Western civilization within the broader socialisation framework (Datta & Garikipati, 2019). The distinction lies in whether individuals identify as "I" or "We"—where "I think, therefore I am" is the key principle embodying individualism, while "I am, because we are" is the key underlying principle of collectivism (*Ubuntu*). This implies that in an individualist society (Western), people are expected to take care of themselves and their family, whereas in collectivist cultures (African), this is not the case.

Table 11.1 Comparative analysis: Ubuntu vs. Western individualism

Aspect	*Western Individualism*	*Ubuntu*	*Ubuntu Implications for Marketing*
Core philosophy	The individual is autonomous and independent	The individual is interconnected and inseparable from the community	Market messaging should emphasise community benefits vs. personal gain
Key principle on identity	"I think, therefore I am."	"I am because we are."	
Emphasis	Personal rights, freedom, self-reliance	Collective well-being, harmony, shared responsibility	
Social relations	Individual as primary unit, defined by personal choices	Group solidarity: an individual is defined by relationships	Campaigns that highlight social belonging and shared success resonate with Ubuntu-oriented audiences
Privacy and openness	Privacy is highly valued, personal space, and boundaries	Openness valued; privacy less emphasised	
Ethical focus	Individual rights, justice based on legal frameworks	Mutual care, empathy, reconciliation, community restoration	Emphasise ethical sourcing, social impact, and shared responsibility
Resource sharing	Private ownership, competition, and personal wealth accumulation	Collective ownership and sharing	Engage customers in dialogue and community events rather than just selling
Sustainability	Often prioritises personal success over community sustainability	Sustainable communal living, local relational focus	
Expression of identity	Identity expressed through personal achievements and autonomy	Identity is shaped through relationships with others	Promote products that benefit communities, local sourcing, and sustainability

Source Compiled for the study

Similarly, Vargas and Kemmelmeier (2013) characterise African culture as socio-centric rather than self-centric, emphasising societal collectivism over individualism. Therefore, it cannot be concluded that individualism is absent from the African experience. Individualism exists; however, there is a stronger emphasis on collective societal values than on self-centredness.

According to Bhatt and Garikipati (2024), African personhood is characterised as ensembled individualism, which features fluid boundaries between self and other, situates power within a field of forces surrounding the individual, and understands the self as inherently relational with others.

Rutsviga (2024) observed that employees of any organisation are expected to conform to specific standards and procedures to attain the designated objectives. Consequently, the African philosophy of Ubuntu is a fundamental and reliable ethical framework that can guide social media marketing towards substantial success and benefit in the African context. Marketing does not exist in isolation; it is inherently a human activity and must therefore be conducted with ethical considerations and a focus on humanity (Rutsviga, 2024). Also, relationality, interdependence, amicability, communalism, and humanness are all value-laden essential notions that render hunhu/ubuntu ethically significant and appealing. Therefore, it is essential for marketers to leverage the underlying principles of ubuntu to effectively engage their primary target market, particularly the youth, who prioritise inclusivity and collaboration (Kupangwa et al., 2024).

The Core Principles of *Ubuntu*

It is important to recognise the principles of Ubuntu, which embody a people-centred approach that underscores communalism and collectivism, emphasising the interconnectedness essential to the well-being of the community (Imafidon, 2022). This fosters a feeling of belonging, unity, and shared success, where individual experiences are deeply connected to those of the group, and in turn, the group's fate inevitably affects the individual. The relationships between individuals, nations, ecosystems, and spiritual beliefs are intricately woven and deeply nuanced. The person might express: "I am defined through my connections with others, and in our shared existence, my own being is validated". The fundamental principles of Ubuntu emphasise community, relationality, respect, and interdependence.

- *Compassion:* Compassion denotes the human capacity to comprehend the obstacles and difficulties faced by others (Ngubane & Makua, 2021). Compassion is essential to the sense of belonging and interconnectedness within African societies. This principle emphasises the significance of acting with kindness and offering aid to people in need.

- *Community:* In many community-oriented tasks, individuals unite as a collective to facilitate task completion, indicating that affection for one's community fosters a sense of responsibility and accountability, which is an underlying aspect of Ubuntu philosophy.
- *Relationality:* Ubuntu posits that individual self-realisation occurs through interpersonal relationships; a person's identity is shaped by their relationship with others (Mayaka & Truell, 2021). Consequently, by supporting others, one improves their own quality of life.
- *Respect:* Respect is essential to the African Ubuntu concept, capturing the essence of human interconnectedness and reciprocal acknowledgement. Rooted in the principle of *umuntu ngumuntu ngabantu*, Ubuntu underscores human interdependence and posits that respect is a fundamental moral obligation vital for communal existence, as noted by Shadrach (2025).
- *Interdependence:* Exemplified by the phrase "I am because we are," articulates an individual's identity as fundamentally connected and inseparable from their social context. According to Maphalala (2017), the communal ethical lifestyle of interdependence promotes societal progress by establishing a foundation for a cooperative economy, defined by sharing rather than accumulation, as well as self-reliance and independence.

Other Relevant Indigenous Ethical Value Systems in Africa

Ubuntu exists as a multifaceted idea, interconnected with various philosophical and cultural dimensions. Throughout the African continent, numerous indigenous philosophies uphold the fundamental principles of Ubuntu, emphasising community, relationality, respect, and interdependence.

Afro-communitarianism holds that individual identity and morality are fundamentally shaped by the community. Thus, communitarians contend that social relationships and community connections are essential in influencing individual moral growth (Chimakonam & Awugosi, 2020).

Community offers the framework that enables individuals to understand and address complex ethical dilemmas while shaping their moral identities. Of note, Reupert et al. (2022), posited that, the expression "it takes a village to raise a child" derives from an African proverb and communicates the idea that a collective effort ("the village") is essential to create a secure and nurturing environment for children, enabling them to thrive and achieve their aspirations. The concept of the village inherently implies that child-rearing is collectively shared by many. The notion illustrates a social reality in which the activities and behaviour of a child are the collective responsibility of the community, rather than only that of the biological parents, particularly in instances of inappropriate conduct. Thus, any adult may have the authority to teach and discipline a child without incurring repercussions from the biological parents. The primary focus is the ethical welfare of the community. Consequently, the Africanism approach emphasises community and collaboration, rather than individualism.

Many African cultural worldviews centre on the idea of community, and *chirere chigokurerawo (Raise it well, and it will do the same for you tomorrow), a* Shona proverb that reflects this idea by emphasising the importance of caring for one another and fostering supportive ties in society. This holds true for the philosophy developed by Julius Nyerere, the former president of Tanzania.

Therefore, it is imperative to introduce another African philosophy grounded in the fundamental ideas of *collectivism*. This philosophy, known as Ujamaa, originated in Tanzania. Julius Nyerere provided a description of *Ujamaa* and clarified his understanding of socialism by stating that it is "an attitude of mind… which is needed to ensure that the people care for each other's welfare" (Nyerere, 1987). This exemplifies the values that are associated with "familyhood" or "brotherhood"—we are all in it together. The emphasis on this philosophy is that mutual care can only be assured if individuals perceive one another as siblings or as constituents of the same community. This aligns with the *Ubuntu* ideology and the principles of relationality and communality. This is because Africans emphasise the significance of relational collectivity, which nurtures moral and spiritual awareness of human existence and of interpersonal connections with others and the environment (Maphalala, 2017). For instance, "we" address each other as brother or sister, or as uncle or auntie, regardless of biological ties, as a sign of respect for the elderly, which is a fundamental principle of Ubuntu.

Ubuntu and its Implications for Youth Marketing

The idea of Ubuntu, which comes from African philosophy, is a great way to think about marketing to young people, especially in markets that are multicultural and value-driven. "I am because we are" is another way to say "Ubuntu," which stresses the value of community, compassion, connection, and our shared humanity (Imafidon, 2022). These ideas really speak to young people today, who are looking for companies that are real, open to everyone, and socially responsible. Section 4 of this chapter explores the implications of Ubuntu for youth marketing.

Applying Ubuntu's Relational Ethics to Engage Young Consumers Authentically

The current generation of youths, known as Gen Z—born between 1995 and 2012—is characterised by significant integration with technology and social media, rendering digital engagement essential for effective marketing strategies (Smith, 2019). Nevertheless, businesses strive for genuine customer engagement across all platforms, within the bounds of marketing legislation and the digital channels they use to reach varied populations. McKinsey and Company (2021) explains that platforms such as Instagram, TikTok, and Snapchat are notably favoured by this demographic. Therefore, when interacting with youths, businesses must adhere not only to marketing and digital laws but also to community ethical standards.

Building a real community requires more than just exchanges between a brand and its customers. It requires people to connect with each other—the interdependence principle of "Ubuntu". As such, having the community work together on bigger issues underscores the organisation's social responsibility. A socially responsible organisation focuses more on good ethical conduct in the environment in which it markets its products. The present youth generation prioritises authenticity and transparency from brands, preferring those that demonstrate a sincere dedication to social responsibility and ethical practices (Prasanna & Priyanka, 2024). For example, when marketing to the youth, the ethical values within that community must be observed. This calls for a cultural approach instead of one based on behavioural or psychological models.

Prasanna and Priyanka (2024) suggested that to successfully connect with the youth market, it is essential to attain a deep comprehension of their cultural complexities, a goal best achieved through collaboration with those who navigate such an environment daily. Accordingly, the ideas of fairness, togetherness, and responsibility for those around us infuse every part even in the most business-like marketing setting. This holds true and is applicable to every generation, particularly within the African context, owing to the foundational philosophies of humanism (Buntu).

Emphasising Inclusivity, Empowerment, and Participation of Youth in Marketing Processes

It is important to involve young people as creators, collaborators, and contributors. This is particularly appropriate when considering South Africa through the lens of how its youth are shaping cultural expression through many online mediums, including but not limited to music, style, language, and social discourse (Mulikat et al., 2025). To remain relevant, youth-led creativity is crucial, not merely valuable. This opens the door to culturally relevant and pertinent art. Therefore, businesses need to emphasise inclusion throughout the production process, from behind the scenes to strategy meetings and decision-making rooms, rather than focusing solely on youth representation in front.

Also, implementing marketing campaigns guided by a clear purpose to empower youth represents a transformative approach that acknowledges their capabilities while simultaneously enhancing community well-being. Organisations may also implement marketing strategies that highlight the aspirations and obstacles faced by the younger demographic through collaboration with youth (Kupangwa et al., 2024). This may also highlight initiatives that advocate for social equity, foster entrepreneurship, and enhance educational opportunities. Beyond fostering awareness, these purpose-driven initiatives encourage youth to assume responsibility and actively shape their own futures through youth empowerment programmes.

Building Trust Through Transparency, Honesty, and Respectful Communication

The core characteristics of the Ubuntu concept are *respect, honesty, transparency, and trust*. As such, businesses are expected by customers to demonstrate honesty and openness if they want to attract and retain more discerning, well-informed customers. Therefore, nowadays, it's more important than ever for companies to earn their customers' *trust* and trustworthiness (Kharouf et al., 2014). In turn, companies have adopted a more transparent, straightforward approach to their marketing strategies to cultivate trust among their audiences, thereby transforming their operational methods.

Transparency, according to Vaccaro and Madsen (2009), entails a commitment to openness and honesty with customers regarding business practices, products, and services. This entails providing precise and comprehensive information, acknowledging errors, and assuming responsibility for one's actions. Consequently, transparency plays a crucial role in establishing a company's credibility, as suggested by Burhan et al. (2023). Thus, the substantial advantages of a company's openness can foster trust, enhance employee engagement and commitment to the organisation's goals, boost productivity, and fortify innovation. Therefore, adopting a culture of work openness is likely to enhance innovation accountability within an organisation (Ezeilo, 2022).

Thus, trust and credibility are of paramount importance in establishing and marketing a brand (Shamim & Islam, 2022). Consumers tend to engage more readily with an organisation that has earned their trust, and they are also inclined to advocate for that organisation within their networks. Conversely, insufficient trust and credibility may result in diminished sales, unfavourable reviews, and a tarnished reputation.

Ethical Challenges in Marketing to African Youth

Marketing in Africa cannot be separated from indigenous ethical systems that prioritise communal welfare, reciprocity, and respect, as these are the most important characteristics of the African population. The African moral philosophy of ubuntu, often summarised as "I am because we are", underlines a collective responsibility that shapes decision-making within communities (Kupangwa, 2025). When applied to marketing, ubuntu obliges businesses to treat youth not only as consumers but also as integral members of a social fabric whose long-term development and cultural identity must be preserved. This is very important, given that Africa boasts the world's youngest population, with 70% of its population under 30 years of age (Ichikowitz Family Foundation, 2024). It is noted that by 2050, African youth are expected to account for over a third of the world's youth and will make up 75% of all Africans under 35 years of age (Ichikowitz Family Foundation, 2024).

This group is technologically active, aspirational, and highly targeted by global and local brands. This considerable youth population offers a significant opportunity to drive ethical practices among marketers for the African continent. It is in this regard that marketing campaigns must not ignore indigenous values, as this ignorance often fosters alienation and erodes trust. For example, marketing that promotes extreme individualism or materialism can conflict with community-based values and disrupt cultural continuity. Therefore, integrating indigenous ethics into marketing strategies fosters trust, legitimacy, and cultural authenticity. Brands that support community initiatives, respect cultural symbols, and highlight collective progress are more likely to resonate with African youth. Thus, marketers who will practice indigenous ethics will build a firm foundation for market innovation that enhances sustainable brand consumer relationships.

Balancing Commercial Objectives with Ethical Responsibilities Rooted in Indigenous Values

The conflict between companies' priority to maximise profit and the cultural expectation to uphold communal and indigenous values is one of the ethical dilemmas that are faced by marketers in Africa. In many African societies, indigenous ethics are deeply embedded in collective traditions, social cohesion, and moral responsibility, with Ubuntu being the most prominent framework. Ubuntu emphasises community, solidarity, and empathy, requiring individuals and institutions to act in ways that benefit the collective (Mbiti, 1990; Metz, 2018).

However, globalised marketing strategies often disregard these values by promoting hyper-individualism, consumption-driven lifestyles, and competitive materialism. In South Africa, for example, advertisements that focus on luxury brands or sexualized imagery appeal to individual desires but undermine broader communal norms of modesty and dignity (Dubihlela & Dubihlela, 2011). Similarly, in Nigeria, digital campaigns frequently emphasise personal achievement, wealth accumulation, and social status, which risks alienating traditional values of communal sharing and interdependence (Jatto et al., 2025).

The challenge and danger being faced by African youths is that they are caught between the global consumer culture and their African cultures.

Due to technological advances, international trends, and imitation of Western trends, they end up becoming disconnected from their indigenous moral systems. Marketing campaigns that ignore cultural ethics may not only harm youth development but also weaken cultural identity. In this regard, Jatto et al. (2025) stress that integrating Ubuntu into marketing communications could mitigate this problem by ensuring that brand messages reflect respect, reciprocity, and responsibility for community welfare. For instance, youth-oriented campaigns could highlight collective benefits such as education, entrepreneurship, or environmental sustainability, thereby aligning commercial goals with cultural ethics. However, achieving this balance remains a major obstacle as the global marketing and advertising industry is heavily influenced by Western notions of individual consumer sovereignty and neoliberal capitalism (Firat & Venkatesh, 1995). Without conscious adaptation, these approaches risk perpetuating cultural dissonance in African markets. The task for marketers, therefore, is to reconcile commercial objectives with indigenous responsibilities, ensuring that business growth does not come at the expense of cultural integrity.

Avoiding Exploitation, Misinformation, and Manipulative Marketing Tactics

Exploitation of youth vulnerabilities through manipulative marketing tactics is another ethical challenge. Young people are widely recognised as one of the most impressionable consumer groups due to their developmental stage, limited life experience, and exposure to peer and media influences. Pollay (2014): Strasburger and Donnerstein (1999) assert that this makes them susceptible to persuasive techniques such as fantasy, idealised imagery, and aspirational messaging. For example, adverts that depict alcohol use and nudity trigger curiosity among the youth audience in South Africa as they depict young, attractive individuals enjoying lifestyles associated with consumption, creating unrealistic expectations and glamorising risky behaviours (Dubihlela & Dubihlela, 2011). Another example is the use of sex appeal, alcohol, and celebrity culture in advertising as a way of exploiting psychological vulnerabilities to influence young consumers without fully disclosing the potential consequences by marketers. Cassper Nyovest, one of South Africa's most prominent hip-hop artists, introduced his own tequila label, Don Billiato. To promote the brand, he appeared in a high-profile television and social media campaign alongside well-known figures such as Somizi Mhlongo and Toss. The commercial portrayed a lavish celebration aboard a private jet, a setting that projected alcohol as glamorous and aspirational. The Advertising Regulatory Board (ARB) later intervened and instructed that the campaign be withdrawn, ruling that it contravened the national Code on Alcohol Advertising by presenting drinking in a manner that encouraged excessive or idealised consumption (Wilson, 2024).

The problem is not limited to traditional advertising; it is also experienced on digital and social media platforms. Influencer marketing, now prevalent across Africa, frequently blurs the line between authentic content and paid promotion. It is estimated that, by 2027, the global influencer marketing industry will reach $480 billion (Rossum, 2024). According to Petrychak and Demianenko (2024), previous studies suggest that youth cannot distinguish between organic endorsements and sponsored posts, thereby exposing them to covert persuasion. According to a recent survey, 60 per cent of consumers trust online recommendations from Social Media Influencers (SMIs), with these endorsements influencing nearly half of all purchasing decisions (Digital Marketing Institute, 2024). Ekinci et al. (2025) asserts that some of the SMIs are involved in fostering deceptive consumption practices through buying followers or promoting products without disclosing paid partnerships. Such unethical behaviour erodes trust and integrity among both influencers and followers. Occasionally, SMIs also promote counterfeit luxury goods, illegal products, or banned substances (Ekinci et al., 2025). These endorsements pose twin risks for the African youth as they help proliferate illegal activities and expose followers to legal and health injuries. In 2020, Amazon sued two influencers for facilitating the sale of counterfeit products on its platform (Palmer, 2020). The above examples show how marketing can cross ethical boundaries by prioritising engagement metrics and profit over transparency and honesty. This type of manipulation by marketers can have long-term consequences on decision-making and identity formation for the African youth, who are both digitally active and culturally vulnerable. In this regard, marketers should practice ethical marketing that rejects exploitative practices in favour of transparency, accurate information, and respect for consumer autonomy.

Addressing Digital Privacy and Consent Concerns with Youth Audiences

An equally pressing concern in youth marketing is the safeguarding of digital privacy and consent. Rapid technological innovation in the twenty-first century has significantly contributed to the uptake of smartphones and the dominance of social media platforms across the continent, exposing young consumers to data harvesting and surveillance-driven advertising. Tchao et al.'s (2017) study in Ghana revealed that online users, and particularly younger groups, often feel both exposed and uncertain about how their personal data is being used, a situation compounded by low levels of digital literacy. On a global scale, scholars (Kezer et al., 2022; Trepte et al., 2017) have shown that youth frequently engage in what has been termed a "privacy calculus", where they exchange personal information for connectivity and participation in online communities yet do so without a clear understanding of the risks involved (Akter et al., 2025). The 2024 political protests in Nigeria illustrate this dilemma. While social media provided youth with a powerful tool for activism, it simultaneously created opportunities for privacy breaches and the spread of disinformation (Adams & Dorcas, 2024). Even though continental frameworks such as the African Union Convention on Cyber Security and Personal Data Protection were established to mitigate these risks, the uneven enforcement of such policies across member states continues to leave young users vulnerable to exploitation within digital marketing ecosystems (Bouke et al., 2023).

Opportunities for Ethical Youth Marketing Inspired by Indigenous Values

Africa's youthful population represents not only a powerful consumer base but also a catalyst for cultural innovation, entrepreneurship, and social change. In recognising this potential, ethical marketing inspired by Ubuntu's communal values calls for strategies that transcend profit motives to promote collective empowerment, sustainability, and shared progress. This section explores how indigenous ethics can guide marketing practices by leveraging youth engagement for community development, integrating CSR initiatives that reflect Ubuntu's ethos of mutual care, and creating youth-led campaigns that embody participation, inclusivity, and cultural authenticity. Together, these approaches position marketing as a transformative force that nurtures both social impact and responsible brand identity within Africa's evolving youth landscape.

Leveraging Youth Engagement to Foster Community Development and Social Impact

Africa's youth represent both the continent's largest demographic group and its most vibrant cultural force, shaping fashion, music, digital discourse, and political activism (Ichikowitz Family Foundation, 2024; Mulikat, et al., 2025). For example, the *Amapiano* music movement in South Africa has not only redefined global music trends but has also created entrepreneurial opportunities for young DJs, producers, and fashion designers who integrate the genre's aesthetics into clothing lines and lifestyle branding. Similarly, in Nigeria, youth-led activism during the #EndSARS protests demonstrated the power of young voices to mobilise communities, leverage digital platforms, and influence public discourse on governance and justice. These examples highlight the potential of youth as cultural innovators and social change agents.

Rather than viewing young people solely as consumers, ethical marketing can position them as partners in community development. By engaging youth in campaigns that promote education, entrepreneurship, and sustainability, marketers can strengthen social impact while cultivating brand loyalty. For instance, Safaricom's *BLAZE* platform in Kenya engages young entrepreneurs by providing mentorship, skills development, and funding opportunities, thereby aligning brand visibility with youth empowerment and social progress. Similarly, Unilever's *Shakti* initiative in East and West Africa has incorporated young women into its distribution networks, creating both employment and community upliftment. These initiatives illustrate how marketing rooted in indigenous ethics, emphasising Ubuntu's principles of interdependence and collective progress, can transform youth from passive consumers into active partners in shaping Africa's future.

Incorporating CSR Initiatives that Resonate with both Ubuntu Philosophy and Youth Aspirations

Corporate Social Responsibility (CSR) initiatives that align with Ubuntu's communal values and youth aspirations represent another powerful opportunity. Young people increasingly seek authenticity and transparency from brands, rewarding companies that invest in social responsibility and cultural sensitivity (Kharouf et al., 2014; Prasanna & Priyanka, 2024). Integrating CSR with indigenous ethics allows businesses to frame themselves as community partners rather than distant corporations. Safaricom in Kenya, for instance, has enhanced its legitimacy by positioning itself as a driver of national development through community-based initiatives, while South African banks that support education and entrepreneurship programmes embody Ubuntu in practice. For African youth, CSR efforts that address issues such as unemployment, inequality, and digital inclusion can resonate deeply, as they speak directly to their aspirations and lived realities. These initiatives demonstrate that profit and purpose can co-exist, creating mutual value for businesses and society.

Ubuntu's principle of interdependence, captured in the analogy *"I am because we are"*, provides a framework for positioning marketing as a driver of collective advancement rather than individual consumption (Kupangwa et al., 2024; Mbiti, 1990). This perspective calls for marketing strategies that emphasise shared responsibility and collective upliftment instead of purely transactional gains. For example, youth-focused initiatives that support environmental sustainability or financial literacy not only resonate with indigenous ethics but also empower young audiences to contribute positively to their communities. In Ghana, the *Plastic Waste Youth Recycling Movement* has partnered with local beverage companies to launch campaigns that allow young people to exchange collected plastic bottles for airtime or school supplies. Such initiatives reinforce both ecological responsibility and communal benefit, aligning commercial objectives with social value.

Similarly, in South Africa, Nedbank's *Youth Financial Fitness Programme* integrates financial literacy workshops with digital banking services targeted at students and young entrepreneurs. By equipping youth with money management skills while simultaneously introducing them to responsible banking products, the bank creates long-term trust and loyalty grounded in Ubuntu's ethos of mutual care and empowerment. These examples illustrate how marketing, when infused with indigenous ethics, can elevate itself beyond transactional exchange and become a catalyst for social transformation. By aligning with Ubuntu's principle of interdependence, brands not only strengthen their reputation but also cultivate a generation of consumers who see themselves as active participants in community progress rather than isolated individuals in the marketplace.

Creating Youth-Led Marketing Campaigns and Partnerships

Ethically inspired marketing also means shifting from representation to participation by actively involving youth as creators, collaborators, and decision-makers. In contexts such as South Africa, young people are not only consumers but also cultural innovators, shaping language, style, and digital culture across platforms like TikTok and Instagram (Mulikat et al., 2025; Smith, 2019). The rise of South African township slang, such as "Kasi lingo", and youth-driven fashion labels like Tshepo Jeans, demonstrates how young people shape national identity and brand culture in ways that traditional advertising agencies could never replicate.

Youth-led campaigns and partnerships embody the Ubuntu principles of respect and inclusivity by giving young voices authority in shaping brand narratives. Co-creation ensures campaigns reflect cultural authenticity, resonate with local values, and empower youth to see themselves as stakeholders rather than passive targets of persuasion (Kupangwa et al., 2024). For instance, Coca-Cola's *#ShareACokeWithSA* campaign incorporated youth names and local phrases suggested by young South Africans themselves, creating a sense of ownership and cultural resonance that drove brand loyalty. Likewise, MTN's *Pulse* youth platform in Nigeria engages young creatives in co-designing content and services that speak to their aspirations in music, gaming, and entrepreneurship.

Partnerships with youth organisations, student networks, or grassroots movements can also extend brand reach while embedding ethical responsibility. For example, in Kenya, *Safaricom BLAZE* collaborates with student clubs and youth-led enterprises to run mentorship bootcamps, enabling young people to pitch their ideas directly to industry leaders. Such initiatives align brand identity with youth empowerment while demonstrating accountability to the wider community (Makhetha-Kosi et al., 2025). By embedding indigenous values into participatory marketing, businesses not only strengthen trust but also foster sustainable relationships with Africa's most dynamic demographic. This approach positions youth as active architects of their futures and aligns marketing with long-term cultural and social advancement. In doing so, brands become more than market players; they evolve into trusted partners in the collective journey of African development.

Case Studies and Best Practices

This section presents practical illustrations of how Ubuntu-inspired ethics can be embedded within youth marketing and corporate social responsibility across Africa. By analysing selected African brands and social enterprises, the discussion highlights how indigenous values such as communal growth, inclusion, and shared responsibility are being translated into authentic marketing practices. It further examines successful youth-driven CSR initiatives that integrate Ubuntu principles of reciprocity, empowerment, and collective upliftment to generate both social and commercial value. Finally, the section reflects on lessons learned from ethical successes and missteps, identifying best practices for brands seeking to balance profitability with integrity, transparency, and cultural authenticity in their engagement with Africa's youth.

African Brands and Social Enterprises Exemplifying the Intersection of Indigenous Ethics and Youth Marketing

Several African brands and social enterprises have successfully integrated indigenous ethics into their youth marketing strategies.

- Safaricom (Kenya): Through its *BLAZE* youth platform, Safaricom positions itself not only as a telecom provider but as a mentor to young entrepreneurs. By offering training, competitions, and access to funding, the brand embodies Ubuntu by fostering collective growth rather than simply selling products. Youth are engaged as co-creators in events and campaigns, making marketing an inclusive, participatory process.
- Tshepo Jeans (South Africa): Founded by a young entrepreneur, Tshepo Jeans integrates African storytelling, community pride, and youth fashion culture into its marketing. The brand collaborates with township communities in production and marketing, reflecting values of Ubuntu, shared growth, and communal recognition while celebrating youth identity and creativity.
- YICE Uganda (Youth Initiative for Community Empowerment): This social enterprise works with young farmers to promote sustainable agriculture. Its campaigns emphasise collective success through youth-led cooperative farming, directly aligning marketing messages

with African communitarian ethics of shared responsibility and ecological stewardship.

Successful Youth-Driven CSR Projects Reflecting Ubuntu Values

CSR initiatives rooted in Ubuntu demonstrate that youth engagement can produce both commercial and social value.

- *Nedbank (South Africa):* Youth Financial Fitness Programme: Nedbank invests in financial literacy campaigns targeted at students and young entrepreneurs. The programme uses relatable youth ambassadors to deliver workshops, blending CSR with Ubuntu values by promoting self-reliance and shared prosperity.
- *Unilever Africa Shakti Initiative:* Expanded to parts of West and East Africa, this initiative empowers young women and men as micro-distributors of consumer goods in their communities. The project reflects Ubuntu by fostering inclusion, local entrepreneurship, and the dignity of work while strengthening the brand's presence at the grassroots level.
- *MTN Foundation Nigeria ICT and Youth Empowerment Projects:* MTN has consistently invested in youth digital literacy, coding bootcamps, and ICT hubs. These projects reflect Ubuntu values of reciprocity and collective upliftment by preparing youth for the digital economy while cultivating trust in MTN as a socially responsible brand.

Lessons Learned from Ethical Successes and Missteps

Ethical youth marketing in Africa has produced both inspiring successes and cautionary tales.

- Successes:
    - *Community-Based Campaigns:* Campaigns that elevate collective values (e.g. Safaricom BLAZE, Nedbank Financial Fitness) demonstrate that youth trust and loyalty grow when marketing aligns with indigenous ethics.

- *Cultural Authenticity*: Brands that embrace local languages, symbols, and youth creativity (e.g. Tshepo Jeans, Amapiano-inspired fashion and music collaborations) build stronger connections by respecting youth identity.

- Missteps:

  - *Exploitative Alcohol Advertising*: Cassper Nyovest's *Don Billiato* tequila campaign in South Africa, which glamorised excessive drinking, faced backlash and regulatory intervention (Wilson, 2024). It highlighted the dangers of glamorising risky behaviours that conflict with Ubuntu's emphasis on responsibility and communal welfare.
  - *Influencer Marketing Deception*: Cases of influencers promoting counterfeit goods or failing to disclose sponsorships (Ekinci et al., 2025; Palmer, 2020) erode trust and expose youth to manipulative tactics. These instances reveal the risks of prioritising profit and engagement metrics over transparency and consumer dignity.

Best Practices:

1. Ground campaigns in Ubuntu's core values: community, reciprocity, respect, and interdependence.
2. Shift from targeting youth as passive consumers to empowering them as co-creators and innovators.
3. Align CSR initiatives with real youth aspirations (employment, education, sustainability).
4. Maintain transparency and honesty in all digital and influencer marketing to build trust.
5. Avoid glamorising harmful behaviours; instead, emphasise collective well-being and empowerment.

Future Directions and Implications

This section synthesises the broader implications of ethical, indigenous-value–driven marketing for Africa's youth-oriented marketplace. It begins by examining how ethically grounded marketing can build long-term brand loyalty and generate enduring social value, demonstrating that moral responsibility and commercial success are not mutually exclusive but mutually reinforcing. The discussion then turns to calls for continued research and culturally sensitive practice models, highlighting the need to move beyond Western-centric paradigms towards frameworks that authentically reflect African ethical traditions such as Ubuntu, Harambee, and communal kinship. Finally, the section underscores the importance of sustaining ethical innovation and indigenous relevance in future marketing practice, ensuring that Africa's evolving marketing landscape remains rooted in integrity, inclusivity, and shared human values.

The Potential of Ethically Grounded Marketing to Build Long-Term Brand Loyalty and Social Value

Within Africa's consumer landscape, ethical marketing functions as both a normative obligation and a strategic necessity. It not only upholds moral responsibility but also establishes the foundation for sustained consumer trust and loyalty. The continent's youthful demographic, which constitutes most of its population, demands particular attention. African youth tend to support companies that project authenticity, cultural sensitivity, and a genuine commitment to social responsibility. Adewale et al. (2025) argue that when digital marketing adheres to ethical standards, it strengthens consumer trust, which in turn becomes a foundation for sustained loyalty and long-term competitive strength. Embedding indigenous ethical traditions into brand identity deepens these connections. For example, Safaricom in Kemya has enhanced its legitimacy by framing itself not simply as a telecommunications provider but as a driver of national development through community-based initiatives. In South Africa, firms that draw on the principle of ubuntu, particularly those banks funding education and entrepreneurship programmes, have positioned themselves as trustworthy corporate citizens, cultivating reputations that extend beyond immediate commercial transactions.

The contribution of ethical marketing to society is equally significant (Matlala et al., 2025). Campaigns that foreground financial literacy, sustainability, or gender equity create benefits that stretch well beyond the marketplace. In Ghana, fintech companies are now embedding transparency and fairness into their promotional strategies, demonstrating that financial inclusion can be pursued in ways that uphold cultural expectations of honesty while remaining profitable. These examples confirm that ethical practice is not a barrier to commercial success but a catalyst for generating both social value and durable brand capital.

Calls for Continued Research and Culturally Sensitive Practice Models

Even though notable advances have been made, research on marketing ethics in Africa remains incomplete, with significant gaps that require attention. Much of the literature continues to privilege Western experiences, while African realities and cultural contexts are often marginalised (Dubihlela & Dubihlela, 2011). This imbalance underscores the urgency for models that not only respond to global marketing frameworks but also integrate ethical traditions drawn from African societies. Concepts such as ubuntu in Southern Africa, harambee in East Africa, and communal kinship systems in West Africa offer rich foundations that could be translated into operational marketing practices. As Adams and Dorcas (2024) observe, the expansion of digital platforms has brought new ethical challenges, ranging from the handling of personal data to the rise of misinformation and opaque influencer marketing that must be examined through locally grounded cultural values.

Equally important is the need for empirical research into how young people across Africa interpret ethical and unethical advertising. Comparative insights from different countries across the African continent on community-oriented campaigns and dynamic digital marketing practices could shape adaptable models for the continent. A critical component is the involvement of youth as co-creators of brand stories, ensuring that marketing strategies resonate with indigenous ethics while protecting consumer rights. As Adewale et al. (2025) contend, ethical responsibility must be embedded at the core of corporate practice rather than treated as a peripheral compliance issue.

Conclusion

Ethical marketing in Africa is not only a moral imperative but also a strategic route to cultivating lasting consumer loyalty and building wider social value. With young people forming most of the continent's population, brands face a generation that is increasingly selective in its affiliations. African youth tend to support companies that project authenticity, cultural sensitivity, and a genuine commitment to social responsibility. As Adewale et al. (2025) argue, when digital marketing adheres to ethical standards, it strengthens consumer trust, which, in turn, serves as a foundation for sustained loyalty and long-term competitive advantage. Therefore, embedding indigenous ethical traditions into brand identity deepens these connections. For example, in Kenya, Safaricom has enhanced its legitimacy by framing itself not simply as a telecommunications provider but as a driver of national development through community-based initiatives. In South Africa, firms that draw on the principle of ubuntu, such as Nedbank, which funds education and entrepreneurship programmes, have positioned themselves as trustworthy corporate citizens, cultivating reputations that extend beyond immediate commercial transactions. The contribution of ethical marketing to society is equally significant. Campaigns that drive financial literacy, sustainability, or gender equity create benefits that stretch well beyond the marketplace. In Ghana, fintech companies are now embedding transparency and fairness into their promotional strategies, demonstrating that financial inclusion can be pursued in ways that uphold cultural expectations of honesty while remaining profitable. These examples confirm that ethical practice is not a barrier to commercial success but a catalyst for generating both social value and durable brand capital.

References

Adams, E. J., & Dorcas, B. (2024). Ethical issues of social media in Nigeria. *Indonesian Journal of Public Administration Review, 1*(2), 25–25. https://doi.org/10.47134/par.v1i2.2295

Adewale, J. A., Abdulquadri, A. O., & Zubair, O. S. (2025). Digital marketing and global shift toward ethical advertising. *Nigerian Journal of Management Studies, 27*(1), 150–174.

Akter, M., Park, J. K., Headrick, C., Page, X., & Wisniewski, P. J., (2025). Calculating connection vs. risk: Understanding how youth negotiate digital privacy and security with peers online. *arXiv preprint* arXiv:2503.22993. https://doi.org/10.48550/arXiv.2503.22993

Bhatt, P., & Garikipati, S. (2024). Feminist ideologies at work: Culture, collectivism, and entrepreneurship among disadvantaged women in India. *Feminist Economics, 30*(3), 185–216. https://doi.org/10.1080/13545701.2024.2383209

Bouke, M. A., Abdullah, A., ALshatebi, S. H., Atigh, H. E., & Cengiz, K., (2023). African union convention on cyber security and personal data protection: Challenges and future directions. *arXiv preprint* arXiv:2307.01966. https://doi.org/10.48550/arXiv.2307.01966

Burhan, Q. U. A., Khan, M. A., & Malik, M. F. (2023). Achieving transparency in business processes by developing and implementing ethical climate: An integrated model of ethical leadership and engagement. *Business Process Management Journal, 29*(3), 757–776. https://doi.org/10.1108/BPMJ-08-2022-0384

Chimakonam, J. O., & Awugosi, C. I. (2020). Afro-Communitarism and the question of individual freedom. *Philosophia: International. Journal of Philosophy, 21*(2), 34–49. https://doi.org/10.46992/pijp.21.1.a.3

Datta, P. B., & Garikipati, S. (2019). Culture, collectivism and empowerment: The role of feminist ideologies in women's work and organization. https://doi.org/10.2139/ssrn.3802519.

Digital Marketing Institute. (2024, April 14). *20 surprising influencer marketing statistics*. Digital Marketing Institute. https://digitalmarketinginstitute.com/blog/20-influencer-marketing-statistics-that-will-surprise-you

Du Toit, A. (2021). Ubuntu for social entrepreneurship education. In *Proceedings of the 24th international RAIS conference on social sciences and humanities* (pp. 10–17). Scientia Moralitas Research Institute. https://doi.org/1044804

Dubihlela, J., & Dubihlela, D. (2011). Youth attitudes towards advertisements depicting nudity and alcohol: Ethical dilemmas in advertising. *South Africa Journal of Psychology, 41*(2), 207–217. https://doi.org/10.1177/008124631104100209

Ekinci, Y., Dam, S., & Buckle, G. (2025). The dark side of social media influencers: A research agenda for analysing deceptive practices and regulatory challenges. *Psychology & Marketing, 42*(4), 1201–1214. https://doi.org/10.1002/mar.22173

Ezeilo, L. N. (2022). Transparency: A guide to practicing good business ethics in Nigeria. *Journal of Business and Strategic Management, 7*(2), 85–98. RePEc:bhx:ojjbsm:v:7:y:2022:i:2:p:85–98:id:947.

Firat, A. F., & Venkatesh, A. (1995). Liberatory postmodernism and the reenchantment of consumption. *Journal of Consumer Research, 22*(3), 239–267. https://doi.org/10.1086/209448

Ichikowitz Family Foundation. (2024). *A turning point for African youth: African youth survey 2024*. Ichikowitz Family Foundation. https://ichikowitzfoundation.com/storage/reports/September2024/GSLcmLTnruHzhTrIuDOV.pdf

Imafidon, E. (2022). *Exploring African relational ethic of Ubuntu for inclusion and solidarity in the humanitarian field*. https://www.salto-youth.net/downloads/4-17-4259/17-Elvis_Imafidon-Ubuntu.pdf

Jatto, A. A., Abdulquadri, A. O., & Zubair, O. S. (2025). Digital marketing and global shift toward ethical advertising. *Nigerian Journal of Management Studies, 27*(1), 150–174. https://njms.unilag.edu.ng/article/view/2567/2073

Kezer, M., Dienlin, T., & Baruh, L. (2022). Getting the privacy calculus right: Analyzing the relations between privacy concerns, expected benefits, and self-disclosure using response surface analysis. *Cyberpsychology: Journal of Psychosocial Research on Cyberspace, 16*(4).

Kharouf, H., Lund, D. J., & Sekhon, H. (2014). Building trust by signaling trustworthiness in service retail. *Journal of Services Marketing, 28*(5), 361–373. https://doi.org/10.1108/JSM-01-2013-0005

Kupangwa, W. (2025). The African philosophy of Ubuntu and family businesses: A perspective article. *Journal of Family Business Management, 15*(1), 57–67. https://doi.org/10.1108/JFBM-10-2023-0216

Kupangwa, W., Venter, E., & Farrington, S. (2024). Manifestations of ethical values in indigenous African family businesses: An application of the Ubuntu philosophy. *IFBRF, 2024*, 237. https://doi.org/10.1080/15228916.2024.2352951

Makhetha-Kosi, P., Matlala, N., Shumba, K., & Shambare, R. (2025). Social media, reference groups, and their brands. In A. Gbadamosi (Ed.), *Brands, branding, and consumerism*. Palgrave Macmillan. https://doi.org/10.1007/978-3-031-80859-3_4

Maphalala, M. C. (2017). Embracing Ubuntu in managing effective classrooms. *Gender and Behaviour, 15*(4), 10237–10249. https://doi.org/10.10520/EJC-c1eb0d3be

Mathebula, M., & Martinez-Vargas, C. (2023). Ubuntu as a valued capability for university students in South Africa. *Journal of Student Affairs in Africa, 11*(2), 17–33.

Matlala, N., Shumba, K., & Chimucheka, T. (2025). The roles of Brands in Consumer Protection. In A. Gbadamosi (Ed.), *Brands, branding, and consumerism*. Palgrave Macmillan. https://doi.org/10.1007/978-3-031-80859-3_10

Mayaka, B., & Truell, R. (2021). Ubuntu and its potential impact on the international social work profession. *International Social Work, 64*(5), 649–662. https://doi.org/10.1177/00208728211022787

Mbiti, J. S. (1990). *African religions and philosophy* (2nd ed.). Heinemann. https://books.google.co.za/books?hl=en&lr=&id=eTUpo9lH-

McKinsey. & Company. (2021). *The role of personalization in winning over Gen Z consumers*. https://www.mckinsey.com/business-functions/marketing-and-sales/our-insights/therole-of-personalization-in-winning-over-gen-z-consumers

Metz, T. (2018). An African theory of good leadership. *African Journal of Business Ethics, 12*(2), 36–53. https://doi.org/10.15249/12-2-204

Mulikat, A., Omoniyi, I. E., & Abdulsalam, T. A. (2025). Digital marketing factors and buying behaviour in the fashion industry: Evidence from gen Z consumers in Africa. *Economic Outlook/Ekonomski Pogledi, 27*(1), 1–42. https://doi.org/10.5937/ep27-51541

Ngubane, N., & Makua, M. (2021). Ubuntu pedagogy–transforming educational practices in South Africa through an African philosophy: From theory to practice. *Inkanyiso: Journal of Humanities and Social Sciences, 13*(1), 1–12. https://www.ajol.info/index.php/ijhss/article/view/212332

Nyerere, J. K. (1987). Ujamaa: The basis of African socialism. *The Journal of Pan African Studies, 1*(1), 4–11. http://jpanafrican.org/edocs/e-DocUjamma3.5.pdf

Palmer, A., (2020). Amazon sues two influencers for peddling counterfeit goods on Instagram and TikTok. *CNBC*. https://www.cnbc.com/2020/11/12/amazon-sues-influencers-for-allegedlymarketing-counterfeits.html

Petrychak, O., & Demianenko, O. (2024). Ethics of marketing communications in the digital age. *Economic Bulletin of Cherkasy State Technological University, 25*(1), 48–57. https://doi.org/10.62660/ebcstu/1.2024.48

Pollay, R. W. (2014). The distorted mirror: Reflections on the unintended consequences of advertising. In *Readings in advertising, society, and consumer culture* (pp. 291–318). Routledge. https://www.researchgate.net/profile/Richard-Pollay/publication/328704606_

Prasanna, M. P., & Priyanka, A. L. (2024). Marketing to gen Z: Understanding the preferences and behaviors of next generation. *International Journal for Multidisciplinary Research, 6*(4), 1–8. https://doi.org/10.36948/ijfmr.2024.v06i04.26612

Reupert, A., Straussner, S. L., Weimand, B., & Maybery, D. (2022). It takes a village to raise a child: Understanding and expanding the concept of the "village". *Frontiers in Public Health, 10*, 756066. https://doi.org/10.3389/fpubh.2022.756066

Rossum, V. D., (2024). *Who wants a slice of the $480 billion creator economy pie?* https://www.flexos.work/learn/who-wants-aslice-of-the-480-billion-creator-economy-pie

Rutsviga, A. (2024). Hunhu/Ubuntu as a social media marketing strategy ethic in post-Covid19 times. *London Journal of Research In Humanities and Social Sciences, 24*(6), 1–11. https://journalspress.uk/index.php/LJRHSS/article/view/719

Shadrach, O. (2025). Respect as a pillar of African Ubuntu philosophy. *Nnadiebube Journal of Philosophy, 8*(2). https://acjol.org/index.php/NJP/article/view/6322

Shamim, K., & Islam, T. (2022). Digital influencer marketing: How message credibility and media credibility affect trust and impulsive buying. *Journal of Global Scholars of Marketing Science, 32*(4), 601–626. https://doi.org/10.1080/21639159.2022.2052342

Shavitt, S., & Cho, H. (2016). Culture and consumer behavior: The role of horizontal and vertical cultural factors. *Current Opinion in Psychology, 8*, 149–154.

Smith, A., (2019). The Generation Z technology report. *Pew Research Center.* https://www.pewresearch.org/report/technology-and-gen-z

Strasburger, V. C., & Donnerstein, E. (1999). Children, adolescents, and the media: Issues and solutions. *Pediatrics, 103*(1), 129–139. https://doi.org/10.1542/peds.103.1.129

Trepte, S., Reinecke, L., Ellison, N. B., Quiring, O., Yao, M. Z., & Ziegele, M. (2017). A cross-cultural perspective on the privacy calculus. *Social Media+ Society, 3*(1), 2056305116688035.

Tynan, L. (2021). What is relationality? Indigenous knowledges, practices and responsibilities with kin. *Cultural Geographies, 28*(4), 597–610. https://doi.org/10.1177/14744740211029287

United Nations. (2025). *Young people's potential, the key to Africa's sustainable development*. https://www.un.org/ohrlls/news/young-people%E2%80%99s-potential-key-africa%E2%80%99s-sustainable-development#:~:text=Africa%20has%20the%20youngest%20population,is%20involved%

Vaccaro, A., & Madsen, P. (2009). Transparency in business and society: Introduction to the special issue. *Ethics & Information Technology, 11*(2). https://doi.org/10.1007/s10676-009-9197-7

Vargas, J. H., & Kemmelmeier, M. (2013). Ethnicity and contemporary American culture: A meta-analytic investigation of horizontal–vertical individualism–collectivism. *Journal of Cross-Cultural Psychology, 44*(2), 195–222. https://doi.org/10.1177/0022022112443733

Wilson, N. (2024). Very much a party vibe: ARB orders Cassper Nyovest's tequila brand to pull ad glamourising drinking. *News24.* https://www.news24.com/business/companies/very-much-a-party-vibe-arb-orders-cassper-nyovests-tequila-brand-to-pull-ad-glamourising-drinking-20240718

Index

A. Gbadamosi et al. (eds.), *Contemporary Marketing Practices in Africa, Volume 1*, Palgrave Studies of Marketing in Emerging Economies,
https://doi.org/10.1007/978-3-032-27126-6

Kolibri 360 GmbH
Ferdinand-Jühlke-Straße 7
99095 Erfurt, Deutschland
produktsicherheit@kolibri360.de